More Praise for

VERY IMPORTANT PEOPLE

"Astonishing. Mears has amassed pages of enthralling, richly human testimony. . . . The anecdotes are hugely entertaining, in a throw-up-in-your-mouth way. . . . Mears's thesis—that nightclubs aren't exceptions to 'real life,' but a distilled, brutal caricature of it—gathers strength as the details accumulate. . . . Elegantly written and genuinely page-turning, with revelations about life that go far beyond nightclubs."
—IONA McLAREN, *Daily Telegraph*

"*Very Important People* depicts a complex world of exchange and exploitation, and warrants praise for doing so without passing predictable moral judgement. More than offering a mere window into the exotic lives of others, Ashley Mears emphasizes themes that should resonate with us all: the labour of marginalized others that lurks behind so much status-seeking consumption, the risks of conflating work with fun and friendship, and the sad fact that 'girl power' remains as oxymoronic as ever."
—ALICE BLOCH, *Times Literary Supplement*

"*Very Important People* was written before the coronavirus pandemic, but Covid-19 makes it more relevant. Lockdown has widened inequality as poorer households lose jobs and rely on their savings. Meanwhile, the rich are getting richer, leading to pent up demand for parties, girls and bottle trains among those who have already missed a season of it."
—OLLIE WILLIAMS, *Forbes*

"Compelling, vivid and curiously poignant. . . . *Very Important People* succeeds in exposing the intriguing and often distressing realities of a culture whose values seem both alien and unpleasantly persistent."
—LISA HILTON, *The Critic*

"Enlightening. . . . A fascinating glimpse into life behind the velvet rope."
—MATTHEW PARTRIDGE, *Money Week*

"With sharp analytical insight and riveting evidence, Ashley Mears takes us backstage into the glamorous global world of parties and nightclubs. Behind the flowing bottles of Dom Pérignon and other

VERY IMPORTANT PEOPLE

Very Important People

Status and Beauty in the Global Party Circuit

Ashley Mears

PRINCETON UNIVERSITY PRESS

PRINCETON AND OXFORD

Published by Princeton University Press
41 William Street, Princeton, New Jersey 08540
6 Oxford Street, Woodstock, Oxfordshire OX20 1TR

press.princeton.edu

All Rights Reserved
First paperback printing, 2021
Paperback ISBN 9780691227054

The Library of Congress has cataloged the cloth edition of this book as follows:
Names: Mears, Ashley, 1980- author.
Title: Very important people : status and beauty in the global party
    circuit / Ashley Mears.
Description: Princeton : Princeton University Press, [2020] | Includes
    bibliographical references and index.
Identifiers: LCCN 2019050389 (print) | LCCN 2019050390 (ebook) |
    ISBN 9780691168654 (hardback) | ISBN 9780691189895 (ebook)
Subjects: LCSH: Young women—Social life and customs. | Socialites. |
    Social status. | Businessmen—Social life and customs. | Rich people. |
    Subculture.
Classification: LCC HQ798 .M447 2020 (print) | LCC HQ798 (ebook) | DDC
    305.242/2—dc23

LC record available at https://lccn.loc.gov/2019050389

LC ebook record available at https://lccn.loc.gov/2019050390

British Library Cataloging-in-Publication Data is available

Editorial: Meagan Levinson and Jacqueline Delaney
Production Editorial: Ellen Foos
Jacket/Cover Design: Amanda Weiss
Production: Erin Suydam
Publicity: Kathryn Stevens and Maria Whelan
Copyeditor: Stephen Twilley

Jacket/Cover image: Stocksy

This book has been composed in Adobe Text and Gotham

Printed in the United States of America

CONTENTS

ACKNOWLEDGMENTS

I wish to first thank the many men and women in New York who let me into their world and shared with me their time and the stories that form the basis of this book.

One positive consequence of taking a long time to write a book is that one gets the chance to discuss it with many people. I am much indebted to the generosity of friends, colleagues, and family who dealt with multiple iterations of the ideas in these pages. Many colleagues read and commented generously on versions of this material: Gabriel Rossman, David Grazian, Bruno Cousin, Sébastien Chauvin, Giselinde Kuipers, Noah McClain, Clayton Childress, Nicky Fox, Viviana Zelizer, Timothy Dowd, Jeremy Schulz, Alison Gerber, Sharon Koppman, Shamus Khan, Frédéric Godart, Francesca Seteffi, Rachel Sherman, Luna Glucksburg, Gary Allen Fine, and Annette Lareau. My colleagues at Boston University, especially Emily Barman, Julian Go, Catherine Connell, Michel Anteby, Alya Guseva, Nazli Kibria, and Nancy Ammerman, shared their brilliance and helped me navigate academia. My student Connor Fitzmaurice gave invaluable feedback early on, and Heather Mooney provided terrific research assistance.

I was able to begin this ethnography with a Junior Faculty Fellowship awarded by the BU Center for the Humanities in 2012 under the leadership of the late James Winn, who was an inspiring colleague. During the early stages of data analysis, I held a research fellowship at the Amsterdam Research Centre for Gender and Sexuality, thanks to the invitation of Sébastien Chauvin, with whom, over many conversations together, I developed my arguments around gender and capital. While drafting the book, I held a visiting professorship at the Central European University, in Budapest, in the remarkable (and resilient) departments of gender studies and of sociology and social anthropology: thanks especially to Alexandra Kowalski, Elisa Helms, and Dorit Geva for their support. I had the opportunity to share and refine various arguments of the book with audiences at several colloquia and workshops in the United States: the Economic Sociology Seminar at MIT, the Culture and Social Analysis Workshop at Harvard, the Center for the Study of Social Organization at Princeton, and in sociology departments at the University of Pennsylvania, Emory, the University of Georgia, the University of Southern California, the University of Toronto, the University of Texas at Austin, and the University of California, Berkeley. In Europe, I presented to and workshopped with colleagues at the Max Planck Institute, in Cologne, Germany; the University of Lausanne, in Switzerland; the University of Padua, the University of Verona, and the University of Bologna, in Italy; L'école des hautes études en sciences sociales, in Paris; and at the Institute of Philosophy and Social Theory at the University of Belgrade, Serbia.

Material from chapter 4 appears in *Poetics: Journal of Empirical Research in Culture, the Media, and the Arts* as "Girls as Elite Distinction: The Appropriation of Bodily Capital" (2015). Material from chapter 5 appears in the *American Sociological Review* as "Working for Free in the VIP: Relational Work and the Production of Consent" (2015). Material from chapter 6 is published in *Actes de la recherche en sciences sociales* as "Des fêtes très exclusives: Les promoteurs de soirées VIP, des intermédiaires aux ambitions contraries." I am grateful for many thoughtful critiques from these journal reviewers and editors.

Thanks also to my careful and thorough editor at Princeton, Meagan Levinson, who is also a patient person. Meagan secured two of the toughest and most helpful reviews my work has ever received; thank you to these anonymous reviewers. On writing, I received valuable feedback from David Lobenstein early on, and Reynolds Richter was an excellent and efficient critical reader to the end. Thanks to Stephen Twilley for the terrific copyedits.

Thanks to friends who sustained me through this work: Olya Zueva, Eileen Lannon, Yulia Vasiltsova, Enrico Corniani, Marie Vaz, Álvaro Sevilla Buitrago, and my mentor Judith Stacey.

Finally, to family. I thank my parents, Kathy and Mike and Edwin and Kathy, for their constant support. My mother-in-law, Slavica Petrović, provided immense help and afforded me time to write. My sister, Jennifer Mears, designed the graphics and even accompanied me out sometimes. Thanks lastly to Vladimir Petrović, a true partner in our transatlantic adventures in academia and parenting Nola and Luka.

Sunday, 5 p.m., Miami

It was 5 p.m. when I woke up in the guesthouse of a villa on Miami's Star Island, mosquito-bitten and sweaty in the afternoon heat. Since coming to Miami three days earlier to follow Santos, a twenty-six-year-old club promoter, to Ultra, the renowned electronic dance music festival, I had experienced a whirlwind of party hopping, from club to club to hotel penthouse to P. Diddy's early morning pool party; finally, Santos, having run out of after-parties on day four, wired up the speakers to keep the party going at our villa. The booming electronic music finally stopped around noon, or at least that's when I fell asleep.

This isn't really *our* villa; it's a rental priced at $50,000 for the weekend, and this weekend, it was home to a group of young men flush with cash from their jobs at a Southern California mortgage bank. The rental agent had invited Santos and "his girls," models mostly, to stay in the bankers' villa for the weekend of parties. The bankers were excited at the prospect of a bunch of models sleeping in the attached guesthouse. Models were such a fixture in the global VIP club scene that the phrase "models and bottles" came to denote a good time. As an "image promoter," Santos's job mostly involved ferrying models to and from exclusive parties well into the night, and even, I was learning, into the next day.

In my muggy little guest room, I gingerly stepped between two twin beds, maneuvering through dresses, high heels, and the other spilled contents of suitcases, to rummage in my Chanel handbag for a cold McDonald's breakfast burrito purchased in a hurry hours ago, between parties, then carried it and my laptop outside to sit by the pool. No sign of the bankers, nor of Santos and his models, only empty beer and champagne bottles scattered around the manicured lawn and palm trees.

It was quiet except for the ringing in my ears that always happened after a long night out. It rarely works to shout a conversation over club music. To hear someone in the thick of a 72,000-watt sound system, you have to press a finger against the pointy cartilage part of your near ear, which, when flattened, drowns out background noise and focuses a stream of vocal vibrations straight into your brain.

This is how I understood Santos when, over the noise at the peak of the previous night's best moments, as crates of champagne were delivered to our table amid cheers and sparklers, he leaned in close to my face, pressed a finger against my ear, and said, "It's amazing! See, I told you. I'm at the best parties in the world!"

Going out with Santos did indeed offer amazing experiences at extravagant parties packed with beautiful models whose bodies were lit up by the fireworks affixed to the trains of expensive champagne bottles coming our way. At one point the previous night, after a rich man ordered a sparkler-lit procession of dozens of bottles to our table, we each got to drink from our own personal bottle of Dom Pérignon. In place of glasses, our high-heeled shoes littered the tables, so we could dance barefoot on top of the sofas. It was an electric couple of hours shared among Santos, myself, and a dozen other girls and promoters, all part of an exclusive world of beauty and money, both present in excess and on full display.

I had come to Miami in 2012 during the peak party season, in March. By that point, the US economy had recovered from the crash of 2008 but unevenly so, with the most gains going to the least-affected share of top income earners. For the rich, it seemed, the champagne flowed freely throughout the Great Recession. So I joined the party circuit for the world's "Very Important People" to understand what they do with their huge and growing pools of disposable income, and how they think about wastefully destroying their money—a phenomenon that, to outsiders, often seems ridiculous and disgusting. From 2011 to 2013, I documented a ritualized form of wealth destruction in the elite club scene, one that repeats around the world, from the Hamptons to Saint-Tropez, but one that does not come easy. It takes an incredible amount of labor to enable conspicuous leisure, and this labor upholds a gendered economy of value in which women's bodies are assessed against men's money. Bottle trains of champagne may seem irrational to a modern economist, but to an economic sociologist they are a type of ritual performance at the heart of hierarchical systems of prestige and masculine domination. Through highly scripted and gendered labors within the VIP space, the absurdity of extreme wealth becomes normal—even, with the right staging, celebrated and honorable.

I got into the scene because I could still pass for a "girl," even though I was thirty-one when I met Santos, far older than the eighteen-to-twenty-five-year-old women that typically formed his entourage. I looked younger than my age and, as an ex-model, I could pass as pretty *enough*, though I was surely more stiff and sober and less desirable than the other girls—a fact that Santos sometimes reminded me of, like when he suggested I change out of my more manageable wedge sandals and into sexier heels.

There was another reason promoters like Santos let me follow them through the exclusive party scene. He was blown away by the idea that a professor, someone with a PhD who teaches at a university, was interested in learning from him. When I first met Santos, at a dinner in New York, I explained my project, telling him about my research on consumption, gender, and markets. He interrupted me in his fast, Colombian-accented speech: "What we do is psychologic. It's psychological. Because you have to work people." He went on to explain the stresses of the job, like when girls canceled on him with excuses to stay home moments before they were supposed to come out. The constant danger, he said, was that you could be left with no one at your party.

But Santos was also full of bravado, bragging about his status in this elite world.

"I'm the best. The very top. Ask anybody. Everywhere in the world, they know who I am, because you do the best party one time in one city, then everybody wants you at their party. They all know me."

I came away from our meeting that night with the impression that he had been waiting for someone to study his world for a long time. As a mixed-race Latino from a poor family in Central America, Santos thought his own story of ascent among the global elite was remarkable, and he believed he was destined to be superrich like his clients. Shortly afterward, he showed me his roster of upcoming summer events and parties planned in Paris, Milan, Saint-Tropez, Cannes, and Ibiza. "They gonna fly me everywhere. It's the top, *top* level. I go everywhere and it's so nice."

And so I joined him with three other women—to Santos, always, "my girls"—on a clubbing trip to Miami where we stayed together in the three-bedroom guesthouse of the Star Island villa. The cab driver at the airport told me it was the fanciest neighborhood in town, a place where the celebrities and moguls live. The guesthouse was probably very nice on most days, but on this weekend it was a mess from transient girls and days of party detritus. The rent was typically $70,000 a week for the villa, but the bankers were paying an inflated price due to the electronic music festival that weekend.

Hannah, a part-time model, part-time Abercrombie clerk, and part of Santos's crew, looked shocked when she heard the bankers paid $50,000 to rent the villa just for the weekend: "Why? What's the point?"

The mortgage bankers didn't have an articulate explanation. A group of four of them regularly came to Miami with their boss, George, the founder of the mortgage bank. We would see George and his colleagues at nearby tables at the clubs, where George told me the table rent cost them $30,000 a night.

"But I didn't tell you that, you know, because I don't want to be the guy that spills out what's really going on."

"$30,000? That's a lot," I said. "And what's that buy you?"

"The best night of your life," he said with a sarcastic laugh. "Okay, not really the best night of your life. It buys you some champagne and vodka." That stuff is relatively cheap, as George knows, before the club adds its markup of 1,000 percent. But there is an experience to be had in these nights that George and his colleagues and Santos and his girls were all seeking.

"If you come, you gonna see," said Santos, about this VIP world. Santos said this often in the days leading up to our trip to Miami. And when I arrived at the first destination in what would become an eighteen-month-long tour through the elite global party circuit, from New York to Miami, the Hamptons, and the French Riviera, I found an intricate gendered economy of beauty, status, and money that promoters like Santos pieced together night and day.

Now, ears ringing, I sat by the pool typing up my notes from last night, thinking about my own weird tangle of enjoying access to this exclusive world of the rich and the beautiful, while also being repulsed by it. The late orange sun dipped behind the palm trees. Soon, Santos and the rest of his girls would wake up, and it would be time to get ready to go out again.

1

We Are the Cool People

Sunday, 11:30 p.m., New York City

Most people think that ostentation comes easy. Dre's life was testament to how much work it takes to get people to show off.

It was nearly midnight, and Dre's table was finishing dinner at the Downtown, a perfectly chic restaurant in SoHo. Dre was flanked on either side by half a dozen beautiful women, beautiful in the way that fashion models are: young and tall with flawless features, their clothes and high heels so stylish, they could have arrived straight from a catwalk. It is hard to look away when they enter the room.

The Downtown is a beautiful sight on Sunday nights. The decor is opulent: plush upholstered furniture, a mahogany bar, an enormous chandelier, and walls adorned with giant iconic prints from famous fashion photographers. There is no music, just the steady buzz of conversations in various European languages, punctuated by laughter and the clink of champagne glasses, immediately refilled by white-coated Italian waiters. Each table is anchored by wealthy men—celebrities and aristocrats, socialites from the gossip pages, actors and musicians and producers, entrepreneurs and bankers— dining in the company of beautiful women.

In the middle of it all was Dre's table. He held court, steering conversations, Bellinis, and plates of pasta among his guests. Whatever else he was doing, he was also always scanning the room to see who sees him, graciously doling out smiles and winks, and standing up to greet passing guests seamlessly in French or English, with two kisses on each cheek.

Dre was a thirty-eight-year-old black man with a gorgeous smile and a near-shaved head. He dressed in leather pants, a crisp white T-shirt, and a shiny new pair of limited-edition Adidas sneakers, a casual but clearly expensive look he called "rock-and-roll chic." He was one of the only black people in the place, where he casually bantered and joked with a mostly white crowd. Even as he charmed the rest of the restaurant, he was careful to keep some attention on the women at his table. He flirted with them and cuddled up to whomever was on his arm, which, for the next several months, would be me.

"I love the job of promoter, because look at all the beautiful girls I'm around," he said. "And some of them like me, which can cause problems." He winked at the woman sitting across from him. She smirked and shook her head.

Dre loved the attention. He had been hosting women in this restaurant every Sunday night for the past six years; before that, he worked in various clubs for three decades, starting in the early 1990s. In the nightlife business, Dre is known as an image promoter. This means he works freelance, contracting with multiple nightclubs and restaurants throughout the city to bring in a so-called "quality crowd," understood to consist of attractive women, rich men, celebrities, and other well-connected people. In theory, the crowd he brings in enhances the image of the club and, ultimately, attracts wealthy clients and their money. Each Sunday, the Downtown's management paid Dre a handsome fee, somewhere between $1,200 and $4,500, depending on the bar spend, from which he took home 25 percent for his five hours of work.

It is a dubious profession. Promoters are widely criticized as pimps and "model wranglers," for whom the fashion industry's surplus of underpaid newcomers, known as "girls," are easy pickings.[1]

Sometimes called "PRs" (as in "*PR*omoter") for short, these men are reviled by modeling agencies, and every few years they are the subject of high-profile exposés in the press.[2] At the center of their work is an uncomfortable reality: they are intermediaries in the profitable circulation of women and alcohol among rich men. Dre knew that his work was disreputable, but it was lucrative. He was making over $200,000 a year. Though his income paled in comparison to those of the rich men around him at night, he was confident that the gap would shrink. Working alongside this segment of the new global elite, he believed, would enable him to one day become one of them.

"Ça va?" he said to a passing gentleman in an expensive suit. Dre stood up to shake hands and speak a little; as he sat back down, he whispered in my ear, "That guy's from a Saudi family. A *billionaire*." He winked to a woman sitting at the bar, supposedly the princess of a small nation-state known for offshore banking. As another man approached the table, Dre whispered to me, "He's really rich, his family. Really rich." Dre gave him a playful shoulder punch and fist bump. "A girlfriend of mine asked if there are any hot guys here tonight," Dre offered, followed by a calculated pause. "I said yes when I saw you walk in!"

This is the elite in Dre's world. It's not the 1 percent, he told me, "but the 0.0001 percent. That's the crowd I want around me."

The women who flank Dre, like myself, only need to *look* rich, not to be rich. Thankfully so, since it's unlikely any of us could even pay tonight's dinner bill. Cocktails, plates of pasta, fresh veggies and salads, fish and steaks, and now desserts and espressos arrived without any of us checking the prices. At the Downtown, I know from my own furtive glances at the menu, one cocktail costs about $20. A salad with beets and goat cheese is $24. I ate dinner here a dozen times over the course of roughly eighteen months researching VIP parties, and I never paid for anything.

As "girls," our drinks and meals were comped; the endless plates and glasses came to us "compliments of the house." To host our table, Dre paid a tip to the wait staff, usually about 25 percent of the bill.

Each Sunday night, the Downtown forwent over $1,000 just for the pleasure of our company. But in the long run our presence generated far greater value to the Downtown, to the men who dine here, and to Dre himself.

Dre's guests tended to be women with fledgling careers in fashion modeling, or they were students, or looking for work in fields ranging from design to finance. The main criterion for sitting next to Dre was that you look beautiful. Indeed, earlier that afternoon, Dre had sent me two playful text messages ensuring that I looked the part: "Dress to impress, Ash," and then a few minutes later, "High Heels."

Or maybe they weren't so playful. He was full of compliments when women looked good, and icy when they didn't. He would turn his back toward women whose looks did not meet his standards—unless they were rich or important in some other way. Once he told a woman of average height, "Go stand over there," referring to a corner away from his table.

I often felt uneasy in these places and out with Dre, even then as I sat beside him in a new silky dress and four-inch heels. When Dre first agreed I could shadow him in clubs for sociology research, in 2011, I began carrying a hand-me-down Chanel handbag from the 1980s. The bag was a loaner from my sister, who had bought it on eBay for $200, and it was in bad shape. I bought leather patches from a shoe smith and glued them onto the worn-out corners; before long they started to peel off. I kept the bag tucked behind my back, displaying only the signature gold-and-black chain across my chair, playing dress-up with the 1 percent.

But I was not alone: Dre was also playing dress-up with the elite, albeit with far greater ease. He came from a suburban middle-class family in France, the second-generation son of a professional family from Algeria. He dropped out of law school in Paris to pursue a music career in Miami, and when that went bust, he waited tables. For a short stint he was homeless, something you would never have guessed then, as his conversations regularly showed off his connections and entrepreneurial potential. He always boasted about the five or six projects he had in the works—his career as a pop singer, his movie production company, branding for a tech company, the reality television show he was developing, the food shipping company "in Africa" (among the most vague of his ventures), the car service company. The list changed depending on the week, but his essential optimism was always the same. Dre described his business model for the car service as follows: "You start with one car. It becomes two. Then ten. That's the American way."

A typical text message from him, when I asked what he was up to on a given day, might read: "I am working on a major business deal! Wish me luck . . . Within 2 days top I'll know!! Millions of $ deal."

"I love nightlife," he was fond of saying. "You never know what's gonna happen." But like a lot of things with Dre, this was just talk.

Soon Dre ordered an espresso, as he always did, before inviting his guests upstairs to the nightclub. "Girls, what do you say we go upstairs for the party?"

Jenna, an unemployed blonde in her twenties searching for a job in finance, stood up with a sigh, and under her breath she mumbled, "Let's go dance for our dinner." Jenna rarely went out—she had met Dre a year earlier, when he had noticed the pretty college student on the street and stopped to introduce himself. Jenna didn't have many college friends, and she found Dre to be an interesting character, whom she would eventually consider a friend. Dre convinced her to come to the Downtown tonight to have a nice dinner for free. "You never know who you might meet," he said to her, a standard enticement among promoters to get a woman to come out with them. Jenna agreed, hoping to meet someone in finance that could help with her post-college job search.

The club upstairs was small and intimate like the restaurant, but darker, louder, and drunker. We repositioned ourselves around a banquette, a long, curved sofa adjacent to two small low tables brimming with bottles of Perrier-Jouët champagne, Belvedere vodka, carafes of orange juice and cranberry juice in silver ice buckets, and neat little stacks of glass tumblers. The table is right next to the DJ booth, where Dre played emcee to his weekly karaoke party. From 12 to 3 a.m., he sang, danced, and cajoled others to do the same, all to ensure the party had a good vibe. As the evening went on, the room turned sweltering hot, as more and more people crowded around the small tables. Women in high heels grew even taller as they perched on top of the sofas, and Dre poured bottomless glasses of champagne and vodka from his table. Models sang Russian pop songs and laughed, businessmen unbuttoned their tailored Italian dress shirts and pulled down their suspenders, and Dre wrestled the mic from an overly drunk "Brazillionaire." Through it all, people jumped up and down to the music. This was the Downtown's famed Sunday night party that Dre made happen every week.

While Dre was paid well for the night's work, his female guests, here and elsewhere, were not paid.[3] Instead they were *comped* in two senses of the word, with freebies of food and drinks, and with the compliment of being included in an exclusive world that did not otherwise welcome people with mediocre status or money, and that prized good looks. Most of the "girls" understood these terms of exchange, as I would learn in interviews with them, though they rarely discussed them when they were out.

Meanwhile, VIP establishments like the Downtown generate large profits. The Downtown is part of a global chain of restaurants in Manhattan, London, Hong Kong, and Dubai that pulls in well over $100 million a year. That's small change, however, compared to the fortunes of the Saudi princes, Russian oligarchs, and run-of-the-mill tech and finance giants who buy bottles here and at other exclusive clubs around the world.

"There's so much money in this room," Dre told me, smiling and shaking his head. He often gestured to me to take notice when a sparkler-lit bottle of Dom Pérignon champagne floated by, held high above the head of a scantily clad waitress. Each one cost about $495.

The bottle buyers were men from the global economic elite. A notoriously difficult population to study and even define, the "elite" here refers to people who command demonstrably large economic resources, irrespective of their influence or political power.[4] The VIP party circuit appeals to mostly young and new money for whom a $495 bottle at the Downtown is the equivalent of a Starbucks coffee for someone like middle-class Jenna, who was now standing nearby Dre's table, swaying listlessly to the music, eyes scanning the room.

Like most of Dre's girls, she usually stayed close to his table and only occasionally mingled about the room. After an hour, she left, not having found any job opportunities amid the loud music and flashing lights.

Everyone in this room has power. Some of it is fleeting—like women's beauty, a short-lived asset that gets them into the room, but not recognition as serious players once inside. Some of it is blunt financial capital, like that of the big spenders, whose sheer pecuniary might is put on full display for everyone to see, and sometimes to criticize. Some of it is convertible, like the promoters' connections to elites around the world. Rich in social capital, Dre could do anything and climb anywhere—or at least that's how it always seemed to him from his vantage point as emcee, concierge, jester, and sometime friend to the world's new global elite.

The New Gilded Age

Maybe you've passed by a nightclub at some point, noticed the long queue behind the velvet rope, and wondered what was going on inside, who gets in, and how. In the various earlier manifestations of New York City's nightclub scenes—be it the discotheques in the 1970s or the legendary downtown dance clubs of the mid-1990s like Palladium or Tunnel—the rules were basically the same. After paying a cover charge, all visitors shared the same space with anyone else who had $20 in their pocket that night, and everyone jostled together to get an overpriced drink at the bar.[5] Most clubs also featured a small, roped-off "VIP" section, where celebrities and friends of the owner could party in visible seclusion.

By the 1990s, the city was in the midst of a major transformation, from the urban blight that characterized downtown Manhattan throughout the 1970s and 1980s to a resurgence of economic investments and cultural growth. More clubs began opening as rates of violent crime fell and the volume of money in the city spiked. In the 2000s, nightlife and entertainment venues began to sprout up in the Meatpacking District. The formerly industrial neighborhood's giant warehouses underwent renovations by fashion agencies, art galleries, and club owners.[6] By the early 2000s, commercial rents in the Meatpacking District had risen to about $80 a square foot, triple what they were in the 1990s.[7]

While New York underwent its renaissance, the global distribution of wealth shifted toward the very top of the economic ladder. The share of money ballooned among the top 1 percent of wealth holders, such that by 2017, the richest 1 percent owned half of the world's wealth—a record level of $241 trillion. Within that top fraction, there emerged vast differences too.[8] The wealth share among the top 0.1 percent skyrocketed from 7 percent in 1979—a year when Studio 54 co-owner Steven Rubell famously refused to let in anyone without enough style—to 22 percent in 2012, when Dre was marveling at all the rich bankers and tycoons buying bottles around him.[9] Sometimes called the "superrich," the top 0.1 percent of families in America now own roughly the same share of wealth as the entire bottom 90 percent.[10] Ours is an era of wealth concentration as extreme as the 1920s, when Jay Gatsby's fabulous parties symbolized the excesses of the Gilded Age in *The Great Gatsby*.[11]

Not only is the share of wealth different; the source of it is, too. America's top 1 percent, for instance, holds nearly half of the nation's assets in the form of stocks and mutual funds.[12] Income is increasingly a source of wealth as well, for those working in the right industries. Sociologist Olivier Godechot has noted the rise of the "working rich," whose fortunes come from booming industries like finance, real estate, and technology, where incomes and bonuses can outpace investment gains among the wealthy.[13] As the financial industry's role in the economy grew, Wall Street workers' pay swelled, leaping sixfold since 1975, nearly twice as much as the increase in pay for the average American worker.[14] The average bonus for anyone working in financial securities in the late 1980s was around $13,000. By 2006, just before the Great Recession hit, it was $191,360.[15] That year at Merrill Lynch, a twenty-something analyst with a base salary of $130,000 collected a bonus of $250,000. A thirty-something trader with a $180,000 salary got $5 million.[16]

Against this backdrop of rising financial fortunes, downtown Manhattan was transforming, as new luxury leisure services emerged to cater to the newly rich. As the amount of money on Wall Street shot up with each passing year, in came more young financiers with huge pools of disposable money who could afford a thousand-dollar bar tab.

New York had long been a destination for moneyed consumers, but as globalization and local policies expanded the city's key economic drivers—finance, real estate, insurance—it became a destination for international millionaires, affluent tourists, and rich businessmen.[17] By the time the financial crisis hit, in 2008, the Meatpacking District had become a millionaire's playground. Posh clubs, designer boutiques, famous galleries, and upscale restaurants and hotels had popped up on seemingly every corner.[18]

Perhaps it was inevitable, then, that amid this surge of wealth, club owners began to approach their spaces like real estate. With increasing rents, operating a huge club on door and drink prices couldn't turn a profit like it used to. The dance floor and the crowded area by the bar remained the same, open to whoever was willing to pay the cover charge and high drinks prices. But the real profits of a club now came from individual tables, which club owners started to "rent" to people with money, who would pay for the right to occupy one for a few hours. After some negotiation at the door—concerning their required minimum spend, for instance—table customers get whisked behind the velvet rope and led to their table. Some clients make reservations to secure a table in advance, while others simply lay down the right credit card at the door to signal their seriousness about spending. Bottles of alcohol are brought to them, and they can serve themselves from their own private space in the club. Everyone else has to stand at the bar and get jostled.

Table service had been the norm in the 1980s at select clubs in Paris, where New York club owners first saw it; in the 1990s they imported it to New York as a way to expedite serving drinks. The club Marquee on Tenth Avenue in Manhattan is often attributed with pioneering bottle culture by hiring image promoters to bring models to attract spenders.[19] Marquee was launched in 2003 by two former promoters, Jason Strauss and Noah Tepperberg, in a 5,000-square-foot former garage. The lounge area adjacent to the dance floor featured thirty-six tables, with couches, ottomans, and banquette sofa seating. Promoters occupied about a third of those tables, which were strategically located throughout the room, placed in the corners and next to big spenders, giving guests the impression they were surrounded by models.

Clubs had long used "mass promoters" to mobilize high volumes of people, at least fifty and usually a mix of men and women, who might get discounted entry or drink tickets. Mass promoters keep a club from looking empty, but they don't attend to the minutiae of looks. Image promoters, by contrast, focus their efforts on "quality" over quantity in terms of the female bodies they bring, so that clubs can attract big spenders. The business model of image hosting is simple: "Let in ten groups for free so fifty will pay," as one manager put it.

In most clubs, tables are placed between the dance floor and the walls of the room, with a bar to one side and the DJ booth usually elevated above the dance floor. Below is a graphic of the interior layout of a typical high-end club in Manhattan's Meatpacking District. This club is on the small side, with a capacity of three hundred people. To sit at a table here, the minimum spend on a Friday night is $1,000. Of the seventeen tables at this club, anywhere between four and eight—between a quarter and a half—will be occupied by a promoter (or team of promoters), each with anywhere from five to fifteen beautiful girls. The owner sometimes also has a table reserved for himself and his guests, often also models or celebrities. Less economically and symbolically important persons, called "filler," order their drinks standing at the bar.

The "table" is an area consisting of a banquette sofa on which a group may sit, or more likely stand, and even dance, and several low tables on which the bottles, buckets of ice, and glasses rest. A table like the one shown in figure 2 typically holds ten to fifteen people; on a crowded night, people may climb onto the sofa's upper back or spill over into nearby tables and the dance floor.

Inside the VIP Club

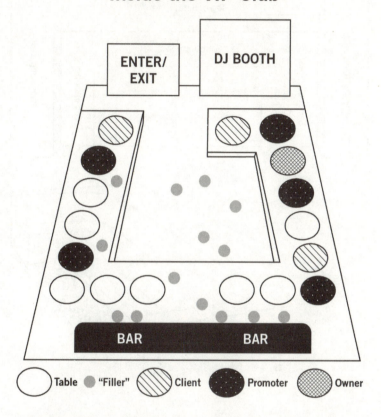

Inside a New York VIP club with a legal capacity of three hundred people and seventeen tables. On any given weekend night, the club can expect between three and five clients to purchase tables; they will hire between four and five promoters to host tables strategically placed throughout the room, with "fillers" on the dance floor and at the bar.

FIGURE 1. Inside the VIP Club

At first, bottle service was a convenience, a way for people who had money to avoid waiting at the bar, but it quickly escalated into a luxury experience. Over the course of the 2000s, prices on bottles soared and clubs began to encourage spending sprees, setting the stage for a new kind of publicly visible "very important person"

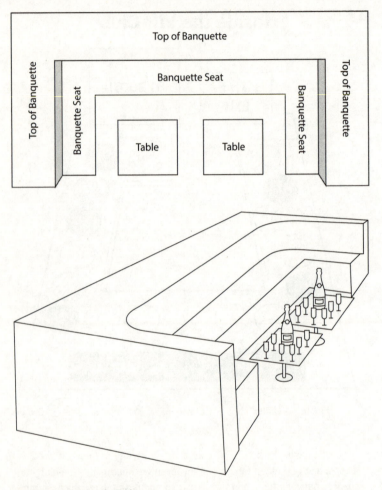

FIGURE 2A AND 2B. At the Table

to show off.[20] When the first bottle service appeared in New York clubs, in the early 1990s, a bottle of vodka cost about $90. By the early 2000s, prices were up to $500 for a bottle of Grey Goose vodka (which retailed for around $30 at the time, a markup of more than a thousand percent).[21] A few years ago, at Double Seven, a 2,400-square-foot space with a capacity of 175 on Gansevoort Street, the average tab for table service was "only" $2,500.[22]

Bottles started arriving at tables with sparkler fireworks taped to their necks; soon you could order champagne bottles up to six liters big; eventually gold-plated and diamond-encrusted bottles appeared on some menus. Within the velvet ropes of Provocateur, a 7,000-square-foot club at the front of the Hotel Gansevoort, on Eighth Avenue in Manhattan, a six-liter bottle of Cristal champagne went for $40,000. With such high prices, some lamented that clubbing had become exclusively for the rich, to the point of being boring; some club owners complained that bottle service had ruined nightlife and predicted that the practice would soon die.[23] Riding the growing popularity of electronic dance music (EDM), club owners have opened larger spaces to host superstar DJs such as AfroJack and Tiësto, whose nightly fees reach six figures. While large EDM-focused clubs charge tickets to a large mass of entrants, a large share of their profits still come from price-inflated bottles of alcohol bought by VIPs.[24]

The city, and especially the city at night, is "where the action is," as sociologist Erving Goffman described it. Today's clubs are the latest in a long line of urban entertainment: first the opera and the penny arcade and the promenade, then the bar, the speakeasy, and the club.[25] In all of these modern urban leisure spaces, there is an endless sense of possibility, the potential for unknown thrills and pleasures in the company of strangers. In the taxi dance halls of the 1930s, working-class men could hire a woman for a ninety-second dance for ten cents; sociologist Paul Cressey observed that the dance hall was just one of many wondrous leisure places in the modern city built to satisfy the human need for stimulation.[26] City dwellers, increasingly drawn away from home into new commercial spaces, have always gone out in search of excitement.

The bottle service club today pitches Goffman's "action" to the world's new elite; it encourages the rich to flaunt their riches, to display wealth for display's sake. Bottle service clubs are predicated on *conspicuous consumption*, a term coined, in 1899, by Thorstein Veblen, the quirky Norwegian American economist. Writing in the Gilded Age, a time of vast economic inequality, Veblen viewed consumption as a competition for social status.[27] He argued that the nouveau riche, lacking prestigious titles enjoyed by "old money," attempted to gain status by flaunting their leisurely pursuits, to indicate that they did not have to work for their money. For instance, Veblen observed, among the rich, a high-class wife has delicate hands and impractical dress to indicate that she is both useless and expensive, a testament to her husband's success. The displays of this "leisure class" were often attempts to outdo one another in a never-ending show of wealth, or "pecuniary emulation"; beneath this extravagance, however, lay deep anxieties about the uncertainty of their status relative to the titled, aristocratic elite.

Today's nouveau riche differ from Veblen's leisure class in at least one important respect. Since the boom of finance-driven salaries catapulted the "working rich" to the top of the income ladder in the 1990s, there has emerged an *inverse relationship* between leisure and earnings, such that elites now have less leisure time than their poorer, less-educated counterparts.[28] With demanding work schedules in industries like finance, the working rich in the United States now work more hours and spend less time on leisure than Veblen's leisure class. Most of the clients I met in bottle service clubs extolled the virtues of their hard work and were proud of the long hours they logged at their jobs. Particularly important to their self-presentation was a conviction that they deserved the occasional breaks that clubbing afforded: they work hard, they said, so they play hard.

VIP clubs offer a stage for this hard-working leisure class to play out conspicuous consumption, and this form of display has spread to cities around the world.[29] The celebration of money in nightclubs also crosses racial lines; hardly a practice of preppy white Wall Street guys alone, the consumption of high-end champagne in clubs is a common reference in rap and hip-hop. Famously, Jay Z initially praised Cristal, until Frédéric Rouzaud, managing director of the champagne house Louis Roederer, publicly fretted over the luxury company's association with a "bling lifestyle," prompting the rapper to boycott the brand and promote his own gold-bottled champagne known as Ace of Spades, now also a fixture on menus in the high-end club scene. The global popularity of hip-hop has meant that its celebrations of extravagant consumption have spread around the world, widely embraced by urban youth culture from London to Abidjan, Côte d'Ivoire.[30]

Even during and after the global financial crisis, displays of excess and ostentation continued among the world's superrich, for whom the recession had little effect on luxury spending.[31] In 2012, Wall Street elites threw a lavish annual party in Manhattan's Four Seasons hotel with parodies making fun of the financial crisis, including a drag performance set to Abba's "Dancing Queen" called "Bailout King."[32] Promoters like Dre weren't part of the superrich, but they felt that they shared their financial immunity. As Dre put it during the economic recovery: "We are fine. There's no recession." Then he filled my champagne glass and turned his attention to the girl on the other side of him. The unemployment rate in the United States at the time was about 10 percent.

Most people, including Veblen, imagined ostentation was an inherent trait of the rich. I found, however, that it takes considerable coordinated effort to mobilize people into what looks likes the spontaneous waste of money, and the VIP nightclub has mastered it. The tables inside a VIP club are carefully curated and controlled. Even though this scene looks like the life of the party, it is the outcome of tremendous backstage labors—the unseen work that makes conspicuous consumption possible. It begins, like all good performances, with the right audience and the right staging.

Models and Bottles

In essence, the promoter's job is to stage a show of two types of power—wealth and beauty—embodied in the form of rich men and girls, respectively.

"Each night is a production," one promoter told me, likening his work to that of casting a theater production. "That's why there's so many players that put it together. . . . It's a show. It's a production. You're the cast," he said, pointing to me. "I'm the casting director. We all play our part."

The wealthy spenders at every VIP club, everywhere in the world, are almost always heterosexual men. Occasionally a woman comes through the scene and buys bottles, but women are the exception in this male-dominated world of sex and money.

The most central ingredient in the success of the club and the promoter's livelihood are "girls." A "girl" is a social category of woman recognized as so highly valuable that she has the potential to designate a space as "very important." While most nightclubs want more women than men inside as a matter of security, the quantity of women does not alone suffice to distinguish a place as VIP.[33] To be VIP, a club needs a high quantity of so-called "quality" women. These are the girls: they are young (typically sixteen to twenty-five years old), thin, and tall (at least five feet nine without heels and over six feet with them).[34] They are typically though not exclusively white, owing to the dominant preference for white women among both elite men and the fashion industry.

The most obvious physical features of the girls—beauty, height, and body shape—take primacy over their personalities or other embodied cues of class such as accent or charm, especially given the low lighting and loud music common at nearly every club, as Eleanor, a white twenty-two-year-old fashion intern who spent most of her nights out in the Meatpacking District, explained: "It's all about how you look, how thin you are, how tall you are. It's all that matters. You could have a horrible personality, and you'll get into the club if you're five nine . . . Basically, the promoters will come and find attractive girls, and tell you to bring friends that are attractive, skinny, tall, you know. And they'll bring you out, and you don't have to pay for anything."

Women in possession of this bodily capital are treated to free nights out in expensive restaurants and clubs around the world, regardless of their financial means, education, or personal qualities.

But not all girls are equally valuable. At the top of a clear hierarchy of girls are fashion models.

"Oh, no, models in New York City are, like—how can I compare them?" Eleanor continued, "I'm not gonna say they're like the royals of England, but I guess—it's not power—but *the praise* they get, is unlike anything I've ever seen in my life."

Exploiting our fundamental human assumption that the more attractive you are, the higher your social status is, clubs and their promoters want beautiful women of a specifically rare sort: fashion models.[35] Or at least women who look like they could be models. Promoters and club owners prefer "real" models—those signed with a big agency—to "Instagram models," or models represented by small, unknown agencies. Of course, a famous model is the best, one that everyone will recognize from magazines and billboards. A promoter couldn't really do any better than bringing Victoria's Secret models, for they are considered the hottest, that is, physically attractive, and the coolest, because of their high symbolic status.

In this field, the model possesses symbolic capital, a particular kind of power that field insiders can immediately recognize.[36] The model connotes the fashion industry's high status and elevates the status of a space and that of all the people around her. Sometimes the bottle service formula is not-so-jokingly referred to as "models and bottles." Explained Claude, twenty-seven, a white male from France and a promoter for four years:

> It is the quality of the woman. It's the perfect thing. It's just so beautiful to see and watch. A model is a model. She goes into a club, and she's, like, *flashlight*. She's here, you know. And the guys next to her, they'll be like, "Damn, this club is hot. Get me another bottle."

As an ironic statement on the importance of models to the industry, one promoter printed "I hate models," embossed in gold, on the back of his business cards; in reality, his business is built on the adoration of models. Most promoters aim to bring at least five beautiful girls to whichever club hires them that night, but ideally promoters will bring between ten and fifteen each. Since every high-end club hires a handful of image promoters each night, this creates serious competition for any given promoter to find models, befriend them, and get them to come out night after night. If promoters get it wrong—if their girls are not beautiful enough or are too few in number—they'll get reprimanded by club managers. They could even get fired.

After authentic models, the next best thing is a woman who looks like she could be a model, a "good civilian." In addition to beauty, she has the two most important bodily cues that signal high status: height and slenderness. Malcolm, a twenty-nine-year-old black promoter in the business for eight years, defined a good civilian as a woman who is maybe a little thicker or shorter than a model, "but you bring her to the club, she look all right." She is "modelesque": not quite the real thing, but close enough.

Below good civilians are just plain "civilians," language that in the military designates people who do not belong in the field. Neither pretty nor wealthy enough, they are largely invisible in this economy. Sometimes they are called "pedestrians"—the ordinary and hence relatively worthless types include, well, pretty much every woman who looks to be above the age of thirty, under five feet seven, and/ or larger than a dress size six.

How do promoters and patrons even see these fine-grained distinctions among girls? One might think that in the context of a nightclub, where the lights are low and shapes are blurred, the slight differences between models and good civilians would not matter. Yet there is a palpable difference between "just a hot girl" and a model, a difference that promoters, clients, and club managers can see. Vanna herself a working model and one of the few women in the business of promotions, could easily spot a working model: "It's the way she carries herself. The way she dresses." Former New York club owner Steve Lewis told me that "only really sophisticated people can tell the difference between models and hot girls." One promoter, twenty-seven-year-old Ethan from New York, likened the difference between them to buying real Chanel and Prada couture, versus the knockoffs on Canal Street. The goods appear more or less identical to the untrained eyes of the average person, but Ethan's clients are not average. "Someone spending $15,000 a night in a nightclub wants the real thing," he said. "Just the peace of mind that he is now part of that A-list, that social elite. I think that is what the actual difference is."

Beautiful women justify the bill. Or rather, they are a part of what it covers. As any business manager knows, women's beauty can change the mood of a place to incentivize spending.[37] Explained Brook, a promoter and an assistant to the doorman at one exclusive club: "So when the guys look around, they're like, 'Oh, shit. I just dropped my last quarter bonus in one night. It's because I'm in a room with the most gorgeous people I've ever seen in my life.'" Clients are less likely to spend if they are surrounded by mere civilians. Promoters have seen clients arrive at a club teeming with "pedestrians," take stock of the crowd, and leave for another club. One club during my fieldwork even hired a handful of "table girls," underemployed models, at about $100 per night, just to stand at the bar, awaiting invitations to sit and drink at clients' tables if requested by managers, who brokered the invitations.

Like many people whose value is based on "bodily capital," models are young and their careers are short; they start as early as age thirteen and peak by their mid-twenties.[38] A lot of girls in the VIP scene meet the legal definition of underage. Many of the girls that I met out were younger than the legal drinking age in the United States, twenty-one, and some were not even eighteen, the legal drinking age in Europe. Twenty-year-old Katia had no problem getting past security; she would just flash her credit card as if it were an ID card and get waved in. Hannah, a nineteen-year-old part-time model, once flashed the driver's license of a promoter, a large black man; Hannah is thin and white. "The bouncer could barely keep a straight face," she said, laughing. On nights that are likely to be heavily policed, or if the club has been tipped off to potential police visits, underage girls won't get in. But most nights the girls breeze through the door, business as usual, with barely a nod from the bouncer.

Other "girls" are nowhere near the age of girlhood, but the term still applies. People inside clubs were shocked when I told them that my true age at the time of my research for this book was thirty-one or thirty-two. I looked younger so I could pass, but it was shocking to them that an adult woman, with a career or a family, would be out with a promoter. There are certainly older women in this scene, such as guests and friends of male spenders, and occasionally there are even women clients who buy bottles. But they are far less visible or important than the girls.

Everything in this economy revolves around girls: How good the club is. How good the promoter is. How much money he can make. How much wealth and power the clients are perceived to have. And how much money they will spend.

For the duration of my time as a girl (and indeed, for several years before and after), Club X (not its real name) was widely recognized as one of the top clubbing spots in the New York exclusive club scene, where $1,000 bottles were regularly purchased. Said Trevor, a nineteen-year-old promoter new to the scene, trying to identify why other clubs weren't as good:

> Other clubs don't have the quality crowd, the girls are a little bit shorter, a little bit heavier. And I don't like that. At Club X, there'll be some shorter and some thicker women there but it's because they're there with men who are spending money.

"Girls" play a central role in elite men's pursuit of status and wealth. Sometimes, the girls at promoters' tables dance excitedly on top of the sofas and tables, or they mingle about the room in search of flirtatious encounters, or they just sit there, forming a visual backdrop to the club's high-status decor. Simply by being there and looking beautiful, they generate enormous value for the club industry, the individual men operating within it, and the larger urban economy of New York City. Their value emerges from the very specific conditions in which they are seen. Most importantly, these "girls" exist in an altogether different social category from women. And because I want readers to experience this difference, I strategically use the term "girl" from here on without quotation marks to refer to this category of women in the VIP arena. Because in this rarefied world there is an unspoken but widely understood logic: girls are valuable; women are not.

Face Control

The greater the exclusivity, the higher the desirability of the club. Door personnel screen carefully to make sure that only the right people—either beautiful or rich—get inside. In Russia, they are called "face control," and that's basically their job in New York, too. One club owner described his door as similar to the "Fort Knox experience."[39] He meant that as a selling point.

Unattractive women, in particular, are carefully screened out.

For a promoter, the worst possible embarrassment is when a doorman turns away someone in the group that he has assembled. Girls' constant requests to bring their friends are the bane of the promoter's work, since girls are never as discerning about their friends' looks as the club world is. The promoter Ethan recounted a recent incident, when one of his girls brought a friend who didn't have the right look, because she was heavier and not as pretty as a model. Ethan was squirming in his chair during our interview as he explained how the scene unfolded: "I've gotta, like, kind of, like, pull my hat below my eyes when the doorman is like, 'No, that fat bitch can't come in here.' I'm like, '*Argh*, that's so embarrassing! Can you be a little politer?'"

Then there was that time at a top Manhattan club when, as Ethan's girls were getting in, the doorman called out one of his girls for her toes, which poked out over the edge of her high-heeled sandals. Ethan tells the story partially laughing and again partially squirming: "The doorman called her out on it so bad. Like, she was already half-way in. He was like, 'No. Look at your toes. Like, what is going on? They're hawking over your shoes. Get out of here.'"

Doormen can be ruthless in their assessment of women. Marley, a black Venezuelan man promoting since 2007, remembered: "Oh yeah, some of them are horrible. I brought a girl, she's a friend of mine. The doorman was like, 'Marley, what the fuck is this shit? Don't bring this fat fucking girl here.'" The doorman eventually let them pass, but Marley's friend ended up crying.

"It was horrible," he says. "I'm like, man, tell me after, you know. Don't tell it in front of her face. And he knows I am always there with quality and it's just this one time, but he doesn't want that inside."

To avoid embarrassing ordeals at the door, potential customers frequently make the decision to go to less exclusive places when they are in the company of women who don't look like models. "Sadly," said one client, himself a big spender, about Club X, "[They] don't care how much money you have. If a girl doesn't fit their look, like, it's not happening." This was especially the case at Club X, which had a strict door policy that specifically targeted women's appearance. Once I invited a girlfriend, a model who was five feet ten, to Club X with me, and the door person remarked about her shoes, "Sorry, we don't really do flats here." Other clubs in the city are less restrictive and hence, less exclusive; here tables of mixed-sex groups of rich civilians, including women of various looks, are common. But Club X had built its reputation, and achieved its status, on the harsh assessment of women's bodies.

Door personnel quickly assess a person's status by sizing up physique, beauty, race, accent, clothes, watch, dress, even handbag. Red-soled Louboutin heels signal high status, but if the girl wearing them stands below five feet seven, matching the height of the "door girl" stationed at one club, she is not allowed inside. Especially if she's a person of color.

The VIP space is a racially exclusive environment. Even if hip-hop is frequently played inside VIP clubs, on most nights out I could count on both hands the number of black and brown people present, not counting the service workers. Promoters know not to fill their table with too many women of color—a couple of black, brown, and Asian girls are fine, but the majority of tables host white bodies, and deliberately so.

Some of the clients that I interviewed, too, were subject to race-based discrimination. On one egregious occasion, a handsome French Middle Eastern man with a lot of inherited wealth and connections was out with his white male friend, to whom the "door girl" leaned in and whispered, "Your friend can't come in unless you go inside and bring out a brown person he can replace. There's too many brown people inside already."

Such outright discriminatory remarks were rare, however, because for the most part nonwhite bodies are implicitly denied on the basis of the quality of their looks. With alarming frequency, such "velvet rope racism" prohibits nonwhites from entering. But unlike its Jim Crow predecessor, this is a softer form of race-based discrimination that articulates race in terms of beauty, status, and "quality." Clubs are careful to admit the right number of exceptions to conceal racial bias, making it much harder to legally prosecute.[40] In this way, the clubs cater mostly to white clientele and appeal to them with the bodies of mostly white girls. The dominance of whiteness is surprising in such a global scene, where we should expect its decline, both symbolically and materially, as the share of wealth continues to grow among nonwhites and non-Westerners. Perhaps because the VIP circuit I followed was rooted in the New York scene, and hence tied to American racial politics, white supremacy remained strong even as big spenders from Arab and Asian backgrounds made frequent appearances.[41]

Yet as much as nonwhiteness lowers the status of a potential entrant in the eyes of the door person, for girls, beauty can override it: a black fashion model, a real model, will always be welcome. A white girl of short stature or large size, on the other hand, will be told that tonight is a "private party" and she cannot come in. Or, perhaps, she will be insulted to her face.

Short women are regularly called "midgets," and heavier women are dismissed as liabilities for the club's prestige and the promoters' reputations. To describe a club that was perceived as lower quality, one promoter flatly stated, "The girls were fat." Another promoter said in our interview, "I will use the term *muppets* or *hobbits* to describe the, like, less-than fortunate-looking girls." Another referred to the women at a nearby table as "ugly dogs."

Midget. Troll. Elf. Hideous. Disaster. Monster.

These are words club personnel use to describe women who do not meet their physical criteria. Their bodies are seen as worthless and contaminating. Their presence is perceived as draining value from the club, its management, the promoters, and their reputations. They lower the quality of the crowd, the fun of the night, and its economic potential. They are fiercely excluded.

Ask a doorman to make an exception just this one time, to let in a girl of perceived lower quality, and you will likely hear this retort: "If we let her in, you won't want to come here anymore."

Hierarchies of Men

Any club, whether in a New York City basement or on a Saint-Tropez beach, is always shaped by a clear hierarchy. Fashion models signal the "A-list," but girls are only half of the business model. There are a few different categories of men that every club owner wants inside, and there is a much larger category of men that they aim to keep out.

The most valuable in this hierarchy of men is the *whale*, a term you might know from casinos and speculative finance. Whales can drop huge sums of money from their vast riches, sometimes over a hundred thousand dollars in a single night. Their reputation is legendary in nightlife.

The biggest whale at the time of my fieldwork was a Malaysian financier known as Jho Low, a name I heard often as soon as I entered the club world. Said one twenty-nine-year-old promoter, drawing on hearsay as much as established fact:

> There's—what's his name—Jho Low, who spends throughout the world a million dollars a night just for the kick of it, just because he can afford it . . . He's Asian, I think he's from Korea. He's making a shit ton of money, so wherever he goes he spends a million dollars and laughs at everyone. Like everyone is underneath him. The guy's like twenty-six years old.

Another promoter, a twenty-three-year-old recent college graduate, spoke of Jho Low with both admiration and ridicule:

> The last time I was out and I saw Jho Low, he bought a bottle of Patron [tequila] for every table at Club L. He spent over a hundred thousand dollars that night. And the guy doesn't give a shit. He doesn't even talk to the girls. He just sits in the back and drinks a beer. He just wants to party—he wants to be like, "Yeah, I did that." It's crazy.

Low Taek Jho was in fact a thirty-year-old financial investor from Malaysia involved in multiple real estate and business ventures in Manhattan and the Middle East. Low did indeed spend hundreds of thousands, even millions, per night at clubs and in private parties with celebrities, and he was even an investor in the 2013 Martin Scorsese film, *The Wolf of Wall Street*. The source of his money was often unclear to those who partied with him; one promoter thought he was an arms dealer, and another believed he was a contractor for governments' construction projects. It turns out that Low was a consultant on the state-owned investment fund 1Malaysia Development Berhad, which was eventually mired in corruption charges.[42] Indeed, at the time of writing, Low had gone into hiding, wanted for laundering billions of dollars from Malaysian investors into private hands. Low is now a fugitive, and the US government has confiscated millions of dollars from his illegal spending spree, including a Picasso he gifted to Leonardo DiCaprio and diamonds to supermodel Miranda Kerr.[43]

But for all the talk about Low, whales of his magnitude are rare. One industry insider said to the press, "A Jho Low comes around once in a lifetime."[44] Though their visits were infrequent, whales drive a lot of the action in the club and they fuel stories of excess, luxury, and excitement, stories that are essential to the club's allure. Whales raise the possibility that you, too, might witness a grand display of wealth tonight.

After whales, club owners hope to attract celebrities, another class of highly valued clients. Sometimes celebrities buy expensive bottles, part of the show of excess that will likely make it into the press, but usually they are comped, since their mere presence adds value to the club. Some celebrities even get paid to make appearances in clubs, notably Paris Hilton, a pioneer in paid club appearances who created her own celebrity through the VIP scene, which she then aggressively monetized.[45]

While exciting, whales and celebrities don't account for the bulk of clubs' profits; they are too rare. Furthermore, very rich men who could spend huge sums are regularly invited to party free of charge, even if they aren't celebrities. An elaborate informal system of prices marks who is important enough to be among the VIPs, and who is actually "very" important. Prices are negotiable, contingent upon the spender's social status; some men pay reduced prices for tables, and some are comped automatically because of their status. In fact, the men with the most riches, either in terms of their social connections, symbolic value, or financial worth, are often comped drinks on the house. One self-described Brazillionaire explained why he rarely paid for drinks in any Meatpacking District club that knew who he was: "They think I'll give something back," such as investing in the owner's next bar or club venture, or holding his next big (and lucrative) birthday party at that establishment.

Free things are a clear marker of status in the VIP world. Free entry, drinks, and dinners signal recognition of a person's social worth.[46] "I always said, in nightlife it's not what you spend, it's what you get for free. That's real power," said Malcolm, the promoter I followed in New York and Miami. "You got a lot of money and you spend a lot, of course you get respect. But if you don't spend a dime, that's power."

Most clubs make the bulk of their profits from smaller and more reliable table bills, the $1,500 to $3,000 sums spent by groups of affluent tourists and businessmen—your run-of-the-mill banker, tech developer, or other upper-class professional with a disposable income. While on the lower end of importance compared to whales and celebrities, they are central to the VIP scene; in fact, they bankroll it. They regularly run up high-volume tabs because they, too, want to be close to power and beauty. Unlike celebrities and higher-status VIPs, these men always pay.

Duke, a former club owner and now a real estate magnate in downtown New York, calls these people *mooks*: "You know, a mook. Someone who doesn't know what's going on . . . It's the dentists that come in and buy the tables, thinking they're in the company of the cool people, and the beautiful people." Dentists with their own practice in New York, I should note, make considerably higher incomes than the national average. But such high-earning professionals are not nearly as exciting as the people at promoters' tables.

One night at Dre's table at the Downtown, a well-known music producer named Jimmy poured our free glasses of champagne. Himself a minor celebrity, he scanned the crowd around him and observed how the Downtown was filling up with rich men, some of them accompanying "women with a lot of plastic surgery," and a lot of girls. He explained, "You only get in if you're really rich or really cool. That's why we drink for free. They sell tables to really rich people who can say they were here with the cool people."

He added, "And we're the cool people."

Jimmy is actually quite ordinary-looking: short and balding, he wore basic jeans and a dress shirt. Dre can't invite unattractive people to his table unless they are very important in some other way. By virtue of his sitting at Dre's table, everyone else will know that Jimmy is valuable; after all, he's surrounded by striking tall white fashion models.

"If you're not good-looking, you have to be somebody," in Dre's calculus. "Everybody brings something to the table. Everybody that gets in has something we want."

At the bottom of the hierarchy is a category of men without connections or money who cannot afford even modest table rents, but they might still have something of value to offer the club. Called "fillers," these men keep the place from looking empty. They look cool enough, and have enough "cultural capital" to be allowed in, but they have to stand at the bar and jostle for their drinks like everyone did in the old clubbing formula.[47]

And then you have the "bridge and tunnel" crowd, people who might have some money, maybe even enough to buy a table, but don't have the right look. To the bouncer of a VIP club, they look like outsiders, people from Staten Island or Queens, who lack the right cultural sense to live on the island of Manhattan. If you give off class-coded cues that make you look like you traveled by bridge or tunnel to the Meatpacking District, you are unwelcome upon arrival. Mike, a twenty-three-year-old promoter who has sometimes worked as a doorman, will call you a "goon," like a comic villain. He described an encounter with one at the door:

> He was a straight-up goon. He was, like, baggy suit, his shirt was all wrinkly, his hair wasn't combed. I was like, why the fuck am I gonna let this kid in here? He has nothing to add. He's not gonna add anything to the room. Like, he's not gonna make it look better.

Also at the bottom of the hierarchy is what Dre called the "ghetto crowd, scary crowd," invoking stereotypes that link the lower classes, criminality, and nonwhite people. Plenty of clubs in New York cater to this crowd, and while they make money in the short term, Dre would never step foot in these clubs. "You can make a ton of money with them," on inflated prices on bottles, "but they are carrying a piece [a gun]. They start shooting and will fight. It's dangerous, scary people." Himself a black man, Dre took pains to distance himself from other black people, whom he understood were stereotyped as lower class, and who therefore posed liabilities for his reputation.

Bridge and tunnel, goons, and ghetto. These are men whose money can't compensate for their perceived status inadequacies. The marks of their marginal class positions are written on their bodies, flagging an automatic reject at the door.

A clever man can try to use models as leverage to gain entry and discounts at clubs. A man surrounded by models will not have to spend as much on bottles. I interviewed clients who talked explicitly about girls as bargaining chips they could use at the door. For instance, Rhys, a wealthy financier and regular Club X visitor, considers that five finance guys in suits, "if they are older and if they are uglier," will have to pay the table minimum, say $2,000, to get in; it's like paying a tax on their own low-status bodies. On the other hand, Rhys reasons, two "decent-looking guys with three or four models" will be welcomed inside with no hassles, and no required minimum to spend. They can stand on the dance floor and order drinks at the bar, as fillers, avoiding the hefty table rent.

Men familiar with the scene make these calculations even if they have money to spend: How many beautiful girls can I get to offset how I look? How many beautiful girls will it take to offset the men with me? How much money am I willing to spend for the night in the absence of quality girls?

How deeply stamped in our bodies is the status structure of a society. You can actually see this hierarchy just by scanning a room like the Downtown, which depicts a topography of embodied statuses everywhere you look. Bouncers, or security personnel, are large black men nearly always dressed in black; they are emblems of physical power but not social status. The busboys who carry trays of empty bottles and glasses are short and brown-skinned Latinos, between five feet three and five feet five tall. Wearing plain black uniforms, they weave through the crowd carrying trays, mops, and glasses almost sight unseen. In the space they are "non-persons," as Goffman would call them.[48] Sometimes they hold flashlights above their heads so you know they are coming through, but you can hardly see the body beneath the light, a contrast to the sparkling bottle of champagne illuminating the tall, stiletto-clad girls. Cocktail wait-resses, called "bottle girls," are tall, voluptuous, and relatively racially diverse, their dresses as tight and revealing as their heels are high; they stand for sex and, according to guys like Dre, they are as much for sale as the bottles they carry.[49] Unlike the seemingly available bottle girl, the fashion model represents not sex but beauty—a prize of far greater status. While everyone else—bouncer, busboy, filler, and even the bottle girl, except when needed—tends to fade into the background, the model is meant to stand out. Tables for models are reserved in highly visible areas of clubs and restaurants, and every-one in nightlife wants to be seen with them.

It is common sense that whales only go to clubs with a high-quality crowd. Promoters are also incentivized to bring in men who buy bottles, sometimes called "bottle clients," for which they receive a commission of 10–20 percent on their drink purchases, which the managers pay to promoters either in paychecks at the end of each week or nightly in cash, depending on their arrange-ment with the club. Sampson, a twenty-seven-year-old promoter in New York for the preceding three years, put the commission sums in perspective like this, "If a guy spends $20,000, that pays my rent. In one night."

To be clear, to refer to a "high-quality crowd" is first and foremost to refer to the quality of its girls: that is, to a crowd full of models or women who look like models. Girls determine hierarchies of clubs, the quality of people inside, and how much money is spent. Their presence or absence has other important effects for certain men in the VIP party scene—girls make or break, especially, the reputations of promoters.

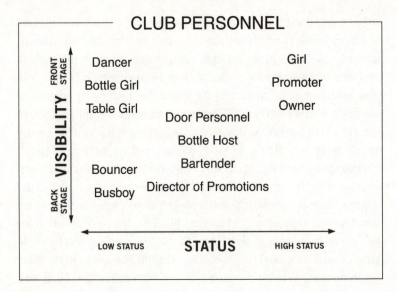

FIGURE 3. Club Personnel

With a consistently high volume of high-quality girls—between five and ten, say—promoters like Dre could demand as much as $1,000 a night. But the kind of symbolic value girls lent to promoters made models seem priceless. When Dre began promoting at Club X, he boasted about it often. In his view, if a promoter worked with Club X, all the other clubs would want him. When Dre got wind that Celia, a rival and one of the few women promoters in the scene, was claiming to work at Club X too, he mocked her. Celia's quality of girls was too poor, said Dre, because she brought mostly good civilians, not models. "I can bring one girl to a party and [get] more than what Celia will get for twenty girls. It's the reputation, you see."

Without models, promoters like Celia could get between $300 and $600 a night, depending on the quality and quantity of their girls, and these criteria are assessed over the course of the night as managers cruise through the club; promoters are only paid at the end of the night. A promoter makes constant loose calculations based on quality and quantity: if he has real models, he only needs four or five of them to have a quality crowd. If he only has good civilians for the night, he will need to roughly double that amount. If he has one bad civilian, he might be able to "hide" her among plenty of high-quality girls, and so on.

Promoters can't get respect in this world without models. "It's crazy," said Joe, a thirty-one-year-old promoter, "when you bring out models, it's like they give you the keys to the city in New York."

The twenty-nine-year-old promoter Malcolm started out as a mass promoter, bringing eighty people to big clubs in the Meat-packing District. But he found that with the same effort, he could focus on fewer, higher-quality people, models mostly, and demand even more money from the owners: "We pitched it to the club, like, 'Listen, you got this promoter who's gonna bring a whole bunch of girls who are five foot three and cute, whatever. Or you want to hire people like us, who are gonna bring you the It Girls? . . . Listen, we gonna bring fifteen of the hottest girls in the place. I want a thousand dollars for it."

It worked. "Put it this way," he said, "I bought two BMWs working in the club. I went from the Five Series to the Seven Series, you know what I mean?"

It Girls turn heads when they walk into a room. They were how Malcolm went from quantity to quality, from mass to image and to the A-list, and eventually to hosting girls at beach clubs in Ibiza and at private parties aboard clients' yachts in the Côte d'Azur.

When Dre quit promoting at the Downtown, about a year into my fieldwork, a younger black man named Abe took over. The talk about him was that Abe was a "loser"; he didn't have enough models in his network. His own girlfriend wasn't a model. In fact, as one Club X promoter told me with contempt, his girlfriend "had a lot of cellulite in her legs. It's disgusting. It's better to close the place than have Abe working there."

Such cruel talk was normal, for promoters routinely cut each other down by insulting each other's girls, joking, for instance, "Who's their modeling agency, Instagram?" On one occasion, I sat with a promoter at the Downtown who denigrated the girls at the table of Enrico, a rival promoter, across the room:

> For us, it's quality over quantity. We have two great girls, that's better than Enrico, he'll just bring anything, girls that look like retarded prostitutes, you know that big boobs, plastic in their lips, you know, cheesy style. That's worse than just one good girl, just bring one good girl over that.

Shortly after this encounter, I started to join Enrico's table. It turned out that he preferred the company of strippers and escorts to fashion models. He was thirty years old and from an upper-class family from Spain, one of the few promoters I encountered who came from money. To him, strippers were sexier and more fun, especially for partying hard late into the night, which was usually fueled by an abundance of cocaine. Models, on the other hand, were more likely to be a "pain in the ass"—they were too demanding, in his view, probably because they knew their value. Enrico sacrificed status for his own personal enjoyment, and he stayed a notch below promoters like Dre.

Thinking about his place in this hierarchy of crowds all the time, Dre was most concerned to stay at the top. He wouldn't dare to take a promotion job at a club that didn't already have a reputation for elite clientele. "You can only go up. You never go back down, or you dilute your brand, and you die slowly and surely. When you cash in, when you chase the fast money, it's dangerous. Your reputation follows you." The status of a club could stick to a promoter, too: working in a low-status place or having a non-model girlfriend was to be branded a "loser."

The more time I spent with promoters, the more I saw how their world was divided between A-list and everyone else. You could be at a party with successful people or losers: "That's what it's all about," said Michel, a promoter for over twenty years. "When you're surrounded with people that are beautiful and successful and stuff like that, you just feel like you're in the right place. When you go to a dump, and it's a lot of losers in the place . . . in your mind, you're not like, 'Wow, I was at this place. It was amazing.'"

The right place, for Michel and other promoters, is only for very important people.

A-List Economics

The cool people don't stay in one place for long, and club owners can both spend and earn a lot of money in pursuit of them. A nightclub usually stays in business for a few years, rarely more than that. During that period, each club follows a similar life cycle. First it attracts high-status guests and excludes everyone else. Over time, as the VIPs gravitate to other, newer clubs in the city, the club opens its doors to the lower-status masses and the crowd gets less exclusive. "If you put it in New York terms," explained a banker and club regular, "it just gets a lot more bridge and tunnel . . . [they are] not nearly as sensitive to if the really high-end crowd is there or not. They're just happy to be there . . . They probably don't know the difference between the hottest place in town and the third- or fourth-hottest place in town." A club may still be profitable at this lower tier for a few years, relying on its former cachet to sell price-inflated bottles to people imagining themselves as VIPs. But to get to this point, the club needs to establish an A-list reputation right from the beginning. To do this, the club needs image promoters to bring in the curated crowd.

For their services, promoters could charge up to a $1,000 a night; in fact, promoters were the biggest drivers of cost increases for Club Marquee in New York, for example, which couldn't afford *not* to hire them, lest they take their networks of models to a competing club.[50] Though they were expensive, image promoters helped to bring in huge profits to club owners.

Marquee was estimated to gross $15 million at its peak, in 2007, and it grew famous for both its hip crowds and its longevity—it closed in 2012 only to reopen, after a $3.5 million renovation, in 2013.[51] Marquee's founders, Strauss and Tepperberg, were called "the most highly regarded nightlife impresarios in the world" in a well-known case study of their company conducted by the Harvard Business School.[52] The pair would go on to found Strategic Hospitality Group and join Tao Group, amassing a portfolio of hospitality and entertainment businesses that would eventually include over thirty restaurants, clubs, and hotels, spanning from Las Vegas to Sydney, Australia.[53] Some they owned; in others they were managing partners with a revenue, profit, or equity interest.[54] Marquee in Vegas was, as of 2017, the third-highest grossing club in the country, pulling in $85 million a year. Strategic Group venues were a key part of the wave of upscale food and beverage businesses that transformed Vegas into a luxury party destination.[55]

Strategic Hospitality Group is one of many blockbusters in the lucrative global nightclub industry. The top-ten clubs in the United States collectively earned upward of $550 million in revenue in 2014.[56] The club XS, in Las Vegas, at one point the highest-grossing club in the country, could make up to a million dollars in a single night.[57] Even Goldman Sachs got into the industry, backing EMM Group, a New York–based competitor of Strategic Group that holds a portfolio of clubs and restaurants in New York, Los Angeles, Atlantic City, and the Hamptons.[58]

Vegas is one of many such places in a global circuit of destinations for rich spenders seeking to maximize their scarce leisure opportunities. With money flowing from emerging finance and energy industries in Brazil, India, China, Russia, and the Gulf States, the world's economic elites are more globally dispersed and more mobile than ever.[59] Elite communities are no longer anchored to neighborhoods or cities, as they flock to prime destinations at specific times of the year in what have been called "rich enclaves": summer colonies like the Hamptons and the French Riviera; St. Barts, Aspen, and Gstaad in the winter.[60] The island of St. Barts transforms from a quiet upper-class resort into a celebrated landing pad for millionaires' yachts during the peak season, in January.[61] The elite business class follows a transatlantic calendar of VIP scenes—St. Barts in January, Miami in March, Saint-Tropez and Ibiza in July—and a predictable schedule of parties crops up along the Fashion Week calendars each September and February, with stops in Milan, London, and Paris.[62] On the one hand, elites are more diverse and geographically dispersed around the world than other classes; on the other, they are so segregated from them that geographers describe their movements as "super-gentrification," characterized by geographic isolation, social self-segregation, and a sense of remoteness. Today's hypermobile elites live in a bubble separate from most people.[63]

Nightclubs have accordingly also gone global, opening franchises that offer satellite parties in Cannes and Dubai or "pop-up" clubs at Coachella and Art Basel Miami.[64] "It's a competitive business where everyone's gunning for the A-list crowd. You have to chase them around the world," says Ronnie Madra, co-owner of New York's 1 OAK ("One of a Kind"), which has franchises in Mexico City, Los Angeles, and Las Vegas.[65] Provocateur, once located in the Meatpacking District, even closed its doors in New York during August, posting a sign that read: "The Provocateur family is in Europe for the annual summer holidays. We will return to open pre–Fashion Week in late August."

Guests who frequent "Provo," as it was often called, in New York will know whom to expect when they converge in the French Riviera for the summer holidays. Many of the people I interviewed used words like "fraternity," "small community," and "tribe" to describe the reappearance of familiar faces in exotic destinations. As Luc, a wealthy forty-eight-year-old restauranteur and a regular at clubs in New York and Saint-Tropez, put it:

> Like in Saint-Tropez, Ibiza, I know exactly where everyone is sitting. Sometimes there are newcomers but I would say 60–70 percent is a network, old school, always there. . . . You know it's funny because it's like a bond, the people that party together all the time, it's like a fake bond but it's a bond. They call each other and they meet together and it's like a tribe, you know.

This closed circuit of migration by the globally nomadic leisure class has created a homogenized look and feel among VIP clubs. Parties in the Hamptons, Miami, the French Riviera, and New York all featured the same chart-topping hip-hop and house music. For drink options, one could choose between a uniform stable of brands such as Belvedere vodka and Cristal, Dom Pérignon, and Veuve Clicquot champagne, all similarly priced.[66]

To access these destinations, you would need both time and either economic resources or personal connections, because transportation and hotels are expensive. In the summertime in Saint-Tropez, a taxi costs about 100 euros for the four-mile trip (6½ km), the distance from the main seaport to VIP destination Nikki Beach Club; many clients simply arrive by small boats from their yachts anchored off the beach. Many VIP destinations are public spaces, ostensibly accessible to everyone. But by design, they are effectively closed off to all but the world's most privileged.

These "dreamworlds for the super-rich," as the geographer John Urry describes them, cater to a very small segment of the world's population, but they enflame general desires for luxury in the popular imagination.[67] As gathering spots for elites, a mostly male and white population, these are prime sites to examine masculine domination and white supremacy, though gender and race are often ignored in discussions of elites.[68] These dreamworlds are important for another reason, too: they provide social space for rich and powerful men to develop a closed global community and cultivate the shared cultural values and beliefs that drive contemporary capitalism.[69] In these places, elites can foster a sense of belonging with each other. And researchers know almost nothing about what happens there.[70]

Joining the Very Important People

It has been over a hundred years since Veblen wrote *The Theory of the Leisure Class*, and the global moneyed classes continue to outspend each other in what is now our new Gilded Age of extreme wealth concentration. This book revives Veblen's original critique and advances it empirically to ask, How does conspicuous waste happen? I document competitive spending rituals as organizational achievements, hugely dependent upon the backstage work of vulnerable women and marginalized men. In so doing, I revisit a second critical insight of Veblen's on the role of women in communicating men's status. In this world, girls function as a form of capital. Their beauty generates enormous symbolic and economic resources for the men in their presence, but that capital is worth far more to men than to the girls who embody it. Finally, I examine how this scene maintains "social closure" in which mostly white and male elites retain privileged access to a valuable global space, especially evident in the blunted careers of the disproportionately minority men who work as promoters.[71]

My analysis unfolds in five steps. First, we meet the promoters who are central to constructing this world in chapter 2. Next, in chapter 3, we witness the clients' spectacular displays of wealth and waste, as well as the backstage labor required to produce the show. In chapter 4, we meet the girls and see how men convert their beauty into profit. In chapter 5, we see the labor process behind girls' leisure, which promoters control and manage. Finally, in chapter 6, we see how promoters, marked as outsiders by their race and class positions, strive but only partially manage to join this privileged space.

Because I relied on promoters for access and I spent the bulk of my fieldwork by their sides, my portrayal of the VIP party circuit attends disproportionately to their perspectives and my critical examination of them. This is not just a matter of access, however, because I found promoters' stories to be among the most fascinating and, sometimes, heartbreaking, in this world. Promoters were crucial to putting these dreamworlds together, and they were heavily invested in the belief that they too fully belonged in them. For all of their dreaming, promoters remain mostly shut out of the elite. Dre was an emblematic case.

"In five years, I'm gonna be a *multi*millionaire," Dre told me one early morning after a Sunday night of karaoke at the Downtown.

This became a familiar refrain from Dre, but the first time I heard it, we were sitting on a bench facing the Hudson River, listening to the breeze on the still water in the darkness around 4 a.m., shortly before daybreak. It was a strange quiet compared to the blasting speakers of the Downtown, where not thirty minutes ago Dre had wrapped up the party belting out his own heartfelt rendition of Michael Jackson's "Billy Jean." Leaving the club, he held my hand, not romantically but protectively, looking over his shoulder from time to time to make sure no one followed us. Sometimes there were disgruntled people who hadn't been able to get into the club waiting for him after closing, frustrated and drunk and eager to harass him and his crew.

At the waterfront, facing the twinkling New Jersey lights, Dre decompressed from the night. The calmness of the water allowed him to process all of the energy of nightlife. "It's not just a business, it's an experience. It can be positive and it can be negative." After a few minutes of silence, he finally went home.

Dre lived nearby, in a small but gorgeous studio apartment in a Tribeca high-rise, a luxury building with a doorman and a sundeck. He paid a little over $3,000 a month for the apartment and was making about $15,000 per month promoting at Club X four nights a week and the Downtown Sunday nights. He had lots of lucrative gigs in between: a rich acquaintance offered him $10,000 to organize his daughter's bat mitzvah; another long-time business friend paid him and his partners $3,000 a week to host a dinner party at a pizzeria in the Meatpacking District. Dre knew he made a lot of money, certainly more than what most people made. On more than one occasion he told me, "There's so much money in nightlife, Ash. People don't realize."

But it didn't feel like much to Dre, who hung around tycoons, celebrities, and plutocrats every night.

Dre had a plan to be as rich as his clients—"I'm building a structure," he liked to say—that he imagined would catapult him into the upper echelons of the class ladder. His plan involved a lot of networking and strategic cultivation of ties from nightlife, which he took seriously. He usually went to bed around 6:30 a.m., and by 10:30 he was awake again. He started his day by watching CNN or *The View*, then was ready to work by 11:30. Work meant going to lunches and walking around SoHo, courting would-be investors in his various projects, keeping up his ties with the girls, and going to the music studio to record. So it was around 11:30 a.m. that I would text him to ask if I could tag along with him during the day.

I followed Dre off and on over the course of three years. After getting to know him in 2010, I first pitched my research project to him in early 2011, and I began going out intermittently with him, each time growing more curious about his aspirational world of ostentation, beauty, and wealth. I started to follow him systematically in 2012, and for roughly eighteen months I immersed myself in his world, taking detailed field notes and conducting interviews with forty-four promoters, twenty girls, and twenty clients.

Dre quickly introduced me to Enrico, the Spanish promoter who came from a wealthy family. I then began following Enrico through his daily routines in lower Manhattan, beginning with breakfast as late as 4 p.m. at his favorite café in Chelsea, and ending as late as 5 a.m. at his favorite strip club after the nightclubs closed.

Also at the Downtown, Dre introduced me to Santos, the mixed-race Colombian promoter who worked in New York, Miami, Milan, London, and throughout the French Riviera and Ibiza. Santos invited me to Miami with him for five nights, and a year later, I met him again in Milan and followed him to Cannes for a week. From Cannes, I took a ferry to Saint-Tropez, where I met up with friends of Enrico, who introduced me as a girl writing a book about nightlife, and they offered to host me for three days aboard their yacht while they docked at the port and partied at the nearby beach clubs.

Through Santos, I met Malcolm and Sampson, both of whom I followed to the Hamptons. A year later, I met a client through Santos who worked in private equity, who also allowed me to shadow him for a weekend at his co-owned mansion in the Hamptons.

To conduct this fieldwork, I became a "girl" and went out regularly with promoters in the global VIP party scene, mostly in New York, with stops in the Hamptons, Miami, and the French Riviera. In exchange for dressing up and wearing my high heels at their tables at night, promoters let me follow them during the day, as they took models to beaches and to lunches and drove them to their castings, and as they hung around on city streets trying to pick up girls.

An ethnography of the global VIP party circuit can reveal a great deal about today's global elites, their practices and rituals of signaling status, their shared cultures of fun, and the gendered expectations of relationships formed within them. This book tells the stories of promoters and the girls who support them, the rich men who pay to be around beautiful women, and the global shifts in capital and consumption among the nouveau riche that make this dreamworld possible.

2

Daytime

Tuesday, 2 p.m., New York

Promoters wove complex social worlds during the daytime, and these proved critical for how their nights would unfold. As one promoter-turned-club-owner put it, "There can be no night without the day."

As he typically did on a sunny afternoon, Sampson parked his black SUV at the corner of Spring Street and Broadway in SoHo, downtown Manhattan. Two renowned modeling agencies are located at this corner; nearby are a dozen casting and fashion studios. It was a warm Friday, ideal conditions for scouting. If Sampson didn't have afternoon plans to take models to lunch or to castings, he came here looking to meet new girls. "This is what I do," he said, sitting in his car, looking through the windshield at the busy street.

Sampson usually woke up around 10 a.m. and headed to the gym. He was trying to work on his body to see if he could pick up modeling work in the fall. At five feet eleven and Caucasian, he could pass as a male model. He had full lips and feline eyes. He had a handsome young face for twenty-seven. It served him well in attracting girls.

As we were talking, Sampson stopped mid-sentence as a young white woman walked by.

"I know her. Let me just say hello—" Before I could respond, he practically leapt out of the car. He stopped her for a quick chat on the sidewalk before returning with a smile. "That was good. I said, 'What are you doing tonight,' and she said okay, she'll come out."

Leaning on the hood of his SUV with a cigarette, Sampson continued to survey the street. He guessed that pretty girls got stopped by guys like him all the time. Sometimes they were rude to him. He heard "I don't talk to promoters" with some regularity. Across Spring Street, Omar, one of Sampson's competitors, occupied a bench outside a café with his "subs," or sub-promoters. Sometimes Sampson and Omar would both start to pursue a passing girl, in which case they played rock-paper-scissors to determine who should get to talk to her.

Sampson preferred the car to the bench. The temperature might not be right outside, or it might rain. He kept the car idling to pull maximum air-conditioning. If he got sick of looking around he could take a break, maybe watch Netflix on his iPad.

A young woman passed and he set off again, tossing his cigarette in quick pursuit. He often left the car running with the doors unlocked, but he was not afraid of theft because there were plenty of police around. He knew because he got tickets all the time.

When he caught up to the girl, they talked for about five minutes, and she gave him her number, then they kissed on the cheek goodbye.

"That one was nice," Sampson said, returning to lean on the hood of the car. "She was older but had a good look, like I can tell if she had her hair down she would look great."

"One sec," he said, interrupting himself again to follow after a young woman walking fast down Broadway, hair bouncing and shiny. When he caught up to her, she didn't slow down but just talked to him sideways as he tried to keep pace. This went on for less than a block before he gave up.

"How'd it go?" I asked when he returned to the car.

"Like shit," he said, still smiling.

Sampson was always good at picking up women. It was his niche, if you could call it that. After the workday at his previous job selling cell phones, he used to hang around Thirty-Fourth Street and practice the pick up:

> No joke, no kidding. I would go after work. I'd be like, I'm bored now, I need new ass. I did this before I started doing this. I've always been comfortable, I've been after girls. Like, that was my thing. I had such a drive for like, women. I don't do my job because I need to do it. I do it because I like it.

Sampson grew up in working-class Queens. He dropped out of community college and was working at a cell phone store when he met a beautiful woman on the subway who invited him out to a club. He declined, apologetically explaining that he was broke. The woman persisted.

"No, she was like, 'It's free.' 'What do you mean it's free?' 'It just is, I'll show you. Come to dinner.' I was like, 'No, I don't have money for dinner.' She's like, 'No, that's free too.'"

The woman, it turned out, was a model and well connected to promoters, to whom she introduced Sampson. The promoters assumed Sampson was a model and offered him part-time work as a sub, $50 a night to help them bring beautiful girls to their tables. This is commonly offered as side work for male models, who are thought of as bait to lure female models. Men connected to beautiful women could easily be fast-tracked to work in VIP clubs.

After that night, Sampson began looking up fashion websites and Facebook profiles of promoters and girls to "learn the look." Sampson himself was drawn to Latin women, which he described as "you know, curvy women, not fat but like, bigger and like, really strong and outgoing type of women." Models were not his thing, so he spent that whole first week on the Internet to train his eye. By the time I met him, two years into the work, he was married to an ex-model and sleeping with a number of other models on the side (he soon divorced).

In forty minutes on the street in SoHo, Sampson had talked to ten girls. Half of the interactions were positive, ending with the agreement that he would send a text message with upcoming party details. At 3 p.m., he noticed the time: "I should be texting." And with that, he began organizing his table for the night.

Dre's Network

While Sampson was soaking up the AC in his car on any given week-day afternoon, Dre was likely to stroll by, also strategically looking to meet people to join his parties. Dre took a different approach. He was aware of the many castings for models going on in SoHo where he could meet new girls. It was easy for a promoter to attend castings with a girlfriend, where he could sit and wait for her in the lobby of the casting studio or stand around outside in front of the building, greeting models on their way in and out, trying to get their phone numbers. But Dre was approaching forty, and he just could not imagine himself or any other forty-year-old man loitering around cast-ings. He kept his eyes on the people around him instead, taking long deliberate walks through the city in a constant effort to groom his network and befriend the right kinds of people.

When Dre walked through SoHo, he took only busy streets like Spring, Prince, and Broadway, even if the quickest way to get to his destination was on a quiet side street, so he could mingle among the retail shoppers and fashionable pedestrians working in the neighbor-hood's creative industries. This maximized his chances of running into people he knew: models, club owners and restauranteurs and their workers, shopkeepers, and famous artists (one of whom took us to his studio and gifted us prints). To get back home to his upscale condo in Tribeca, Dre rarely walked on the same streets he had just traveled. He was on the lookout for something new. "As a promoter, you're always looking for information," he said. As Dre walked, some-times cars honked and their drivers waved or stopped to greet him. Dre is a public character, in the sense outlined by urban theorist Jane Jacobs, who studied the cultures of cities and observed that such a person "need have no special talents or wisdom to fulfill his function . . . His main qualification is that he *is* public, and he talks to lots of different people."[1] Unlike most anonymous urban dwellers, when Dre takes to the streets, he connects with people.

When Dre lunched at the fashionable Café Mafa in SoHo, with its big sidewalk terrace which made it a favorite spot of his, he usually got his preferred corner seat facing the crowd. The times I joined him there, he constantly looked up to engage passersby. He would pause often in our conversations to give a wink here, flash a smile there, or smile big and give a double "thumbs-up" to someone. As acquaintances approached, he stood, shook hands, and was easy with all of them, jovial and joking, moving between French, English, and Spanish.

"We go here," Dre said about Café Mafa, "because this is where all the action is. We go here to see people, to get information."

At one point during lunch, he said to a woman, beaming, "The sun is out, do you see? It's now shining because you are here."

Then as an aside to me: "I know how to talk to girls. That's why they like me. I make them feel good. And I'm being honest."

Eying a very thin young model at a nearby table, Dre pointed her out: "That's the kind of girl we are after. That's the kind of girl we want with us."

"Why?" I asked. "Some men might not think that's attractive."

"It's true, she's too skinny," said Dre. "I like a woman with more curves on her. But to most people, models represent the dream. They represent the elite, trendy world, the high-end world of fashion and beauty. They are the dream. I am not attracted to her, but she is my target; if I see her on the street I'll stop her and talk to her. We need those girls."

Many promoters worked against their personal tastes in women, at least initially. A promoter named Joe, a thirty-one-year-old black man, was in disbelief when he first saw fashion models: "I was like, that's a model? You gotta be kidding. You know some of them in fashion, they look really strange and super-skinny. Not my thing." After five years in the VIP scene, Joe realized, "My eyesight changed! Now when I see a super-skinny model, I think that it's normal. And when I see someone normal, I think she's fat!" Likewise, a New York club owner told me that models weren't even that pretty. To him, they were strange, but "it pops in the club because they're seven feet tall." Promoters' own tastes in women may have been different from that of the VIP look, but their work necessitated a restructuring of their vision around four key indicators: height, slenderness, youth, and facial beauty. This vision of beauty defines the VIP field as a high-status space, crowding out and even belittling alternative visions of beauty.

By specifically targeting top models—and he dropped their names frequently—Dre aimed to build a reputation for having the very best girls. A Victoria's Secret model came to see him at Club X a few times that year ("Nobody could believe it when she walked in to see me") and when she was there, she attracted all the other models and top clients to Dre. With the right girls, everyone else showed up for Dre.

It's easy to see why women were drawn to Dre. Five feet eleven, fit, stylish, and handsome, he had worked for a short while as a male model. Ten years ago, Dre had long dreadlocks that he sometimes wore tied up; he could be spotted in a crowd instantly. As he has grown older and more established, his look has grown more understated. Today his hair is closely cropped, and his typical outfit consists of designer jeans and a blazer or leather jacket, mostly in tones of black, white, and gray.

In fact, Dre says he has always had a certain talent for meeting beautiful women. This is how he became aware that the job of promoter even existed. He had been partying in clubs in France since he was a teenager, always in the company of beautiful women. He was fifteen years old when a club owner invited him to work as a promoter. When the owner paid him a few hundred dollars after his first night, he hid the bills under his mattress, terrified that his mother would think he was dealing drugs.

Dre grew up in a middle-class neighborhood of Paris, France, after his parents left North Africa. The son of a diplomat and a housewife, he had professional aspirations. After high school he briefly pursued a law degree, but dropped out to chase his dreams of music stardom, in the early 1990s heading to Miami with his brother to join a boy band.

Miami in the 1990s was a gold rush of fashion models, parties, and expanding real estate developments that would shape what is today glamorous South Beach. While the boy band floundered, Dre worked as a waiter and male model. It was then that an established promoter in Miami noticed him crossing the street and invited him out. Dre went to the club, which was packed with models, and there he met what would become his future network of nightlife collaborators. In 1999, he moved to New York, initially to live with a girlfriend, whose offer to house him quickly fell through. For a year he was homeless, either crashing on friends' sofas or sleeping at the apartments of girls whom he had picked up at the clubs. He supplemented his irregular promotions work by cleaning apartments and tutoring French. After a year, one of his contacts from Miami offered Dre a room in his mother's house in Harlem; before long, Dre teamed up with four men in the nightlife business who became known for hosting some of the best nights in the most exclusive clubs in the city, right at the moment that bottle service culture took off. Dre's niche in the business became top-quality girls: he specialized in bringing models to the men's parties.

Like Dre, most promoters unexpectedly fell into their line of work. They tell a remarkably consistent story: of the thirty-nine male promoters I interviewed, only one sought out the job on his own initiative.[2] Rather, the job had a way of finding *them*. It's easy to see why: they are charming men, flirtatious, stylish, and persistent.

Now, walking down the street in SoHo, Dre wanted people to recognize him and think, "There goes Dre: that's the girls, the access, the network." To get the very important, high-quality people, Dre invested in long-term relationships with them. He knew various celebrities, mainly actors and musicians, from going out over the years, and he knew which girls liked which celebrities. He connected the right kind of girls to the right kinds of powerful men at his tables; at one point, he kept a handwritten list of the men's preferences, a way of supplementing memory like he did in his law school days. I continually shook hands with strangers while out with Dre, who seemed energized by the constant chitchatting, joking, and inviting to the club that night.

"Ash, when I think about where I came from, and now I am going to be a millionaire. It's the American dream, my story."

The Pickup

Just a few blocks east of Café Mafa, Trevor, twenty-one, and Malcolm, twenty-nine, hung out a few afternoons each week when the weather was nice. These two promoters, both black men, sometimes worked in partnership with Sampson and Santos. Trevor was just one year into the job, and Malcolm, eight years in the business, mentored him in recruiting the right kind of girls.

Malcolm was a six feet three black man from Flatbush, Brooklyn—not the upscale part of the borough—and had made it to places unimaginable to his school friends. "I'm a statistic," he said about the people he grew up with. "Ninety-five percent—well, to be realistic, it's more like 98 percent—have not traveled in Europe. At least not like me."

Malcolm's rise to international club promoter began when a friend at the gym invited him out and, noticing his sociality, offered him a position as a sub-promoter. Promoters typically began their career as subs, making $50 per girl that they bring out, or about $100–200 per night. Malcolm had been working at a public relations firm, having majored in business marketing at the City University of New York. He kept working his day job part-time while working the clubs at night, eventually branching out on his own and climbing up in nightlife. By the time I met him, Malcolm was working for clubs and private clients in Saint-Tropez and Ibiza, and his cash flow was evident in his studded Versace belt and oil-based Dolce & Gabbana perfume that smelled like citrus and herbs ("Hold up, that cost a hundred pounds!" he scolded when I tried to spray the bottle he showed me.)

As a large black man, Malcolm liked to be around girls because they made him look like less of a threat in the predominantly white VIP world. He had been practicing how to pick up girls since high school, when he rode the subway each day between Brooklyn and Manhattan with his friends, and they played a game called "You've Got to Talk to This Girl":

Imagine being fourteen, fifteen years old, walking up to random girls on a train, how mortifying that is . . . Just a random stranger . . . Just the long walk to the end of the car . . . How do you approach, you know? So that's done wonders for my confidence now, because it like, just trained me in being able to speak with strangers and trying to break down girls' defenses. I learned that at an early age.

When Malcolm approaches unknown girls now, he cracks a joke, or makes something up. "I'll pick up a piece of paper on the floor, and I'll be like, 'Hey, you dropped this.' She'll go, 'You sure?' 'No, I just needed to get your attention. I figured this would work.'"

Some girls find his tactics cute, especially when he flashes his dimpled smile. "But," he acknowledged, "some girls find it repulsive. You're playing the odds."

With its high concentration of fashion studios and modeling agencies, SoHo was a great training ground for Malcolm to show Trevor how to target models. Sometimes they walked on specific streets, like the one with a frozen yogurt shop: "Models love Pink Berry. They always in there," Malcom said. Walking down the busy street, Malcolm pointed out models versus good civilians. His head followed as a blonde woman walked by.

"She's hot," he said casually as we kept walking. "She's not a model but she's hot, I'd definitely get with her. That's what we call a good civilian. There's models and there's good civilians. A good civilian is a girl who fits the description of model but is not really a model. Like she's not as slim or, you know what I mean, she's not five eleven, but she might be five eight. She's just a pretty hot girl, something that the clubs will see and say, 'Ok, she's pretty hot.'"

"But you can tell the difference?" I asked him.

"Oh, everybody can tell the difference. You look at her and you look at her"—pointing out two girls standing outside the trendy restaurant Balthazar on Spring Street—"and you know who's the model. Right or wrong?"

I conceded he was right. One woman, the model, was just a little bit thinner, taller, and poised in a way that invited slightly more of a gaze than the woman standing next to her.

"Some girls are street pretty and some girls are models," Malcolm concluded.

At the time, Trevor couldn't quite tell the difference. Sampson was constantly reprimanding him: "He's bringing me girls all tits and butt, you know, girls he likes. I'm like, 'That's not what they want. That girl is just taking up space. Don't bring that. No tits and ass. Just skinny and tall.'"

A pretty young woman walked by. "Look over there," Trevor said to Malcolm. "She's a model." The woman he pointed out was wearing very high heels and an elaborate outfit.

"She's not a model," dismissed Malcolm. "She wouldn't be wearing shit like that."

"What do you mean?" asked Trevor.

"Shoes like that. No book," meaning she didn't carry a model portfolio. "She's not working; she's just styling. She's not a model. Models don't style during the day . . . like wearing high heels all day. It's pointless. They gotta go from casting to casting." And so we continued down the SoHo streets, playing this game of dissecting the differences between models and good civilians to help Trevor sharpen his eye.

Once he knew what to look for, Trevor was generally pretty smooth in meeting girls. Trevor was cute and had a "good personality," according to Malcolm. That's how he found out about the job. His main source of income was on the retail floor of an Abercrombie & Fitch in Midtown. A coworker invited him to help promote at a lower-level club, because, according to Trevor, "He saw that I had personable characteristics and people are comfortable with me. You do have to be a good-looking or fairly attractive guy." And working at a place like Abercrombie ensured he had access to a large volume of young women shopping for clothes whom he could invite out.

Why do women accept these unsolicited invitations from complete strangers?

For some, the decision is well informed, even instrumental. Such was the case for nineteen-year-old Catherine, who was a "fresh face," in modeling industry parlance, with platinum blond hair. When she was first recruited by promoters, at age eighteen, she was prepared for it. Catherine had heard much about the club scene from her roommates during her first year in New York, where she modeled after finishing high school in Oregon, but she wanted to get her bearings in the city and focus on her career before heading out to clubs. Catherine didn't really like going to clubs anyway. But when a promoter approached her on the corner where Sampson regularly parked his car, she found his offer compelling.

She was rushing to the hair salon when a "random guy" approached her and very nicely asked to talk, but she brushed him off to make her hair appointment. Three hours and blonder hair later, he was still out there on the sidewalk, and he came up to her again with this pitch:

> Well, me and my friends, we throw a bunch of cool parties and, like, brunches and we go to the movies . . . and we go to the Hamptons and we all hang out. We have a really great bunch of friends. If you ever wanna hang out with us, we are a bunch of really cool people.

Catherine figured he was just one of those promoters she had heard about, but she took his number. A couple of weeks later, when she did feel like checking out the club world, she met him in the Meatpacking District, and thereafter became a part of this promoter's group of "really cool people." Within a year, she made plenty of connections to other models and promoters, including a promoter team run by Vanna and Pablo, with whom she would end up going out five nights a week and forming a group of "the most amazing friends" that helped her navigate the city as a teenage model.

Other girls had more inchoate reasons to join promoters, and their choices were shaped by the fact of living in the city in close proximity to power and wealth while only being partially aware of its grandeur. Consider Leila, a twenty-six-year-old Parisian who first arrived in New York for an internship with a French fashion company. Upon arrival, Leila went out for a walk, energized by the city. She didn't know Manhattan except for the famous Fifth Avenue, where she saw the Abercrombie store. Right away, Trevor greeted her.

"He was very confident," Leila recalled, "talking in that 'Trevor talk' way, you know, like 'Hi, where are you from? Welcome to New York.'" He told Leila that he organizes fun parties in the city and he'd like to invite her.

"They know how to talk to women," Leila said.

She went out for the first time dressed in a T-shirt and jeans, her standard Parisian look. At the velvet rope to a Meatpacking District club, she mentioned Trevor's name and was whisked right in to his table. She was amazed. The girls were so sexy, so dressed up, and so tall in those high heels. "I was really struck by the beauty around me," she recalled. Leila began to go out regularly with Trevor, Malcom, and Santos for the next six months. As a newcomer to the city who did not know anybody, "it was a great way to meet people." She found a network of friends among the girls at promoters' tables, since "a lot of them are very bright and down to earth."

She had also been single for several months prior to meeting Trevor, and she was "wondering if anyone finds me attractive." In the VIP, Leila found validation. She took pleasure in rarefied experiences like early morning house parties with millionaires in the Hamptons. She wouldn't trade those experiences for anything.

Leila was an ideal pickup for Trevor, since she was new to the city, lacked her own friends, and had never heard the criticisms of promoters before. While plenty of young women were put off by promoters and their street scouting tactics, girls like Leila were pleasantly surprised to learn that promoters and their exclusive parties existed, and for free.

Reba was another pickup who was glad to be invited into the world of high-end parties. Promoters first spotted her a few blocks north of SoHo, outside the Astor Place subway stop on her way to class at NYU. "Someone approached me and said there is a great party tonight, wanna come? I was new to the city and didn't know anyone, so I was like, 'Okay, sure.' I was a little bit apprehensive at first, but once I looked up the place, I knew it was legitimate." A good civilian, Reba was five feet ten and curvier than a model, with "a booty," as she put it, and a strikingly pretty face. She loved to dance, especially to hip-hop. Lacking the know-how and the finances to get into a club, promoters offered her an attractive opportunity. That night in the Meatpacking District club, Reba experienced a "hot night," meaning a fun crowd, and within two hours, it seemed like all of the city's promoters had introduced themselves and given her their numbers. She was nineteen years old.

Thus began Reba's tour through VIP nightlife. On a student budget, Reba was treated to free nights out including dinner and transportation. Perhaps best of all, she got to be a part of the exclusive club world, so different from her life back home. "And I had so much fun," she told me later, when she was twenty-eight. "I come from a small town in North Carolina where there really isn't a nightlife. I thought meeting all these people and all that stuff was great."

Promoters were hoping to pick up girls like Leila, Reba, and Catherine, to whom their offers of free luxury entertainment and friend networks would appeal. But as Malcolm had said, they were playing the odds in talking to girls on the street, and not all targets responded well to the pickup.

Walking in SoHo that afternoon, Trevor passed a sidewalk café where he and Malcolm both spotted three models having drinks together. After some deliberation, Trevor decided to approach them. Malcolm coached him to come up with a good opener: "The first line, the opener, is so important, because they're gonna know you're a promoter. You have to overcome that and make them feel comfortable, make them laugh."

Trevor backtracked to the café, walked up to the women's table, and interrupted their conversation to say:

"Excuse me, hello. I'm Trevor. This is—um," and he paused, forgetting my name. "Ashley. How are you guys?"

The women unenthusiastically replied hello, and Trevor asked where they were from.

London.

He asked, "What are you guys doing here?"

After an awkward pause, the women replied that they were models, here for work. Trevor launched into the pitch: "Well, I'm new in town too, and she's new, and I'm new. I'm always looking for friends and people to hang out with. How long you guys in town?"

"One month." They were clearly not interested in talking to him.

"One month. You guys like bowling? We could go bowling. And movies. You guys like movies?"

"Um, sure," they replied.

"Okay, I go out too, to clubs and parties and stuff, so let's hang out. You got numbers?"

After two refusals—"I can't remember my American number, sorry"—Trevor ended up with one of the women's phone numbers.

Back at his car, Malcolm laughed as we recounted the story to him. Trevor admitted, "That was not my best," and he sighed loudly.

I asked him if he would really take them bowling.

"Yeah," he said. "That's how it works. You have to establish the relationship."

Among the dozens of girls that promoters approached daily on the street, perhaps only a few of them would eventually join them at the club. Street scouting was just one of many techniques to recruit girls into the promoter's network. Other promoters found ways to get close to girls from within the fashion industry.

The Man

Cruising around SoHo any given day of the week were Thibault, Felipe, and Nicolas, each in a big SUV, spacious enough to fit several girls in the backseat. They drove models to their castings and on various errands, and they sometimes met up for lunch at a trendy restaurant in Union Square, several blocks north of Café Mafa.

Thibault was a forty-five-year-old Dominican man, usually dressed in stylish baggy jeans and a T-shirt, with bright sneakers and a backward baseball cap. Felipe was his forty-four-year-old cousin, also from the Dominican Republic, and Nicolas was a fifty-six-year-old Jamaican man who looked much younger. They also worked with a sub, Jack, a racially mixed twenty-one-year-old from Brazil. They went out four nights a week with at least ten girls, sometimes up to fifty, and each night they typically worked at two or three VIP clubs owned by the same corporate group. The team was making upward of $3,000 per night, plus an additional 20 percent of what their clients spent on bottle service. One night a week, they threw a popular party from which they earned a large share of the bar's profits. They had been in the business for over twenty years.

"Those guys are the best," said one promoter at a table near Thibault's one night. It was a sentiment echoed by several promoters and girls. Within the hierarchy of the nightclubs, everyone agreed that Thibault's team was at the very top. They were idolized as role models in the business. Some people even believed Thibault and Felipe were the original masterminds behind the business formula of models and bottles (though there are several claimants).[3]

Their success spawned competitors, like Ethan, the twenty-seven-year-old promoter from New York. He was wowed by Thibault and Felipe's reputation for having such high-quality girls, which brought them other spoils: "I feel like those were the guys who always were sitting next to the celebrities, and always had the most beautiful girls, and always had, you know, the houses in the Hamptons and the superrich friends," he said. "They just were the—you know, they were just *the man*, so to speak. Like, if you wanted to aspire to someone, you had to aspire to be those guys, 'cause they were the best."

It was Ethan's goal to be their competition; he even told them, "Listen, guys, I want to be like you."

I met Thibault in the way that many models do. Back when I was studying the fashion modeling industry, I was waiting in line for a Fashion Week casting that he attended with a girlfriend, a typical strategy of his to meet more models. He told me he was throwing cool parties, and that I should come. He even invited me to dinner at an upscale restaurant beforehand where I could dine for free and meet all of his friends who also worked in the modeling industry. I gave him my number. This was in 2005. I have received text message invitations to his parties at least once every couple of months ever since. A sampling:

In 2005: "The bad news is that all the models are back in town and the good news is I'm taking them all out 2nite. Come to Club Alive 2nite. Thibault"

In 2008: "Join us 4A very chic bday soiree 4 our dear friend top model HOLLY . . . the biggest party 2nite at Club Alive . . . let me know if wanna come for dinner b4. Thibault"

In 2011: "Oiii bella . . . We're doing a very classy hotel rooftop party 2nite . . . So many celebs coming . . . u'll see! Then CLUB X later . . . Hamptons [we] leave 2moro 2pm . . . Coming? Thibault"

After years of ignoring his invites, in 2010 I finally replied to one of Thibault's texts messages. I wrote that I was now living in Boston, I worked as a professor, and I was eager to catch up with him for possible research on the VIP scene. He replied that absolutely, I was welcome to come out with him anytime.

He added, "I'd love to shake it with a professor." And just like that, I was back in Thibault's orbit.

Thibault and Felipe welcomed me to research their world; in fact, they were familiar with ethnography from their college courses in sociology. Thibault finished at the City University of New York with a degree in political science. Felipe had studied law in the Dominican Republic, but when he immigrated as a young man to escape economic instability, he couldn't get his official transcripts and had to start college anew. He went to Baruch (after turning down Yale because of the unaffordable tuition), where he studied communications and marketing. Despite their playful demeanors, both were deliberate men who approached nightlife as serious work. They made a lot of money, supported families in America and back home in the Caribbean, and planned major investments in hospitality projects they talked about often.

Like other promoters, Thibault and Felipe questioned the intrinsic beauty of fashion models while wholeheartedly embracing their economic value. Both men were sensitive to the cultural relativity of beauty; for instance, when I asked Thibault why it was important that his girls always wear high heels, he explained: "When a woman puts on high heels, it does something to make her more elegant. It's the way she walks is more elegant, and how she looks. It's just a fact."

"It's not a fact," interjected Felipe, who was seated next to us. "Thibault, all the travels you've done, you should know a woman can be elegant without heels. What about a woman in Africa in a long dress and barefoot? She's the most elegant, more so than a girl in high heels." Their ensuing discussion of the relativity of beauty standards and their origins in Western hegemony ended with the cousins reaching the conclusion that in a nightclub, tall girls in high heels conveyed high status. In this world, if "you can see the girls, like how tall everyone is, it's like, 'Wow, look—*models*.'"

Thibault had seen how the presence of models had an immediate, tangible effect, which translated into their own high-status reputations:

> When we bring in the models, and people see us in the club, like a table full of models, it's like making the club cool, that's where everybody wants to be, where the models are, where the fashion people are. They'll pay more to be by us. When clients book a table they want to be around us. If we do a club, other promoters want to be there too. If we're not there, and the models aren't there, the crowd is like bridge and tunnel.

Shortly after we reconnected, Thibault invited me to observe a model casting he was holding on behalf of an Arabian client who was throwing a huge party on the rooftop terrace of an upscale downtown hotel. The party was masquerade-themed, and the client would pay models to attend and mingle among the crowd. There would be professional makeup artists there to cover most of the girls' faces, but the client still wanted them to be pretty and, of course, very tall and thin. To the models, it looked like a casting for a professional modeling job, but it was in fact an audition for the role of paid party guest, and a ripe opportunity for Thibault to meet agencies' new faces, since agencies would not send their more established models to audition for such an arguably disreputable gig. The hotel front desk directed the models to where Thibault was sitting, and as the girls dropped by, he took their model cards, explained the job to them, and let them know of his other, unpaid but nonetheless valuable, nightly outings. We sat on the plush sofas in the hotel lobby as the last of the auditions wrapped up.

"I wanted you to come here," Thibault told me, "because when you work in promotions, you want to be where the right people are. Where you'll see them." The lobby was buzzing with men in sharp suits, models, and people who looked rich. Inserting oneself among them and into the fashion industry was one of many strategies for being a promoter, which, in Thibault's case, required the disciplined reorganization of his life around attracting models and wealthy men.

"There's so many small, little pieces of this business," he said, "and if you do all the small things, it adds up. You have to be doing something all the time that is related to work. A promoter has no time off, night or day."[4]

Thibault showed me the ropes over the next few months, and I was welcomed to come out with them each night. Naturally, I would need to wear my high heels.

Travis in the Masses

At a Starbucks in Union Square one midafternoon, not far from where Thibault was busy buying lunches for models, a twenty-five-year-old promoter named Travis sipped his coffee as he sent out hundreds of text messages, many of them to virtual strangers, inviting people to come to whichever club he was working at that night. In the world of nightlife, Travis knew he was of lower status than Dre and Thibault. As a mass promoter, he brought out a mix of men and girls, sometimes models but mostly fillers. On a good night, he could bring sixty people out; on a slow night the number was closer to fifteen. Not all of these people he invited would get in, since the doorman filtered out those who didn't have the right look. Travis got paid a flat rate of $300 a night on weeknights, about $500 on weekends. Image promoters, he knew, got paid more, and their scene was far superior. The A-list clubs where Dre and Thibault hosted simply drew better crowds, he said. "You walk inside, you see way more beautiful people. You see more sparklers. You see more bottles being purchased." Beauty and money: that's what Travis lacked.

Travis didn't mind his lower-status position. "Sometimes it's less hassle and stress. Because right now, as you can see, I'm just, like, literally sending a text to everybody in my phone," he said as we sat in the Starbucks. It would be a headache trying to please models, or to chauffeur them around town to their castings. He sometimes didn't bother when a beautiful girl walked by him on the street, as happened that very moment during our interview.

"Like okay, like this lady"—he pointed out a woman walking by. "She's very beautiful. She's tall, she's pretty. You know, blue eyes. She would probably go with an image guy to an A-list club. I would still approach her, but I may be working a place where she might not want to go. You know? . . . So I could take her to a B-level club, but she's more fitted for A-level. So she could come to B-level, not like it, [and] she will meet a better promoter at that place, and the next day go to the better place because her friends recommended it." A better bet for Travis were tourists and foreigners, because "they're unaware of what a good spot is." He preferred good-looking tourists, but average-looking ones would do fine for his purposes. He helped them get in; they mostly paid for their own drinks at the bar.

Mass promoters like Travis are at the bottom of the hierarchy, bringing in filler for B-level (or worse) clubs. This kind of promoter might even hand out promotional fliers to students at the city's colleges and universities to bring in a crowd. His goal is to get as many people to come out as possible.

All promoters are connected to a wide range of people. They spend a good portion of the day texting, calling, and sending Instagram and Facebook messages to girls and prospective clients. The sheer volume of people they know is impressive. They have between fifteen hundred and five thousand numbers in their phone contacts, and with the numbers they store key points of information that sometimes they glean from the Internet, like a client's industry and which companies he owns. One promoter showed me his text history; he had sent text messages to 4,600 people in the last two weeks.

But the image promoters are connected to more powerful people, especially models and higher-status clientele, those who buy bottles. They can earn $200 per night when they start out, and $800 per night on up as they get more established—depending on the quantity and quality of their crowd.

As promoters climb the nightlife hierarchy, their parties become increasingly exclusive and global, and they attract more models (see table 1).

By the time they reach the level of international VIP host, they have learned to turn down lucrative opportunities to promote at B-list clubs, alongside guys like Travis, or to throw parties for clients they perceived as lower status. At the highest level of the career, they travel

TABLE 1. Mobility among VIP Party Promoters

Promoter Type	Nightly Earnings ($)	Exclusivity	Social Capital	
			Girls	Clients
Mass Promoter	500–1,000	Low	"Civilians"	"Fillers"
Image B-list	100–800			
Sub	100–200			
Independent	200–800			
Image A-list	400–1,200			
Image Global VIP	1,000–2,000	High	"Models"	"1 percent"

the global VIP circuit, partying exclusively with models and catering to rich clients. These promoters collect commissions from their clients' bottle sales at clubs. At this level, said one promoter, "Everywhere you go, you have a table."

Enrico's Ease

At Café Mafa, where Dre was often lunching, I would also likely find Enrico, the white Spanish promoter. Enrico had a different style than Dre, Sampson, and Thibault. His preferred look—suspenders and fine Italian shirts embroidered with his initials—broadcast his upperclass background and contrasted with other promoters' uniform of designer jeans and T-shirts. He would never chase after models at their castings or their apartments. "I'm thirty," he said. "I can't stop a girl in the street and say, 'Hey, come party with me.'" He laughed dismissively at the thought of guys like Sampson out there chasing girls on the street.

While Dre's movements throughout the city strategically cultivated his network, Enrico frequently strolled through the upscale streets of SoHo simply because he liked it. He lived in a spacious one-bedroom apartment on a posh corner near Café Mafa, where he liked the pricey food so much that he sometimes just sat there all day, for lunch and an early dinner, too. Or he might take a walk to a designer boutique, where he could try on a $2,000 sports jacket and not bat an eye at the price. Promoters deliberately frequented upscale shops and restaurants in search of the kinds of rich men that were vital for their networks, but in Enrico's case, it was easy to be in these places. He belonged there by birthright.

Unlike most promoters, Enrico came from a rich family, one with properties and wineries in Spain. In his early twenties, in the early 2000s, he left home to study at a private university in New York, but mostly he was spending thousands of dollars of his family's money to party in clubs. The weekly $500 allowance he received from his parents wasn't enough, so his dad told him to get a job. He worked as a waiter in a Thai restaurant in Times Square for about six months, and he liked hanging out with the immigrant busboys. They ate the free "family meal" provided by the restaurant before the evening shift. One time during the family meal, Enrico ordered the lobster off the menu, and the manager reprimanded him, saying that Enrico should not eat lobster in front of everyone else. "I was like, 'What's the problem? I'm paying for it,'" he said. It's a story Enrico tells to reveal both his privilege and his uncritical ease with it.[5] That job didn't last, and he found his way into club promotions.

Like most other promoters, Enrico found the job by way of his lifestyle. One night out, he asked the doorman at an exclusive club how to get in without having to buy bottle service. The doorman told him to come with four or five hot girls, "and you're in for free." Enrico brought fifteen of his most beautiful European girlfriends, a crowd that attracted the attention of a promoter who offered Enrico $400 to bring them every week. Enrico thought it was a scam. "He was black, and I come from Spain, so I didn't know; I thought it wasn't true or was something scary," he said about the promoter, referencing stereotypes of black criminality. But when Enrico did it again the next week, the promoter handed him a big stack of twenties. He remembers being in disbelief in the cab on the way home, handing the cab driver a twenty-dollar bill and asking, "Is it real? How about this one, and this one?" Like almost every promoter I met, Enrico was invited to the job when someone took notice of the beautiful girls around him. With his wealth and preexisting connections, he started working at the top clubs and stayed there.

Six years later, Enrico was going out at least five times a week, making between $500 and $800 a night. He didn't worry much about money. His mom still paid his credit card bill; she liked to do it as a way to take care of him while he was so far away from home. He sometimes turned down payment from the club manager at the end of the night if his table was too sparse and not worth a paycheck in his view, as a matter of his own pride. When he got focused on the work, he could make about $3,500 a week—$180,000 a year—in tax-free cash, so what was it to him to decline $600 once in a while?

Enrico didn't often post about his parties on Facebook, and he didn't email or text mass invitations. "I don't like to bother people," he said. Rather, he tapped into his network of wealthy men. "My network is pretty good now," he told me, because he personally knew many of the top *Forbes*-ranked Spanish business families. He met his best friend, who owned a major sunglasses and sportswear conglomerate, while out in New York, but they soon found out they shared family connections. Enrico regularly showed me pictures in his phone of his "good friends" and "best friends," like famous soccer players from Spain, business tycoons, and their college-aged sons and daughters. This was part of the appeal of going out with him, which he played up in the individualized text messages he sent to invite girls to expensive dinners with wealthy and powerful men:

> I have a client wants to do dinner w/ owner and manager of [an entertainment company] Thurs in W hotel. And he asked me can u bring some beautiful girls and so I thought of u

To find beautiful girls, he often relied on word of mouth among his girlfriends, some of whom were models, but most of whom were good-looking civilians. I met strippers, escorts, students, and professional young women at his table, all recommended by mutual friends in his vast international network. His own girlfriend, Olga, was a twenty-three-year-old model from Russia, and she frequently brought out her model friends. But Enrico wasn't particularly interested in recruiting models. Enrico found that models tended to expect too much: "I think if you look like that," he said, "you get treated better in life. It's normally how it works, right?" It happened a few times that a model stretched her arm across the table to hold an empty champagne flute in front of Enrico's face, not breaking from the conversation she was having with someone else, waiting for Enrico to refill her glass. His face would contort into annoyed disbelief as he glared at the girl who, from his perspective, saw him as little more than a waiter from whom she was entitled to quick refills.

For these reasons, Enrico preferred to party with people he genuinely liked and mostly considered friends. He was known by other promoters for bringing out "hot Europeans," not necessarily models but a good-looking crowd. One promoter described his crowd as "the blazer brigade," new-money Europeans that two decades ago would have been disparaged as "Euro trash"; now, with strong and abundant euros to spend, they were welcomed to the prime tables. As Enrico himself described it, he liked to hang around different types of people, from strippers to athletes and European politicians' daughters.

Thus Enrico's job and his lifestyle meshed well. He frequently shared his drugs and hung out at strip clubs after the VIP clubs closed. Fueled by cocaine and fun-loving women, Enrico's life sometimes seemed to mostly happen at night. He told me one evening at dinner that he was exhausted, having gone to sleep at 4:30 that day. "You don't understand," he said when I nodded in sympathy, thinking he meant 4:30 a.m. "I went to sleep at 4:30 this afternoon."

It could occasionally be a headache trying to get beautiful girls together for dinner and clubbing five nights a week. At one point, he even offered me a job as his sub-promoter. If I could build up a good network of reliable girls to bring out each night, he would pay me as much as $400 a week, cash. I turned it down, but I invited my own friends to his table when I could.

Sitting beside him at one restaurant at 11 p.m., we were at a large table with ten chairs, four of which were empty. I asked him if there were more girls coming for dinner. "I hope so," he said with a little laugh. Was it hard to find ten pretty girls every night to go out with him? "You have to work for it," he said, and winked.

Dreaming

By the time I met Santos, he had such a strong global network of girls that he didn't need to scout in the streets of New York; instead he slept late during the days and preferred to spend long lazy afternoons smoking pot and texting girls. Like Enrico, Santos genuinely liked to party and chased after parties well into the next day. New York was just one of many cities he worked in; he spent a couple months of the year each in Milan, Miami, London, Ibiza, and the French Riviera. He owned an apartment in Milan that he offered as free housing to models, in exchange for their company at the clubs, and the rest of the time he lived in borrowed flats from his "friends"—the rich men whose parties and yachts he filled with girls.

Santos is tall, with long dreadlocks, sleeve tattoos, a great smile, and distinctive style: when I met him at the Downtown, he was wearing ripped jeans and a baseball cap embellished with metal spikes he added by hand, and he wore silver rings on each hand—big skulls and heavy crosses. He almost always had his phone in his hand, since he was almost always working somebody.

Dre introduced us. Though they were friendly, Dre kept his distance and drew a boundary between himself and Santos. "In my opinion, Santos is too into the girls and into the party. You have to be smart and use the nightlife for the access and the opportunities it gives you." Santos, in contrast, seemed too focused on the fun of the night rather than long-term career moves. One night at the Downtown, Dre insulted Santos in the worst way, though not to his face. "Santos is supposed to bring girls tonight, but he didn't. Not really. I don't know *what* he brought," he said, nodding over to Santos's table full of girls. "One of them is cute," he concluded dismissively.

Yet Santos professed often, like every promoter does, the beauty of his girls and the greatness of his parties.

One of eight siblings, Santos grew up poor in Bogotá. His father wasn't around much, and he was mostly raised by his mother, grandmother, and extended family. He remembers having no money for books or shoes for school. He started early in the drug trade, delivering little baggies in his underpants, and he was a practiced thief by sixteen. When his cousin was shot in a drug dispute, he followed an older brother to Milan, Italy, where he did not speak the language and where he was an outsider marked by brown skin and immigrant status.

He picked up Italian fast, first as a busboy in a bar, then as a bartender. Tall and good-looking, with almond-shaped eyes, he was quickly recruited into fashion modeling, which he did for a few months but was put off by the advances of gay men. The advances of women models, however, he welcomed, and at the bar where he continued to work, they came to see him for drinks after their modeling jobs. The manager took notice, and offered Santos a salary to move from behind the bar to the front to continue bringing in a fashionable crowd. Like most promoters I met, he didn't know the job existed until it was offered to him.

Ten years later, Santos had traveled throughout the jet-set world, sometimes via yachts and private planes. He spoke four languages (Spanish, Italian, English, and rough French) and a smattering of half a dozen more; "I can talk to anybody!" he claimed. He picked up languages easily through his travels and girlfriends, never having undergone formal education. He talked often about whom he knew and to which pools of power he was connected.

"They are friends but also clients. Corporate guys, business owners. I meet a lot of guys in finance," he said. In the French Riviera, he said, he knows a lot of princes.

Saudi Princes? I asked.

"Yes, Saudis. I know all of them," he offered casually.

He met them each summer in Saint-Tropez, in the clubs, when they descended for the season, before or after stops in Sardinia, Ibiza, and Monte Carlo. When I asked if he went to the Hamptons as well, he gave me a dismissive look: "Why would I go to the Hamptons? It's just New York people. If I want New York people, I'll meet them in New York."

With access to some of the world's richest families, Santos liked to say, "I'm gonna make it so big." For men like Santos, Dre, Malcolm, Sampson, Enrico, and Thibault, girls were their ticket to the upper echelons of the American Dream. They were systematic about recruiting girls, whether from the street, from within the fashion industry, or from intense networking, and they shared the goal of using girls to pursue ambitious dreams. Girls brought them valuable connections to the club's rich male clientele, from which they believed they could secure investments in their future projects. As in any dream, anything seemed possible.

3

The Potlatch

Saturday, 12 a.m., Miami

Walking through a darkness lit up with pulsating splashes of colorful strobe lights, enveloped by pounding house music, Santos made his entrance to the famous Ace Nightclub on Miami's South Beach strip. The Ace was one of the hottest places to party when the Ultra Music Festival, the famous electronic music event, brought the VIP crowd to Miami every year during the last weeks of March.

"Girls, stay with me!" Santos shouted as he guided us through the crowd to the client's table, where for the next three hours we would sit, stand, and dance on a U-shaped tufted-leather banquette. Some people even stood on the sofa's upper back; I climbed up there too, for a better look at the party. Our table was located in the center of the club, one of two dozen others in the cavernous space. When you looked toward the DJ from any position in the club, you could see us.

From where I stood, the crowd looked huge, maybe a thousand people, mostly white, mostly young, more than half women; at our table, the ratio was three girls to every two men. Most of the crowd was jumping to the music played by a famous electronic music DJ, a regular on the club circuit whose set everyone seemed to know. It's hard to dance in four-inch platform heels while perched on the top of a banquette, but the girls were all shaking hips and shoulders. As the crowd pulsated, jumping in sync, they waved glow sticks the club had passed out, whose neon lettering read "F*** Me I'm Famous."

Our table was stacked with large bins filled with bottles of liquor and champagne, little Evian waters and juices, and rows of champagne flutes and glasses. Almost everyone held a drink. Standing on the floor below me was Santos, his long dreads bobbing to the beat. He caught my eye, tipped his glass with a nod, and gestured around, like, "See? I told you it would be amazing."

The client, a well-known whale, stood nearby. This whale would be fairly easy to miss in the crowd: medium height, black T-shirt and jeans. He looked like a regular guy, except that he held a famously expensive pink bottle of Cristal champagne in one hand and was surrounded by towering, thin, beautiful girls. A few men stood nearby, including an imposing personal security guard who never left the whale's side, and who stood out because he wore a dark suit and tie. Only security and club management dress like that. Most of the men were in jeans and T-shirts, and some even wore shorts on this balmy Miami night—a sharp contrast to the stilettoed girls in svelte mini dresses.

The whale stood confidently in the center of the crowd, slapping hands with acquaintances who came to greet him, sometimes taking a picture of the crowd with his phone. He surveyed the room and the guests at his table. At one point he reached out with two bottles of Veuve Clicquot champagne, extending them as gifts to two girls nearby, who danced and drank directly from the bottles.

His next round of purchases arrived: two bins full of green champagne bottles lit up with sparklers, carried high above the heads of strong bouncers, followed by a procession of scantily clad bottle girls also holding sparklers and bottles up in the air. The bottle train is a magnificent sight that captures the attention of the room. The waitresses were required to wear five-inch-minimum stilettos, and their cleavage was almost always prominently displayed and then illuminated by the glow of the sparklers. The sparkler is a live firework that shoots out as high as eight inches. It burns for up to fifty-five seconds.

People cheered and held up their phones while the glow of sparklers lit up their faces. "Take pictures," Santos had told me earlier. "You gonna see so many places; you have to record it all and write about it." A table facing ours across the dance floor was also buying bottle trains, and the cocktail waitresses took turns walking back and forth carrying bottles and sparklers to each one. After a while it got old, and became a hassle, even, to rummage inside my bag for my phone to snap pictures of the bottle-buying sprees.

Soon there were champagne bottles everywhere. People stopped drinking from glasses, and instead they passed whole bottles to one another, holding them in one hand while dancing, sipping from them like beer.

A guy standing next to me and looking quite blasé about it all passed me a bottle of Cristal to swig from and pass on.

"Wow, how much does this cost?" I asked him.

Seventeen hundred dollars, he said, of this Cristal rosé from 2004. The other, green bottles of Veuve Clicquot sold for $800 apiece. I held the pink bottle of Cristal in my hand and marveled: it was worth exactly one month of my rent in Boston.

Next, the whale played a game. He held out his Cristal bottle to nearby girls' faces for them to drink from. This caught most girls by surprise: they paused for a second, registered his invitation, and accepted a drink. Most did this by holding onto his bottle with one hand as he pushed it to their lips. But one girl, who looked like a model, declined his bottle by turning her head away. In an instant, he grabbed her chin and pulled her face to the bottle of Cristal. She frowned, but he held her face in place and managed to dip the bottle into her mouth. She swallowed some of it, but the fizz was too much, and she had to spit it out with a little spray, wiping her face and scowling. The client quickly turned away and ignored her, pumping his fist into the air to the DJ's set, the bottle of Cristal in the other hand, while the girl sat down, shaking her head and wiping her face, looking disgusted. She left shortly after this.

This scene of masculine domination should give anyone pause. When scholars like French sociologist Pierre Bourdieu use the concept of masculine domination, they usually do so to describe the subtler registers of the symbolic realm, those small ways in which women come to view themselves as inferior relative to men.[1] But here, with a $1,700 bottle of champagne, brute masculine power can be symbolically and physically wielded over a woman. As I thought this, the client turned to me and held out his bottle. I put a hand on the side to steady it, drank, and said "Thanks!" in as chipper a tone as I could muster.

This was one of only two interactions we had while I was a guest of this client at three parties in Miami. On the other occasion, he nodded his head to me when I stood across the table from him, and I gave him a thumbs-up.

"Who is the client," I shouted over the music into Santos's ear.

"He is the biggest spender! Each day, he is spending $200,000, $250,000 on parties. *Each day.*"

What does he do for work, I wanted to know.

"I don't know. I don't like to ask this of people."

By night's end, the whale had purchased a dozen bottles of Cristal champagne and, according to Santos's estimate, two hundred bottles of Veuve Clicquot. For his part, Santos was paid $1,600 by the club to bring his crew of six girls, mostly models and good civilians, on both Friday and Saturday nights. That night, he also got $500 from a Brazilian whale for bringing girls to his after-party on the rooftop of a nearby luxury condo.

I had been in Miami for six hours, and already I had lost count of how many bottle trains I had seen. It went on like this for the next four nights with Santos in Miami, where I trailed him and his girls in a sleep-deprived daze through a series of clubs and their showcases of wealth going up in flames.

Potlatch

Rituals of displaying and squandering wealth have long been objects of fascination to anthropologists. Franz Boas, the pioneer of modern American anthropology, was among the first ethnographers to document wasting rituals, in late-nineteenth-century tribes along the Pacific Northwest Coast in what is now Canada.[2] With his key informant George Hunt, Boas depicted competitive gifting and feasting rituals called potlatches. In a potlatch, a tribal chief or noble lavished gifts of considerable riches upon his guests to advance his title or rank, doling out large quantities of food, woolen blankets, or silver bracelets. Potlatch ceremonies often began as a feast and culminated in a fire, sometimes with the outright destruction of property, like tossing blankets into a fire, breaking canoes, or throwing heirloom coppers into the ocean. This had an element of fun to it, as French anthropologist Marcel Mauss observed: "In effect, and in reality, not only are useful things given away and rich foods consumed to excess, but one even destroys for the pleasure of destroying."[3]

Potlatch was a highly variable practice across societies, and the term has been applied to a wide range of ritual prodigality, from slave sacrifice among the Aztecs to the "big-men" described in Marshall Sahlins's study of social order in Melanesia. Despite its variations, potlatch is typically enacted by a group leader seeking prestige and status.[4] Status was most obviously generated when a nobleman gave gifts so large that his rivals could not reciprocate, provoking their humiliation and establishing his dominance. Giving away treasures seems to be, on the surface, an act of social equalization. In a material sense it is, but it also creates status inequalities. That is, the host loses a lot of wealth but gains recognition among his peers.[5] A successfully magnanimous host gains the status of a "big-man," whose social bigness makes him a man of renown, albeit only in specific factions of a society.[6] As the anthropologist David Graeber notes, he is "infinitely heavy, from which blankets and other wealth flow down like an avalanche of property, simultaneously enriching and imperiling everyone around"; the feel of a potlatch, writes Graeber, exudes this strange combination of aggression and generosity.[7] In ceremonial squander, anthropologists saw not just a curious or irrational practice, but profoundly meaningful ways of representing and building the hierarchy of a society.[8] Potlatch is about rank. It can be playful and transgressive, but it is always rooted in systems of prestige and power.

While classic studies of potlatches now feel dated, ethnographies continue to reveal them in a surprising range of contemporary settings. Sam Quinones, a journalist chronicling the opioid epidemic in America, discovered potlatch as one motivating force driving the labor supply of Mexican drug dealers.[9] Farm boys from a small southern Mexican village called Xalisco made their way north to the American rust belt to deal black tar heroin for their relatives, only to return home after a few months flush with cash and eager to show it. They built new houses, bought new cars, sponsored festivals, and brought home suitcases full of Levis 501 jeans to distribute to their reverent family and friends. This reverence then propelled other men to seek profit in dealing heroin across America, and then return home to squander it.[10]

Displays of ostentation also turn out to be central to business dealings in parts of Asia.[11] Anthropologist John Osburg has documented how rich businessmen in Chengdu, China, establish themselves by lavishly entertaining state officials in upscale restaurants, karaoke clubs, and brothels.[12] At dinner, more dishes are always brought to the table than can ever be consumed. The Chengdu potlatch forges masculine solidarity among business networks and underworld gangs, which, in post-reform China, amount to the same thing.

Potlatches can also be seen in the globally widespread displays of largesse at weddings and in casinos. They are the defining logic of fraternity parties at the start of the school year on every college campus with a prominent Greek life. They are captured in lurid detail on *Rich Kids of Instagram*, a website full of images posted by young rich people from around the world explicitly wasting their wealth— burning dollar bills and soaking in bubble baths of Dom Pérignon champagne.[13]

The economist Thorstein Veblen scandalized elites at the turn of the twentieth century by likening high society to the "primitive peoples" he read about in Boas's anthropology reports. To Veblen, the natives and the elites shared the impulse to show off through "invidious consumption," seeking status among their respective audiences. But Veblen was too reliant on a shaky assumption: that the nouveau riche naturally act this way. Potlatching is hardly a defining feature of the rich; it goes against competing understandings of consumption that view showing off as vulgar. For instance, wealthy seventeenth-century Dutch families were inconspicuous consumers who tended to downplay their fortunes. Today, similar norms of restraint and muted luxuries characterize much of Silicon Valley's newly rich consumers. Among New York's upper classes, sociologist Rachel Sherman has documented discomfort with extravagance. In many contexts, wealth is something to be hidden. A potlatch therefore requires a huge collective accomplishment to orchestrate such enormous waste.[14]

Like any potlatch, the VIP club dramatizes the relationship between subordination and domination. By studying the organization of the show—the gendered entourage, the staging, the props, and the cues provided by the club—we can learn how rich men get transformed into "big-men" over the course of a night.[15]

Staging Waste

For a place that seems to be about spontaneous fun, a club is a highly regimented space, one that provides scripts for wasteful behaviors to unfold in patterned ways, from Miami to Cannes. To begin, the club tries to appeal to rich spenders by looking luxurious. Club decor exudes extravagance, with state-of-the-art lighting and sound systems and meticulous attention to furnishings and fixtures. One club had imported mature birch trees and wrought iron patio furniture to give it the feel of an exotic café. Another was furbished with dark suede ceilings and rich amber light, and customers walked through an arched golden tunnel to get inside. It made the club's entrance feel like a portal to a secret rich world. A few of these spaces cost upward of $2 million to design and build.[16]

Next, managers pay close attention to seating arrangements. Not only are image promoters strategically placed at tables in corners of the room to give the illusion of an abundance of beautiful girls, but clients, too, are carefully placed at tables that correspond to their importance. Big clients are seated near the DJ booth, the center of attention in the room, from where the music and the night's energy emanate. Especially since the rise of superstar DJs and electronic dance music, people come out specifically to see the DJ. At some dance clubs, DJs' fees can be more than $50,000 per night; even six-figure fees are now common.[17]

Big spenders become the focus of the room, so that when their spending happens, all eyes are fixed on bright lines of sparklers snaking through the space. Most clubs situate the tables on slightly elevated platforms, so that clients overlook the fillers on the dance floor by at least a foot, sometimes several. Additionally, guests at tables are likely to stand on the sofa seats, or sit perched on the sofa's upper back. It's a seating arrangement that recalls a court society's staggering of table heights according to nobles' rank.[18]

Perched up high on the upper back of the sofa of his table at Club X, Dre once observed the swelling crowd, in which people could barely walk through the room to get to the bar. "You can only be in here if you are rich or are hot," he said about the club. "That's who has access here. You're not rich, you don't belong here. You don't have a table, just look around here—" and he motioned to the crowd from his elevated position. "Where you gonna go? You can't stand at the bar all night. Where do you go without a table?" Of course, a man may stand all night at the bar or around the edge of the dance floor without a table, and in doing so reveal his subordinate social position. Anyone can recognize high-status guests based on their location and elevation, thanks to a fairly consistent topography of status in the club scene, from Miami to Saint-Tropez, and thanks to a number of the same interior designers who work internationally.[19]

Perhaps the most important status symbol of all is the girl. Girls are displayed in key corners of the room and encouraged to dance in the most visible places: on top of chairs, tables, and the highest banquettes surrounding clients. Sitting down is quickly met with, "Baby, what's wrong?" or "What happened?" from promoters.

For the value of the girl to shine through, not only should she be positioned centrally, she should look the part. Crucially, she should be very tall. With the current fashion of platform heels of at least four inches, nearly all girls at promoter tables stand at least six feet tall. The height of the girl, like the size of the bottle, conveys crucial information. Sampson explained: "It makes an impression. A woman walking in taller than everybody else, it catches your eye, and the men want to talk to you but they're intimidated."

Some clubs charge clients more for tables next to models or celebrities, while others offer this as a perk for well-known whales. Often a promoter's large group will suddenly move to another table, across the room or maybe just sliding over to the next one, sometimes to join a client's table, if he has requested to host a group of girls. "A big client is coming and they want us to be there," next to him, said Felipe when I asked one night why we were migrating, this time to be closer to the DJ. He explained later, "A lot of guys have money or a bonus, but they got no swag, so we bring them the party and make them look good."

Like girls, champagne bottles are put to work in the service of showing off clients' expenditures. Champagne has been associated with exclusive celebrations for at least a century and associated with elites since court society monopolized its consumption in prerevolutionary Europe.[20] Champagne lends itself well to parties: the liquid is clear and fizzy, such that bottles can be shaken and sprayed with fanfare yet minimal damage, unlike, say, red wine.[21] The champagne house Moët & Chandon releases only about six vintages of its prestige champagne, Dom Pérignon, per decade, and each bottle is held for six or seven years before release. Throughout my fieldwork, bottles of the 2009 vintage were frequently purchased, gifted, wasted, and left unopened, in the process demonstrating status through the destruction both of property and of the time symbolized in those green bottles.

Bottles depict their expensiveness by design. In 2002, Dom Pérignon champagne issued glow-in-the-dark labels, specifically designed to broadcast the iconic brand in the low lights of a nightclub. Promoters regularly posted selfies with the neon green glow all around them. Some have used stacks of the bottles as their banner photos on Facebook. People regularly took pictures of the bottles piled high in buckets on the tables. Liquor bottles are likewise decorated with blinking flashlights. Bottles of Belvedere vodka and Patron tequila are lit from within the glass bottle with a dark light, to make the bottle appear an iridescent jewel floating above the crowd en route to its table.

Size also matters in bottles. Larger and larger bottles have appeared on club menus, most with biblical names like the jeroboam (3 liters) and methuselah (6 liters), which is the equivalent of eight regular bottles, priced at $40,000 for Cristal champagne at Club X. As bottle sizes increase on the menu, their prices rise exponentially, not linearly, as the display of the bottle size, not its liquid content, makes it valuable.[22] Sometimes bottles are too heavy for the waitresses to carry, so large security guards bring them to the table and hoist them over a shoulder in order to pour the liquid into delicate champagne flutes. Because spirits are consumed more slowly and in smaller quantities, handles max out at 1.75 liters.

Clubs deploy these valuable champagne bottles and enact rituals around their consumption in choreographies of play and display. To set the client's spending in motion, a manager or owner may send a gift to his table. A gifted bottle of champagne necessitates reciprocity on a grander scale. Don, a forty-five-year-old owner of a VIP club in Hong Kong, was also a bottle client at other clubs around the world. To him, it's all in the timing: "I start ordering bottles in the club when I see other people do it." In his own club, to get bottle purchases going, he explained, "If I give a bottle of Dom to a customer at a table, what do they do? They have to buy one, or two, or buy one that's bigger! That's how it works, and it goes up and up and it can't go down." By setting the process in motion, club owners are personally involved in producing and directing expenditure.

Club owners usually know the biggest clients at their club, and they are in constant communication with them. The club owner in Hong Kong explained, "Those guys, they want to show off. I always say the club is a boxing ring. You get them in so they can do this"—he flexed his bicep muscles. So he came up with the idea of shining a bright flashlight, he called it the "torch," onto the head of whoever settles the bill at the end of the night: "It's so everyone can see who's paying."

"It's on tonight," read a text message sent by one club co-owner to a whale sitting nearby, alerting him to the arrival of another whale and thus rousing the spirit of competition. Competition makes the night's action more exciting, something Hemingway observed in bull-fighting, too ("Bullfighting is worthless without rivalry").[23] Managers deliberately place whales at tables opposite each other near the DJ booth, to fuel rivalry through the public comparison of their purchases. Club managers hope that a large purchase at one table will encourage a larger purchase at an opposite table. Clubs give whales the ammunition of bottles, and whales fire away at each other figuratively. This can escalate into a "champagne war," a ritualized potlatch with bottles as the idioms of rivalry.[24]

Sometimes the VIP potlatch takes the form of magnanimity without rivalry, as when whales gift bottles of champagne to every other table in the club. Partiers sometimes walk out of clubs with unopened gifted bottles of Dom Pérignon, whose prices range from $500 to $1,500 on the menu but cost $240 at the liquor shop down the street. Santos's girls had a few unopened Doms in the back of the SUV one night after the leaving the club in Miami. "Take it, honey," a promoter had told us on our way out, "It's gonna get thrown out." They gave one to a guy dancing on top of his parked Jeep Cherokee as they pulled out of the club's parking lot. He was pleased.

Bottle trains often bring more alcohol than can be consumed by clients, who then destroy the excess. Like the Pacific Northwest potlatch that begins as a feast and culminates in a bonfire, bottle purchases sometimes escalate into "champagne showers," where excess bottles are shaken, sprayed, and dumped onto nearby revelers, thus also potentially destroying designer shoes and clothes.[25] Such spending becomes the center of attention in the club, frequently photographed and video-recorded by other revelers, who cheer and toast the show.

Champagne purchases, wars, and showers take on an aura of playfulness, making displays of excess seem unserious. To build up the fun, club managers sometimes offer clients packages that include extra, cheaper bottles of prosecco or sparkling white wine for spraying. Some patrons shake stacks of dollar bills from on high, letting the green paper fall in the air to the floor below, a practice well known in hip-hop music as "making it rain." Some clubs are renowned for their dramatizations of spending, called "bottle staging." At one night-club in Los Angeles, big spenders reportedly received bottles from "flying midgets" hooked to aerial cables.[26] At the Saturday afternoon brunch at Club Jewel in Manhattan, expensive bottles were delivered by costumed characters including Superman, Batman, and Wonder Woman.

Clubs further manipulate the crowd's attention with music and theatrical tricks. To mark a big purchase, in addition to deploying sparklers, the club may have the DJ interrupt the music ("Alex from London is in the house and he just spent 100 K on Dom!"). One twenty-four-year-old client showed me pictures on his iPhone of his bottle-buying sprees in LA, where his finance software company is based, and boasted about spending $500,000 on champagne in the last six months. His pictures showed the nearby tables' crowd hold-ing white placards with letters spelling out his initials, which they raised in the air when he made a large purchase, while the DJ played "his song," a hip-hop track called "I'm a Boss," by Meek Mill. Not incidentally, the lyrics include the line: "You a boss; he don't care what it cost."[27]

Even the leftovers and detritus are put on display. At Nikki Beach Club in Saint-Tropez, crates of empty bottles are displayed next to their buyers' tables for the duration of the party, evidence of the destructive show that took place. Sometimes girls take off their shoes to dance, putting designer high heels like the iconic red-soled Louboutins in the buckets alongside the champagne bottles, a veri-table bouquet of excess sex and money.

But for all of their wild fervor, these are scripted organizational achievements. There is an interactional order to them, a fairly pre-dictable one that unfolds in sequence night after night: an entourage gathers, a stage ensures visibility, props are procured, and as the vibe builds up, bottles are brought out with an increasing fervor among a cheering crowd. Consider, in striking contrast, a real fight that broke out between two VIP club spenders. Early Thursday morning in June 2012, a physical fight with bottles broke out in a bottle service club called W.i.P., in SoHo, between two rivals, the R & B singer Chris Brown and the rapper Drake, and their entourages.[28] Well-known tensions between the two artists, stemming from their mutual involvement with the singer Rhianna, escalated from ice cubes thrown between the opposing tables, located near each other, followed by whole champagne bottles lobbed as missiles into the rivals' entourages. At the end of the bloody fight, several people were injured, including an Australian tourist needing sixteen stitches after a bottle grazed her head. Police investigated, charges of reckless engagement were filed and three lawsuits were filed against the singers and the club. The real bottle war underscored just how the VIP club sublimates competitive behavior, rendering it allegorical and symbolic, with no real danger beyond, perhaps, that of momentary status loss.

The status of the spender is clearly marked in bodies, space, and money as objectified in the size and quantity of his bottles, and the height, beauty, and abundance of girls around him. "If you have a table, then you're a person of value," said the CEO of a food company, a man in his fifties who was a regular of VIP clubs since the late 1990s. Though he didn't go out much anymore, and he certainly didn't spend on bottles like he used to, he distinctly recalled all the ways that a club could help him project status and impress women.

"If you have nice shoes and a good watch, then she knows. But other than that, when you go to the club and there's hundreds of men there, how do you separate yourself from everybody else? You know how. You buy three hundred bottles of champagne and you shoot it all over the walls. They need everybody to know that 'Hey, I'm the top dog.' You have a lot of girls, a lot of champagne; you have the prime table, not the one all the way in the corner; you have the prime table in the VIP. Then you're the top dog."

Top dogs, big-men, bosses: these performances are organizational achievements. As it turns out, being a part of the show is itself highly appealing to the filler, affluent tourists, and businessmen whose smaller table bills bankroll the show.

The Whale and the Lettuce

For the most part, the big spenders that drop tens of thousands of dollars in a single night are not regular visitors. "They come around once every three months and then they disappear," one club owner told me. Accordingly, clubs don't count on the exceptional excesses of whales for their profits. Their target clients are affluent city residents, tourists, and visiting businessmen who are a reliable presence night after night. These regulars spend relatively modest but consistent sums. "It's like making a salad," continued the club owner. "What's the most important ingredient, the biggest ingredient in a salad? Lettuce. That's our affluent New Yorkers, guys with small bills of three to five thousand."

Over the course of my fieldwork, I came to expect "bottle trains" with between three and six bottles of fireworks-illuminated champagne heading to different tables several times a night. Even with six bottles of Dom Pérignon, the bill added up to only about $6,000 at Club X. I saw just one "champagne shower," which involved the shaking and spraying of champagne onto revelers during a weekend trip to Saint-Tropez, and I observed two instances of competitive one-upmanship of bottle buying, or "bottle wars," while in Miami. A six-figure bill was most likely to occur at high-profile parties during peak season, like Cannes during the film festival, or Saint-Tropez in the summer months.

But I heard a lot about the potlatches. Promoters spent a lot of time talking about the presence of big spenders in the VIP scene, but few of them witnessed the champagne potlatch more than once a month, partly because big spenders travel frequently.

People in the scene delighted in sharing stories about big spenders, whether they had personally seen or just heard about them. The most prominent whale during my fieldwork, Jho Low, was legendary. He had an infamous bar tab in Saint-Tropez, estimated to be over $1 million for a single night, and photos of that night showing him at a table with dozens of magnum bottles, sparklers, and Paris Hilton have appeared everywhere from local Malaysian press to the *New York Times*. That was a night that involved relatively few people, but everyone seemed to know about it. For instance, in a casual conversation between Dre and Rhys, a finance investor and a bottle client, while walking down the street in SoHo, Rhys began:

"Saint-Tropez is ridiculous. One guy alone spent 1.2 million euros on tables."

"That's Jho Low," said Dre. "He's Malaysian. He spent one night $1.5 million in the club. It costs them $1.3 million to make the club, he paid for it in one night. The club is now just profit."[29]

Despite the infrequent appearance of big spenders like Low, clubs orient their spaces to appeal to men like him, keeping stores of expensive champagne bottles on hand and plenty of sparklers at the ready. While their reputations are built by catering to whales, the bulk of the clubbing business is won by appealing to "the lettuce."

To see how this works, consider a consumer like Bryan from Arizona. Bryan is a financial advisor I met at a Saturday brunch party at a VIP Manhattan restaurant and club called Club Jewel. During weekend afternoons, Jewel offers tables for brunch, featuring a resident DJ with loud party music, promoters' tables full of girls, and bottle service—a daytime clubbing experience sometimes called "boozy brunch," epitomized by the "Day and Night" parties in the Meatpacking District.[30] Promoters work the day brunch at Jewel, and by evening, they head to a club owned by Jewel's partners to keep the party going late into the night. Bryan and his five colleagues were in town for a work retreat for his financial firm. Twice a year, his boss rented a brownstone in midtown Manhattan for the team to spend time relaxing and working on New York deals. Bryan was thirty-two; his boss was thirty-five. Their brunch tab came to $6,000. This was a modest sum, Bryan reasoned, compared to the splurges of the really rich people he's partied with. Once, in a Vegas casino, an old friend with a large inheritance threw $25,000 worth of poker chips up in the air, bequeathing them to nobody in particular. Those kinds of really big spenders were foolish, Bryan thought, just "guys wanting to be a baller." Bryan and his colleagues, in contrast, were working professionals just looking to have some fun.

Bryan was as curious about the whales as I was, especially since he would never enjoy bankrolling whole tables full of strangers at a nightclub. He certainly wouldn't pay thousands of dollars for a night out unless he was splitting it with people. "Where do these people come from?" he asked rhetorically.

Though Bryan expressed disdain for the whales, he enjoyed being a part of the show that the clubs put on for them. At Jewel's brunch on Saturday, for instance, sparkler-lit bottles were delivered by the club's manager wearing a gladiator costume, carried to a client's table by a busboy-drawn chariot, cheered on loudly by the crowd. "The chariot blew my mind," said Bryan. Our promoter table was next to his as the brunch party transformed into bottle-buying sprees. "I didn't know it was going to be a nightclub!" Bryan told me. "I loved it." He even sent out pictures of the chariot in a mass text to his friends around the country. "I was like, this is insane, it's out of control! I'm thinking that stuff's not like actual pyrotechnics because I'm looking for the exits," he said, laughing.

"That chariot, though," he said, shaking his head in amazement, showing me the pictures on his iPhone. A carefully staged potlatch produces a dynamic of recognition between spender and audience: his spending rouses the crowd, and meanwhile the club strategically ratchets upward this collective euphoria to maximize and normalize conspicuous excess—the decor, the beauty, the theatrics, and those idioms of masculine power, bottles. The room breathes in the buzz and rejoices in the excitement shared among everyone: girls, the big-men, even the lettuce from Arizona.

Effervescence

Like any social ritual, the champagne potlatch brings people together with the possibility that they might share in something special. It is difficult to convey just how incredibly seductive and thrilling these nights could be. Moments of delight may build up over an evening, beginning with a lavish dinner in an upscale restaurant with beautiful people who don't have to contemplate paying the bill, followed by being whisked past the velvet rope, ahead of everyone waiting out-side in line, to enjoy bottle service in the club. Inside, the pleasures of the group are spurred on by bottomless glasses of champagne, shots of top-shelf tequila, and, depending on the table, sometimes MDMA and cocaine.[31] These intoxicants are consumed amid elaborate light and sound systems with famous DJs delivering beloved house and hip-hop beats, which inspire friends and strangers alike to lose their inhibitions, to shout and dance on the tops of tables and sofas, to flirt with a promoter or kiss a handsome stranger, while snapping selfies that instantly appear on Facebook and Instagram for the admiration of new friends and the envy of old ones. All of it can culminate in an exhilarating feeling of transcendence within an extraordinary world of privilege—money and beauty and fun in excess.[32]

So many people seek this feeling of transcendence. They seek it at sports stadiums, protest marches, Mardi Gras, Burning Man, and homecoming parades—anywhere people come together for a group experience.[33] They seek it in sacred ceremony and religious ritual, as French sociologist Émile Durkheim noted, because this feeling is the basis of religion. This feeling is at the core of human connectivity.

Durkheim studied accounts of rituals among Australian indigenous communities to understand how collective ritual works in modern societies. In his early twentieth-century writings on totemism, Durkheim argued that aborigines lived between two rhythms of life. There were seasons when small groups were scattered across the land, focused on work, hunting, and fishing. And there were times when the population came together for religious ceremony. It is in these ceremonial times, when people come into close proximity in great numbers, that members of the crowd can experience *collective effervescence*, an intense social experience understood as a social emotion, the excitement that comes from feeling close—both physically and emotionally—to others.[34] Durkheim ([1912] 2001, pp. 162–63) described a totemic ritual:

> Once the individuals are assembled, their proximity generates a kind of electricity that quickly transports them to an extraordinary degree of exaltation. Every emotion expressed is retained without resistance in all those minds so open to external impressions, each one echoing the others. The initial impulse thus becomes amplified

as it reverberates, like an avalanche gathering force as it goes. And as passions so strong and uncontrolled are bound to seek outward expression, there are violent gestures, shouts, even howls, deafening noises of all sorts from all sides that intensify even more the state they express.

This is dramatic prose for Durkheim, whose otherwise laconic writing style reflected his desire to study the social world as a scientific object.[35] In this passage, Durkheim is also trying to convey just how powerful effervescence feels once it erupts in a crowd. The very fact of being surrounded by a lot of people propels an energy throughout, lifting each member into a collective greater than the sum of its parts. This energy can transmit feelings of intense highs. It can lead to periodic moments of abandon: throwing your arms in the air, losing yourself in the rhythm, a feeling like falling in love or taking drugs.[36]

Nightclubs are in the business of channeling a crowd's emotional energy toward collective effervescence, which some called the nights' "energy," or "vibe." Different clubs on different nights curate different vibes, by changing the music, the lighting, and even props like glow sticks and sunglasses distributed to the crowd. Some clubs hire dancers wearing exotic and sexy costumes and place them in prominent locations to boost the room's energy.

Promoters similarly boost the crowd's energy at the level of the table. The vibe can be especially strong among tables full of friends, since "letting go" is easier with lowered inhibitions among familiar people. This is one reason promoters aim to build relationships with and among their girls. They are reluctant to bring out a girl if she consistently is in a bad mood, or if she looks out of place, as she is likely to throw off the vibe of the others. "Like a couple times some girls will complain about one girl, like if she's negative or is doing stuff that bothers people, and so I'll say sorry you can't come out with us," explained Trevor.

To work up the energy of their guests, promoters pour shots, refill glasses, and make toasts. They give hugs and fist bumps and lots of kisses on girls' cheeks. They introduce everybody to each other at the table, bringing the group into cohesion. They dance, sometimes slowly grinding with one girl, sometimes jumping up and down on the sofas with the group to a fast beat. When I was out with Thibault, Felipe, and their sub Jack, I saw how they divided and conquered their large group of girls to maximize fun; each promoter took a corner of the clique to ensure a good time, twirling at least one girl in a dance. Felipe was an expert at getting the most reluctant girls to dance; he could flip a dance partner over his shoulder with ease, even if she didn't know the moves.

Intimacy and the vibe went hand in hand at the tables run by Vanna and Pablo, who operated a "model apartment" in New York, where I temporarily lived along with Catherine, nineteen, and Renee, twenty-one, both American models. As a condition to live in the apartment rent-free, the girls were obliged to go out at least four nights a week with the promoters or their sub. This took a toll on their daytime plans and spirits, but when Saturday came around, they renewed their shared love of the group and nightlife.

"It's the most insane night for our group. We all just let everything go and *literally* we have just so much fun and everyone in the club, when we start yelling and screaming, they all turn and look at us like, 'What the hell?' . . . We get *crazy*. We have so much fun," said Catherine.

"It's like family, for us," chimed in Renee.

Their high energy caught the attention of club managers, who frequently joined their tables to share in the fun.

"The managers love us," said Renee. Catherine added: "We bring the energy."

Between Catherine and Renee and their promoter friends, the collective effervescence is a cooperative social production: girls join with promoters to produce the vibe, which is engineered and staged by management.[37]

When it comes together—the crowd, the music, the vibe—such moments of unrestraint can border on danger, since "going crazy" can lead to unpredictable or outlandish behavior. It can be destructive. Passions running through a crowd can violate taboos: people vandalize at sports events and disrobe in public at Mardi Gras.[38] In the VIP scene, rich men buy dozens of bottles, shake and spray them onto each other, and squander in direct violation of widespread cultural norms that showing off is, well, tacky.

Stupid Money

Rich people are ridiculous.

That was Sam's assessment of the bottle-buying sprees he witnessed in clubs. To a guy like Sam, the bottle trains epitomized everything he hated about being rich: the too-obvious attempts to show off, the ability to buy access to anything, the random fashion models inserted at dinner parties. A thirty-three-year-old hedge fund manager who specialized in energy commodities, Sam was used to being around money. Most of his clients were rich men, and though he described his Asian immigrant family and upbringing as middle-class, he grew up with rich friends in Southern California and went to an elite private high school. But in his time around very rich people in the VIP club scene, he felt like an outsider.

After graduating from MIT, he spent several years in New York, building up his business and going out. In the early 2000s, in Manhattan's Meatpacking District, he noticed that probably half of the clubs' tables were filled with finance guys, and most of their tabs would be covered by their corporate expense accounts.

He could imagine how exciting the scene was for those guys. For "someone like me"—not for himself personally, he clarified—who "went to MIT," he began. "You've seen the girls on that campus? Okay, so you know what I mean. In finance, these guys come to New York after four years of being in schools like this, and they start working at Goldman Sachs making tons of money, and they can go out and get bottle service and you get to hang out with models. So the club scene is basically giving them something that was never attainable for them." Sam liked Club X, because it had the best electronic dance music DJs and, he admitted, the girls were very pretty. "Well, every man would be lying if he said he didn't like to be around a bunch of beautiful girls."

But sometimes the excesses of clubbing were just *ridiculous*, a word I heard often in interviews. Sam explained that when he visited Saint-Tropez with his girlfriend, in 2011, he was at first charmed by the unique feel of the French Riviera. There are people from all over the world there during the summer season, international elites and the newly rich from emerging markets. But the nightlife there often turned into gross displays of money, with competitions over who could spend more in shows of waste so spectacular that Sam still had pictures of them saved on his iPhone two years later. The fact that Sam took photos means that he was fully participating as an audience member of these spectacles, which he described with a mixture of repulsion and fascination.

One night at a renowned club, he recalled, the DJ interrupted the music to announce that "Shamir from Dubai has ordered this rare bottle of champagne, it's only the *third* time this season someone has ordered it!," at which point the United Arab Emirates flag theatrically dropped down from the ceiling. Then the DJ played the Emirates national anthem before returning to his set. On another night, the DJ announced, "It's the Bottle Olympics in here; we have a war going between the table from India and [the one] from Pakistan!"

"I'm sure you're aware these countries have a long-standing territorial dispute," Sam said as he smiled and shook his head, scrolling through his pictures.

He showed me how the Indian and the Pakistani clients faced off at opposite tables in the club. With each big purchase, bottles dropped down from cords in the ceiling into the center of the club, and from there they were carried off by bottle girls with sparklers to the rival tables. "It's a circus act!" Sam said, of a night that he estimated cost upward of 300,000 euros.

"A real show of wealth is to buy everyone bottles," Sam told me, still flipping through pictures from Saint-Tropez. He showed me an image taken from another night out, this one of a clubgoer reaching into a box full of Dom Pérignon bottles with their recognizable green glow-in-the-dark labels. On that occasion, a whale had gifted dozens of bottles to strangers. "One guy was walking around with two bottles, one in each hand." This went beyond a display of generosity, to an expression of charity, one of the purest ways to convert wealth into status: if someone cannot recompense the gift, the giver reaps a return in prestige from everyone in the room who has just been made a dependent.[39]

"I've never seen anything like it," Sam said, laughing and slowly shaking his head at the scene. He then turned serious.

"It's disgusting, kind of. I thought about this before, like is this wrong? Is this a bad use of money? And I don't think it is, because it's money spent that creates a lot of good. The money's not better spent on, like, welfare; I mean I just told you I love Charles Murray"— the social scientist known for his racially charged critiques of social welfare, widely embraced by conservatives—"but really it's money that's going back into the economy. . . . and I don't think it's better to just give that money, like, to a homeless person or anything.[40] So when I say it's disgusting, I'm not approaching it from the lens of 'Let's feed the starving babies.'

"The reason is because it's meant to show. It's the status aspect that is disgusting. They're doing it for the sake of being seen. And it's for the attention and fanfare and that's why everyone photographs it and posts pictures of it. That's the part of it that I could not stand." Implicitly, then, Sam did not object to large sums being spent on status objects; rather, the deliberate performance of that status bothered him. The display of wealth, to rich people like Sam, is a violation of decorum.

Most people think, as Thorstein Veblen did, that ostentation is a natural outcome of being rich. Hardly. In fact, showing off can violate modern Western social norms like the virtue of asceticism and hard work, the ideal of equality of people, and the common discomfort people feel with blatant social hierarchies and exclusions.[41] Herein lies the key organizational problem that clubs must overcome. VIP clubs have to go a long way to mobilize people to break these norms, to show off, and to create an environment where such behavior is normal, even applauded.

Furthermore, status is a sensitive thing.[42] It exists only when an audience recognizes it, and it cannot be bought outright without, of course, a loss of status. VIP clubs have to construct the potlatch in a way that suspends the deliberateness of status-seeking, primarily by making it fun and seemingly spontaneous. Clubs are spaces designed to sublimate people's criticism of clients' wasteful displays and refashion them as play. But outside the high-end party, beyond the walls of the carefully orchestrated VIP space, rich customers talk about the scene in a more reflexive and critical way, recognizing that spending can seem silly, tacky, or even offensive to the very people whom they intend to impress.

In interviews, I found that girls, club owners, promoters, and clients themselves frequently critiqued lavish nightclub spending and, in particular, those clients whom they perceived as spending solely for status. The words they most commonly used to describe rituals of bottle buying were "ridiculous," "stupid," "waste," and "crazy." Jane, a twenty-eight-year-old actress and philosophy master's student, said she was not impressed by a recent $11,000 bottle buying spree at her promoter's table. "It does not impress me. It makes me think this guy is irresponsible to buy so many bottles. It impresses the other men. They're having an antler fight while they're all in there, and we're just the lucky witnesses."

In interviews conducted outside the club context, in corporate boardrooms and quiet cafés, clients invoked norms of restraint and described conspicuous consumption as vulgar. They talked with regret about their former recklessly spending selves. As A.J., a thirty-eight-year-old white entrepreneur from Latin America who had inherited wealth, explained:

> I was young. I was stupid. I just threw money away. When I think back on it now, I think it's so stupid, going out like that, buying bottles. It's retarded . . . I mean, do you know how many people you could feed or give water to in Africa?

Clients were especially critical of other rich men whom they perceived as spending specifically to gain status—to "show off" with deliberate acts of striving for recognition. To them, showing off was a hallmark of the nouveau riche and betrayed one's lack of true elite belonging. The very act of displaying one's economic power marked them as not culturally elite, explained Rhys, thirty-five, a

French financial advisor descended from European aristocracy. He described the whales like this:

> I think they're more after social status. It's social status but also more of a culture for them. . . . I think it looks stupid. It's fine, it's good business for the guys owning the clubs, but it doesn't do anything for me. I don't know what their backgrounds are, those guys, I think they're like, "Ok, look, I made it. I'm successful."

It was remarkable, in fact, how almost every client I interviewed took a critical stance toward these staged displays of waste, regardless of whether or not they came from money. They described whales as consuming for the wrong reasons—to show off with forced, unnatural acts of striving. These men, all of whom could be described as "working rich," even when they came from wealthy families, voiced clear justifications for their own large bills in clubs. They minimized their own expenditures by drawing symbolic boundaries between themselves and *other* clients. In the VIP arena, where vast financial resources are on display, even the biggest spenders could see their purchases as relatively modest. There is always someone spending more, given the extent to which the world's wealth is concentrated in the hands of men like the whales. Several clients explained that this is the nature of wealth in a city like New York, where their own riches might seem paltry compared to those of someone else in the same room. As the sociologist Rachel Sherman similarly noted, this is a common discursive strategy through which wealthy New Yorkers minimize their material privilege in order to feel more comfortable with their own economic superiority.[43]

When describing the excesses of VIP club spending, Saint-Tropez was a frequent topic, especially as the site of the extravagances of the most infamous whale, Jho Low. Luc, the forty-eight-year-old French restauranteur and wine salesman who comes from a long line of family wealth and titles, described Saint-Tropez as "the epitome of bottle service," and invoked Low as a universal standard of comparison:

> Saint-Tropez, a *billion* dollars. This guy Jho Low, you know Jho Low? Yeah, he spent a million dollars, and there was a competition

between Jho Low and the Pakistanis. So he was taking a 20,000 euro bottle and the others were taking it, and they were paying for the other tables, "Send that guy a bottle!" . . . That's why I don't go out any more, because . . . there's no limits anymore.

Using the language of waste and stupidity, Luc and A.J. simultaneously relativized their own expenditures, such that their club bills of $1,000 or even $10,000 seemed small compared to "crazy" expenditures on dozens of bottles. In comparison to the "ridiculous" whales, clients' own spending looked reasonable, even modest.

Whales' lavish spending was frequently called "stupid money" or "crazy money," and occasionally "fuck you money." Its quick destruction in nightclubs suggested that such money was not earned through legal or morally legitimate means like hard work and effort.[44] Clients that I interviewed tended to view "modest" bottle purchases as the harmless expenditure of legitimate money. However, they viewed the most extravagant displays of wealth as money poorly spent, and the scale of the destruction of stupid money raised questions about its origins.

The most dubious of big spenders were non-Western outsiders, like Russian, Arab, and "crazy rich Asian" spenders who jointly manifested as the specter of irrational status-seeking. Clients took pains to distinguish themselves from these whales. Luc described Saint-Tropez as ruined by these outsiders from the nouveau riche:

The Russians came in, they destroyed the scene. Before it was family, it was always friends gathering in the same place, spending a little bit of money but not crazy kind of money. But now it's these Russians or these Arabs . . . So the tables we had for so many years, now it's given to Russians. And they don't know how to have fun, these guys. I mean, fun for them is spending as much money as they can, but it's not fun. To have like two hundred bottles coming to you. . . . It's hard to find people who actually have class. Now it's all about money. [He sighed.]

Russians and Arabs were routinely invoked as outsiders who bought their way into the VIP scene. However, the very act of displaying their economic power marked them as not culturally elite, explained Aldo, a thirty-three-year-old finance associate from Italy:

> Someone that can spend $100,000 dollars on a table in a night, first of all must be a billionaire. Secondly, I don't think he's earning that money. Generally, people that earn their money by working hard don't spend money like that. They wouldn't spend it on tables. It's usually the sons of the very wealthy that would do something like that, they just inherit it. . . . It's usually oligarchs; it's Russians. Arabs. People that can spend 100 K on a table are usually people that have an oil rig; they must have some connection to oil, or like the oligarchs. It's people that have not earned their dime.

Aldo was hardly alone in invoking the cultural inferiority of non-Western ethnic clients. One client joked with friends about their expensive afternoons in restaurants as "brunching like a Russian." The most ridiculous of spenders were often those perceived as nonwhite or non-Western, like "the Russians," or the Saudis and others with "Arab money." These discourses may be a response to the global crisis of whiteness, or even "white panic," which describes anxieties of changing class and racial hierarchies in American society and around the world. At least in East Asia, which is now the most economically dynamic region in the world, whites are no longer considered the most elite customers of VIP clubs, nor are white women the most central signifiers of status.[45] Far from recognizing the growth of global financial players and the superiority of their financial assets, these discourses of white supremacy emphasized the cultural inadequacies of non-Westerners and, in particular, their poor work ethic. They haven't earned their dime, as Aldo put it, which allowed him to looked down on other big spenders, who didn't deserve the elite status they sought to purchase.

Hard work was a salient trope that clients used to justify their spending. An interview with the son of a wealthy hedge fund CEO is telling. I met Ricardo, twenty-three, in a club in Cannes, where he was with his family on their annual summer holiday, cruising their yacht around the French Riviera. A few nights later, in Saint-Tropez, I passed by Ricardo in a club, this time without his parents and uncles; he was at his own table and surrounded by girls, friends, and about half a dozen champagne bottles. When I interviewed him a month later in his luxurious Manhattan apartment, he downplayed his own spending in the French Riviera by invoking the whales of Saint-Tropez, and he repeatedly mentioned how hard he worked now that he is employed at his family's hedge fund:

> I saw in Saint-Tropez a guy alone spend 1.5 million on that shit, buying like twenty bottles and they cost $30,000 each one . . . These Arabs have a big oil rig in their backyard. My perception is that if they're spending that amount, they've never worked for that money, so they don't know what it takes to get that money . . . That's not me, I work my ass off, and yeah I go out after, not on weeknights because I wake up at 5:30, get into the office by 6:30. I gotta show them I'm not some lazy rich kid.

Despite securing his enviable hedge fund job at his family's firm after having just graduated from an unexceptional college, Ricardo insisted and seemed to genuinely believe that his income reflected his hard work. He, like other clients that I spoke to, portrayed himself as deserving of occasional indulgences. This was a common trope. In fact, when I described my research interests to one of Ricardo's family members, he summed up his relationship to leisure: "I work hard, so I play hard. I have three companies. I have to take a break."

In addition to emphasizing their hard work, clients legitimated their club spending by describing the utility of bottle service for their business endeavors. Not only was bottle service an efficient and even economical way to get drinks, they explained, but being in the VIP club was important for clients seeking to network with potential business partners; for instance, a lawyer met potential clients; a cosmetic dentist met celebrity patients, and so on.[46]

Clients in finance justified expensive bottle purchases as investments in future business deals. Some expenses could even be billed as work entertainment. Two clients who worked as self-employed commodities traders explained that shared clubbing experiences helped them cement relationships with investors. Similarly, George, a twenty-four-year-old tech entrepreneur from LA, claimed he had secured business deals with other VIP men specifically by spending large amounts on bottles:

> Sometimes, if I think about it, I'm like, why did I spend that? But actually, because I did a quarter-million deal out of a guy I met at a club, that time I spent 50 K, okay, it's a lot of money but I can write off some as a corporate expense.

Even Jho Low, at one time the club world's biggest whale, used similar justifications. In 2010, Low fielded questions from the local Malaysian press specifically about his infamous night in Saint-Tropez, and he, too, framed his expenditures in relative terms and stressed his deservingness and hard work:

> REPORTER: Was there a US$160,000 bill in Avenue [nightclub]?
>
> JHO LOW: I think factually there was a party being thrown for a friend's engagement which I was told cost around US$160,000. Left to me, I would not spend that kind of money. . . . I think there is a pattern of trying to paint me as this person who orders a lot of champagne excessively. But I think the fact is to realise that these are special instances where different events have been held and in many cases not organised by me. One point I want to clarify for certain is neither me nor my brother spent in excess of US$2mil in St Tropez. That is 100% factually not true, for sure. It was 40–50 of us friends who ordered some drinks and had a good relaxing night. For me, we all work very hard. Of course, we have a disadvantage where at our age, people may perceive it differently. At the end of the day, I run my investors' money prudently. I generate returns for them. I am not an excessive person but I do have my breaks for relaxation with friends.[47]

It is striking how Low, a symbol of reckless spending, the ultimate whale whom clients invoked as the specter of ridiculousness and ostentation, uses their same discursive strategies: he describes his own spending as restrained ("I would not spend that kind of money") and he works hard, hence he deserves occasional "breaks."

The VIP club carefully orchestrates the collective production of status, in which rich men are encouraged to enact the display of power through elaborate consumption rituals. But beyond the club walls, there are multiple and competing meanings of conspicuous consumption, and the men I interviewed were conflicted about such extravagance.

This became very clear in talking to Luc, who was a club regular in the early 2000s, buying bottles in clubs in the Meatpacking District and in Saint-Tropez during the summer season. At his peak, he was going out in New York every night, and sometimes he spent upward of $10,000 on bottle service. It was almost as though he didn't have a choice in the matter. If you went out to the right spots, you had to buy a bottle, he explained. If not, "First of all, try to get in. If you have no table, no girls, no nothing, good luck." Even if you made it past the door and got inside, you'd have to fight your way to a drink at the bar and then try to pick up girls on your own. With bottle service, girls and drinks flowed freely to your own semi-private space.

Once at his table, Luc would feel a pull to spend more and more money, especially being surrounded by such beautiful girls. He could sense people sizing each other up on the basis of their bottle purchases, all marked with sparklers. The bottles at your table brought you better service, more fun, and better-looking women. The crowd was the reason to spend, the reason he went to Saint-Tropez and Ibiza year after year each summer.

"You wanna be where everyone is," he explained as we sat at a sidewalk Mexican café near his apartment in midtown Manhattan, drinking a beer at happy hour. "You wanna show off. That's the point of the show. I'm not gonna come *here* and order a bottle of Dom Pérignon. So everyone goes to Saint-Tropez. Why do people go there? Because they wanna be in the same place. These jet-setters, they wanna be in the same place because they feel more comfortable, they know who's who, and then they can show off. So it's a game."

For a display of wealth to be meaningful, the right people have to bear witness to it.[48] Even the fillers have a role to play, since they look high-status enough, with the right clothes and the right svelte bodies. Though they can't afford a table, they are a suitable audience for the night. A purely private competition between two whales would be as meaningless as one staged for mere civilians.

But the good-looking crowd cherry-picked by door personnel and promoters comes with risks. Luc described the people coming to his table looking for a free glass of champagne as "flies." The men were often wannabe entrepreneurs looking to build relationships with him and talk to him about a wine or restaurant deal. "I lost so much money like this. They go, 'Oh I have this great deal, this and that,' and you trust them because you party with them and you're party friends, you think you have this big bond. . . . And you realize when you don't go out anymore you don't see them anymore." Luc brushed his hands together at this point. "You are just out of their life." Women especially were like flies, flitting from one table to the next, one yacht to the next, and though Luc claims he was taking a new girl home two or three times a week during his peak years of partying, he always regretted it the next morning.

"Because first of all, the hangover. Second of all, you don't even know the name of the girl in your bed. You just want her to leave your house and you don't know how to tell her to leave your house. And that's it. The only thing you can do is brag to your friends."

Later in our interview, Luc grew weary. "It's kinda sad when I listen to it, you're like my shrink now. When I listen to what I'm saying it's pretty pathetic actually . . . It's horrible, everyone has in common an awareness it's superficial but at the same time there's something really powerful and attractive. It's power. It's fake power, but why do you take drugs or cocaine? It makes you feel invincible. When you [get] to the club and you take a table, all the doors are open to you."

I asked him why he didn't quit a long time ago, when he was still in his thirties, during the peak of his partying, well before he settled down, got married, and had a new baby. He smiled unhappily, "You have to play the game or you're not part of it."

Wasting Beauty

A high quantity of models—fifteen, twenty, thirty models squeezed together at a table—is considered a necessary condition for spending sprees to happen. It's not just their individual beauty, which is indeed attention-grabbing; the sheer volume of girls delivers a visual impact.

"Why do you think he's spending a thousand dollars on a bottle of Cristal?" asked Pablo, a twenty-nine-year-old promoter from Brazil who worked in a team with Vanna, about one of his biggest clients:

> Not because he loves the Cristal. The guy that is spending 120,000 dollars at the club, we didn't drink it even. You think we can drink a hundred bottles? No way. So it's attention, you know? And he's sitting at a huge table, with thirty models around him. And he's like this [raising his arms high in the air, pretending to hold bottles].

I would have thought Pablo's statement was hyperbole if I hadn't myself been one of thirty or so girls standing around a client in Miami in four-inch heels on top of the banquette sofa, holding my own bottle of Veuve Clicquot champagne. I too observed with amazement the ratio of women to men. It would have been impossible for the client to get to know each of them, or even to catch their names, given the loud music and what appeared to be his disinterest in even starting a conversation with any particular girl at his table. He was surrounded by an excess of girls, more than any man could realistically consume.

There is an easy, though misleading, explanation for why clients might spend such huge sums of money in these clubs. When I asked clients, managers, and promoters about the rationale behind such grand expenditure, I frequently encountered a dismissive laugh and a smirk and a quick, reflexive answer: sex. One club owner humorlessly mouthed the word "vagina" to me when I asked why he thought expenditures in his club ran so high. Santos, when first explaining the centrality of girls, reduced them to a single body part: "If you fill the place with girls, everyone is gonna wanna come. You know about men, you study men, you know they need pussy. So that's how it works." Santos had a crude way of putting into words what many were thinking about the logic behind VIP clubs: sex sells.[49]

The phrase "sex sells" is a deceptively simple way of alluding to the historically entrenched ways that femininity can stoke desire for commodities, turning the female form into an indispensable tool of capitalism.[50] The phrase assumes that women, not men, are the sex available for sale. With the rise of commodity capitalism and its marketing via visual culture, women took on a quality that film critic Laura Mulvey famously described as "to-be-looked-at-ness." Women became objects before a male gaze, not unlike the expanding array of consumer goods displayed in bourgeoning promenades and department stores.[51] When "shopgirls" appeared selling merchandise in department stores in late Victorian England, they raised a titillating ambiguity before the male gaze: Was she, perhaps, also for sale?[52]

With shopgirls, department stores could harness what historian Peter Bailey termed, in his history of Victorian sexual culture, *parasexuality*. Writing about bar maidens, Bailey conceptualized parasexuality as feminine sexuality that is "deployed but not fully released."[53] Parasexuality drives contemporary entertainment and service industries, with sales floors designed to harness men's attention with sex even when the goods and services are far removed from sex: "gallerinas" in art galleries, "booth babes" at tech conferences, flight attendants on airplanes, hotel concierges, even office secretaries.[54] Entertainment, retail, and hospitality industries tap into the value of girls all around the world. At a recent meeting of the World Economic Forum in Davos, Russian oligarch Oleg Deripaska hired beautiful young women to serve as "translators" for the guests at his lavish party—a reproduction of traditional femininity so entrenched that the irony likely went unnoticed by world leaders who had gathered to address systemic inequalities.[55]

This visual economy of feminine display governs the VIP world, and when people say sex sells, they don't mean sex acts. They mean sexiness. Promoters emphasize the visibility of beautiful bodies, not the quantity of sex acts that can be consummated among them. Thibault explained as much, emphasizing that the visible display of high-status femininity, not sex, is of prime importance.

"Like the guy last night, you should have seen it. The last few days he's paying $100,000 at the club every night and he wants us around, like just to be around models. That's like at the dinner, you saw."

I did see it. There were about thirty models with Thibault and Felipe crowded around three tables at an upscale restaurant where a wealthy client paid the bill. After dinner, there were so many girls when we arrived at the club that people stared at our tables, and one woman passing by paused, confused, and looked at me and asked, "What, did a fashion show just get out or something?"

"Does the client get to sleep with any of them?" I asked Thibault. I asked this of all of the promoters, who cringed at my phrasing and its implications of pimping, something from which they took pains to distance themselves: "We don't do it like that," Thibault said. "We're never involved in that kind of thing, because as soon as we do everyone will talk and we'll get a reputation for being like that and we won't have any more girls. If a girl likes the guy, that's her own thing, but we don't do it like that."

Another promoter, thirty-three-year-old Luca, from Italy, had hosted private parties for a Saudi family, and though he brought dozens of models to these events, he said, "They even never touch one girl. That is important for me, because I don't want to be in the middle of things weird, like pimp stuff." Luca thought his clients were mostly married, and anyway, he reasoned: "It's not actual sex, because if you think of the money they have, they can buy expert company. They can have the best bitches of the world," he said, referring to sex workers. Rather, with Luca's services, they want the best-looking girls in their party, where they can say to their friends and cousins, as Luca put it, "Look, I have a top model!"

Girls likewise pointed out that they didn't necessarily speak to the clients, even when they dined together. Petra, a twenty-five-year-old model who frequently went out with promoters and their clients in Milan at the start of her teenage modeling career, described these dinners:

Well, a lot of times they don't even wanna talk to girls . . . I remember only one guy, and he was just like some really rich Italian old rich guy, who wanted to go out and be seen in public places, like really cool restaurants, because people know him, and he would want the girls around.

While the "really rich Italian old rich guy" seemed odd to Petra at the time, she was glad to accept a free meal in a trendy restaurant on his bill.

Sex between girls and clients is not the main point of having so many models in attendance; rather, it is the visibility of sexiness in excess that produces status. A high quantity of girls is visual testimony to the client's importance; it enables him to show off an *excess* of beauty. The display of so many girls' bodies is parallel to the displays of empty champagne bottles whose contents were shaken and sprayed; these are parallel displays of waste.[56]

The Labor of Leisure

For a chance to be a part of the show, girls accepted precarious arrangements, the potential difficulties and dangers of which became most evident when they traveled out of town with promoters. At the Club X outpost in Miami where I met up with Santos, Petra was dancing at a nearby table. The twenty-five-year-old model was invited by the promoter Nicolas and his partners Thibault and Felipe, who were hired to bring girls for the week to surround the whales. Petra was supposed to stay with another girl, nineteen-year-old Rose, in an apartment that was paid for by the club and arranged by Nicolas. It was a large penthouse condo in a luxury condo building, but to everyone's surprise it lacked furniture, so Petra and Rose ended up having to share a different multiroom unit with the whale and his friends for their first two nights. This arrangement ended badly.

First, both girls missed several meals, since the whale, whom Petra described as a "Brazilian mafia guy or whatever," was not very attentive to their needs. "Just not being able to eat on time, you think that's okay, but when it happens, it's not," said Petra. That first night, Rose got left behind as the group went inside the club. She felt ill and wanted to go back to the condo to rest, but no one would take her back, and she didn't have a key to get inside the penthouse on her own. Rose waited outside the nightclub for several hours, into the early morning, until the clients were done partying and brought her home. Meanwhile, that night Petra went with the group to the club by herself. As she described it:

> I had to go there alone not knowing these people, and then I did feel like a piece of meat, like totally, I had to be fun. I had to be fun because if I'm not fun, then they won't take me [back to the condo]. So I was like dancing and laughing and hating my life at the same time. So, of course, when we got back to hotel and got Rose into her room, she was crying . . . It was disgusting, it was so bad.

The club, via Nicolas, had paid the girls' plane tickets to Miami. Petra had the money to book a new ticket and fly home to New York, but Rose couldn't afford that, and Petra didn't want to leave her behind. In the end, the girls found better accommodations after two days, and Petra summed up her experience: "Overall it was a good trip and good experience. Would I do it again? No."

Santos had bragged that Miami would be the "best" parties in the world. From my vantage point, the trip with him was also a good experience, and no, I would not do it again. I was never so tired as I was with him in Miami, where we never got home before 5 a.m. But there were also pleasures to be experienced alongside the instability of being in his company.

Santos had four girls with him in Miami: myself; nineteen-year-old Hannah, a white part-time model and Abercrombie clerk from the Californian suburbs; Katia, twenty, also white, a model from a small Ukrainian city; and Tanya, a part-time model from upper-class Colombia. Atypically old, at thirty-one, Tanya was a long-time friend of Santos; the rest of us had met him only in the last couple of months.

Two nights after arriving in Miami, the five of us piled into the car as the sun set to head out for another all-nighter. Tanya joked that we were like vampires. When I asked her if she knew where were going, she laughed. "I don't know what's going on! I wake up, I get high, I get in the car, and we go!" Tanya didn't mind. She was here to party hard and she loved dancing through the night, especially on ecstasy and cocaine.

Hannah, on the other hand, was at her wits' end. She had stayed in Miami for two and a half weeks already, spending just $40 of her own money all this time. Santos paid her airfare, and she stayed for free in the various accommodations he arranged. It was Hannah's dream to go to the mainstage of Ultra, the internationally renowned music festival with all-day lineups of the world's biggest DJs. Ultra was the reason she came to Miami, but so far it hadn't happened. She was supposed to go back to New York the day I arrived, but she overslept and missed her flight. Her parents and her manager at Abercrombie were eager for her to return, but she was waiting for Santos to book her return flight as he had promised. Santos did the flight bookings and changed them according to his needs. He was delaying Hannah's rebooking because he claimed he was awaiting payment from the clubs and didn't have the funds to cover it. Meanwhile, he continued to bring her everywhere except to Ultra—to Club X, to clients' dinners, to house parties. Finally, after three weeks in Miami, Hannah's stepdad paid for her return ticket. She never did see the Ultra mainstage that year.

Finally, there was Katia, Santos's favorite. She looked like a top model, with long blonde hair and green eyes. Heads turned when she entered the room, and men stopped mid-sentence to watch her go by. She appeared not to have much money, and aside from occasional modeling trips to China, she didn't work. She came for a holiday in Miami with a girlfriend and ended up staying for a month. She had heard of Santos through friends, and she contacted him on Facebook to ask if he could help her buy pot. Santos connected her to a Miami-based photographer, who ended up letting her live in his house for free until, for reasons having to do with her being drunk and rude, according to the photographer, he kicked her out. When Santos arrived in Miami, he let her stay with him at the Star Island villa, and soon they shared a bedroom and a brief romance. Everywhere that Santos went in Miami, Katia followed, partly because she liked hanging out with him, and partly because she didn't have anywhere else to go.

Trouble started in my relationship with Santos right away. As soon as I arrived at the waterfront villa on Star Island, nestled between the rich and famous, I met Jonas, one of Santos's associates and a real estate broker, who arranged our housing. He was going to meet up with Santos later, he said, so I should just go with him. Jonas was going to Ultra, near the pop-up Club X where Santos was working.

When I arrived at the Ultra parking lot and called Santos, he was outraged. He shouted over the phone, "What I told you to do? You just stay and wait for me, and you don't! You go with some other guy!"

I had committed the single biggest offense a girl can commit: going to someone else's party, especially if the promoter is counting on her. Santos accepted my panicked apology, and I met him at the right venue where he was, to my surprise, warm and welcoming.

Two other girls staying in our Miami villa were less fortunate. They did not come out to join Santos but instead stayed home and, according to Santos, even had the audacity to make plans to go out with a different promoter. When Santos returned home, he assessed the situation: disrespectful girls staying in the house he arranged for them, in Miami on tickets he booked for them. He kicked them out of the villa.

It was a terrible scene, with Santos shouting at times at the top of his lungs, "*Everybody out!* . . . I lost my fucking party, now I'm pissed. Who the fuck they think they are? . . . I don't give a fucking fuck!" The girls apologized, said it was just a misunderstanding, but Santos didn't relent. "Did they ever come with me, and now they was ready to go with someone else again. So they pick up their stuff and they go with someone else, because I don't give my room to someone who's not supporting me." The girls cried as they packed and left in the early morning hours, each on their phones trying to find accommodations for the night.

Twenty minutes later, when Santos regained his cool, he headed off with Tanya and myself to another party, eager to show the clubs and clients that he was still at the top of the VIP scene. Tanya did bumps of cocaine in the backseat while he drove through Miami picking up girlfriends that could join him. We did make it to a club that was, as Santos described it, "sick," full of beautiful models and lots of bottles. It was an electric couple of hours, and a sharp contrast to what happened later that night.

When we left the club shortly after closing at 5 a.m., Santos and Tanya got into a terrible argument in the taxi over which after-party to attend. To add to Santos's fury, his phone died, so he couldn't find the address of the after-party he preferred.[57] The euphoria of the cocaine and the MDMA was long gone and there, in the middle of downtown Miami at 5 a.m., the taxi was a cacophony of screaming voices, ending with Tanya in tears and Santos exiting the car.

"Follow me," he said to me, looking down the dark and empty street. "You have flip flops in your bag? Put them on."

We walked the rest of the way from downtown Miami, almost one hour, to the Star Island villa surrounded by celebrities and moguls.

Back at the villa, I took stock of our guesthouse. There were roller bag suitcases splayed open on the floor, and crumpled clothes spilled into the corners of the rooms. An air mattress lay on the floor with a dirty plate on top of it. Upstairs the toilet was clogged, the bidet had become a rubbish bin full of cans, and dirty towels and toiletries were scattered across the bathroom floor. Girls dried off after showers using a roll of paper towels. The beds were unmade and who knows if the sheets were clean, but I crawled into an empty one and quickly fell asleep as the morning sun shone through the windows. He may have been at the very top of VIP nightlife, but in daylight, Santos's world looked pretty rough. In following the production of a potlatch from night to day, I realized that conspicuous leisure took an inordinate amount of labor. The value of women's labor, I would come to see, went disproportionately to men.

4

Trafficking at Model Camp

Saturday, 2 a.m., the Hamptons

By 2 a.m. the dozen or so guests of the nine-bedroom mansion in the Hamptons finally headed to sleep. There were plenty of spots to choose from: most of the bedrooms had bunk beds, up to four single beds per room. The mansion was co-owned by Donald, Grant, and Paul, wealthy businessmen from Manhattan, who ranged in age from forty to sixty. They were not promoters, but they shared a collective aim to host as many girls as possible each weekend. As many as twenty girls could stay overnight during the peak summer season. The house was tastefully decorated but mostly it had been outfitted with girls in mind, with plenty of towels and a fridge stocked with champagne and snacks. When the men noticed that girls wouldn't swim in chlorinated water, for fear of spoiling their blonde highlights, they changed the pool to salt water.

Last summer they hosted three hundred girls, an impressive sum, as Grant mentioned often in conversation. At the start of this season, Grant and Paul went to Bed Bath & Beyond to buy towels and sheets for all of the beds, and they joked at the checkout line that it looked like they were furnishing a sorority house. One weekend they hosted twenty-six girls, so many that they didn't have enough beds, and they had to use their contingency plan: girls slept in tents in the backyard on the manicured green lawn. That's when Grant started calling the house "model camp." And they weren't just any girls. They were beautiful, tall and thin, mostly real models and good civilians.

It took a coordinated effort among the three men to fill model camp each weekend. If a girlfriend wanted to bring her friend, they asked for her full name to check her Facebook or Instagram, to make sure she was tall and pretty enough. Grant would only invite a girl after seeing her first. If a guy friend wanted to come out to the house for the weekend, he was only welcome if he brought at least three high-quality girls with him. Most of Grant's guy friends had houses in the Hamptons anyway, so if he wanted to see his guy friends, he just drove over.

"You're a smart girl," Grant told me when I first met him, so maybe I would understand. "Some people think it's just about the sex. But it's not. It's having all the girls in the house. Having the right ones."

Grant, forty-six, was an entrepreneur in tech. He was about five feet seven, bald, and beginning to wrinkle, a strikingly different kind of body than those of the girls around him. Despite his small stature, he idealized girls' height, and preferred to be eclipsed by women towering high above him in heels. "I love it," he said one night in a Meatpacking District club, looking up at the girls standing half a foot taller than himself, "because I love women."

Soon after meeting Grant, I interviewed his friend Donald, who co-owned their Hamptons mansion. Donald invited me to the house for the weekend. I thanked him and assured him that participation in the project was confidential, meaning that I wouldn't use their real names. He cut me off. "Oh, you don't get it. You think you're invited for being a writer. You're invited because you're a hot girl."

"I'd like to use the weekend as a research experience," I said.

Donald shrugged. "You can use it as a suntan experience."

We kissed cheeks and parted ways. That weekend, I boarded a Midtown Hampton Jitney express bus and headed to model camp. Once there, I discovered a variety of men's strategic uses of girls.

The Hamptons has been a destination for rich New Yorkers since the late nineteenth century, when the city's old moneyed aristocrats and newly minted tycoons transformed the quiet farmland and salt-boxes into a summer colony of mansions for high society.[1] It was in this context that F. Scott Fitzgerald wrote the character of Jay Gatsby, the dubiously nouveau riche businessman with infamous parties, thrown to broadcast his greatness across northern Long Island for everyone, and especially his lost lover, to see.

The Wall Street booms of the 1980s and '90s created a new Manhattanite bourgeoisie with an appetite for expensive properties and cultural capital, making the Hamptons a prime location for financiers and business elites seeking second residences. Today the Hamptons are teeming with seasonal homes of billionaire financiers (e.g., George Soros), political elites (e.g., the Clintons), and entertainers (e.g., Russell Simmons).[2] Parties have continued across the South Fork of Long Island since Gatsby's fabled nights, but with greater restrictions to access.

"You can't get in unless you're a tall, pretty girl or you have wealth. It's a caste system," Donald explained about the Hamptons social scene. He didn't feel completely right about it, but he has also benefited a great deal from his access.

Donald was a professional businessman, and his interests in girls were largely pragmatic. The fit sixty-year-old worked in private equity on Wall Street. He was not a whale, just an upper-class single New Yorker and a regular in the party scene, which served his business well. As an institutional investor, he was always on the lookout for companies worth investing in. In two days in the Hamptons, Donald attended one luxurious outdoor house party hosted by Lou Fallow, the chief executive of a private equity firm, one VIP nightclub late into Saturday night, and a catered brunch pool party at Lou Fallow's mansion. "It's always good to get invited to these things," Donald said, about the importance of the Hamptons parties for his career. Throughout the weekend, Donald shook hands with fund managers, entrepreneurs, and CEOs of small start-ups and big businesses.

It's not that Donald came out to the Hamptons or to the clubs looking for clients. If you want to broker deals, Donald explained, you take them out for dinner and drinks. Perhaps he would take prospective clients out to a nightclub or bond with them over a few games of tennis. These were all ways he strengthened social ties with guys he was already in business with. If someone was spending a lot on bottles at the club, Donald thought, it was most likely a young guy showing off what he didn't have. "I wonder if they really have money, or how much do they really have?" he said about the men he saw spraying champagne in Saint-Tropez.

Being in the Hamptons, for Donald, wasn't about showing off or deliberately seeking out new business opportunities. It was about belonging in an elite world. It was the ability to go from one party to the next in his Porsche SUV along the Southampton coast, clinking glasses with hedge fund managers, philanthropists, and fashion industry moguls. Donald got into almost any event he wanted. He had a special ticket that gave him access to other men perched higher on the social and economic ladder.

"Can you guess the currency?" he asked. "Girls."

With lots of girls, he was assured a steady stream of invitations to the most exclusive parties in the Hamptons VIP scene. The presence of girls also ensured that important people were likely to accept his invitations to his mansion and his chlorine-free pool parties. With girls, he exclaimed, "It's like, okay, every dinner party, you are in!" This included dinners and parties hosted by Lou Fallow.

Lou, fifty-one, was the CEO of a wealth management firm and a playboy in the Hamptons social scene. His interests in girls were largely romantic. I first met Lou at a dinner party organized by Jonas, the luxury estate broker who had arranged Santos's Star Island accommodations in Miami. At an upscale restaurant in midtown Manhattan, a mix of twenty girls and men sat in the deliberate seating arrangement of "boy-girl-boy-girl," which, according to Jonas, discourages girls from gravitating into conversation with each other. In addition, every thirty minutes Jonas announced that the male dinner guests should change seats to refresh conversation partners.

An hour into dinner, following a seat change, Lou sat down next to me.

I began to introduce myself when he interrupted: "I know, let's forget the biographies and tell me, what's your favorite position?"

"Center-left," I said.

He chuckled. He proceeded to explain that he preferred sex on his back with the girl on top, so he could admire her fully.

This went on for a little while, interspersed with light banter around politics, his family, and his divorce, until it was time to change seats again. (Later I understood that Lou Fallow is a donor to the Republican party.)

A few weeks later, Lou hosted a lavish outdoor party in the Hamptons. Divorced and superrich, he was spending the summers in the Hamptons in a palatial vacation home worth several million dollars. Some have described him as a Jay Gatsby type, hoping for the right woman to walk through the door at one of his parties. But in the meantime, he sought the sexually charged company of a lot of girls.

Jonas, forty-seven, was a fixture at Lou's parties, and he used girls to climb up the ranks of elite business circles. Jonas made his fortune renting luxury vacation properties like villas and yachts to rich people, and he invested in many other ventures, from oil to restaurants. But mostly, Jonas would say, he's in the business of knowing people.

"I want to be known as the guy with the most connections. If you need something, you come to me. It's what I do, I put people in touch with each other. You wanna meet a head of state or government official? I can do that," he told me over dinner.

Jonas had always loved going out, ever since his college days as a political science major at an elite university in Paris. He quickly realized that by hosting parties, he could build a web of connections to his classmates' wealthy families. He made sure he always walked into an exclusive event with a few beautiful girls on each arm. He didn't do drugs or stay out as late as guys like Santos, who was always chasing the after-parties into the early morning. And he didn't "fix" men up with girls; he made it clear that he wasn't a pimp, either. Rather, he cultivated relationships with girls and with promoters he could count on to make him look good at social events. In this way, he built connections that morphed into business ventures in restaurants and real estate.

Jonas made a show out of his access to girls' bodies. He pulled girls into his chest too tightly for hugs, and he gave them intense shoulder or neck rubs at his dinners, gripping their bodies in front of all of his guests. He was handsome, tall, and muscular, but his aggressive affections could be repulsive; I once saw a girl grimace in disgust when he went in for a hug.

Jonas was hardly unusual in his interactions with girls—men often took liberties with girls' bodies, assuming their availability in the ways they touched, grabbed, and talked about them—but sex wasn't his main interest in surrounding himself with beautiful young women.[3] Jonas was strategically building a career through his use of girls' bodies. And because he offered them all-expenses-paid trips to destinations like Cannes and Ibiza, Jonas maintained a large Rolodex of girls he could call on to attend events with him.

"Girls are always important, yeah," he said. "It's good to have a lot of pretty girls around you. Especially in the beginning, you know everyone needs decoration." But now, with his formidable social network cultivated through years of VIP parties, everyone in the "jet set" knows Jonas. "I have a reputation, so girls are not the main thing."

Jonas was a lot like the promoter Dre in that he was always bragging about being on the cusp of huge business deals. He was just about to be a multimillionaire, about to make it *really* big.

Donald had his doubts. To Donald, the VIP world was full of Jonases—schemers who boasted that they had a lot of money but actually were just trying to pick up crumbs from the real wealth around them. The deals didn't ever seem all "buttoned up" for Jonas, Donald said skeptically about an impending "huge" one that Jonas spoke about often, a deal involving oil imports from Central America, and Donald didn't believe anything would come of it.

Here we have three men: the professional (Donald), the schemer (Jonas), and the playboy (Lou). Though they came to the VIP scene with very different interests, each of them saw the value of girls to advance their goals. Both Donald and Jonas used girls to get invited to places like the Hamptons, and to get ahead in business. Lou, meanwhile, surrounded himself with a lot of pretty girls as a way of creating what sociologist Erving Goffman called the "chance" of sexual interlude.[4] Donald and Jonas were also interested in meeting girls for hookups and even long-term relationships. Donald had met his previous girlfriend, a nineteen-year-old Brazilian model, when she came through the house one weekend. About Jonas, well, Santos had warned me early on to beware of him, because, as he put it, "Jonas is always trying to fuck the girls."

Beyond sex, Jonas and Donald had strategic goals that the right kinds of girls could help them achieve. Girls got them invited to Lou's parties, and they opened the door for business talk—for Jonas, about yacht rentals, and for Donald, about private-equity investments. For these men, girls functioned as *decor* in two senses of the word: they were an embellishment that made the men look better than they were; they were also a mark of honor, a status signifier that caught the attention of other men.

Toward the end of the weekend with Donald, we stopped by a private beach, and Donald ran into an old friend, a rich Manhattan restauranteur and hotelier. He had owned a fashion model agency back in the 1980s (and he was apparently himself a renowned playboy, too). There on the beautiful Hamptons beach, our toes digging into the fine white sand, they talked about business ventures and Donald casually asked the restauranteur if he knew of anything worth investing in these days. As an aside, Donald mentioned: "You should come to the house one of these days. It's quite the menagerie, if you want to relive the old days."

That men could use girls to advance their social and business aspirations was obvious, everywhere from Miami dinner parties to sandy beaches in the Hamptons. What was less obvious was how girls themselves could capitalize on their beauty. As it turned out, female beauty was worth more to men than it was to the girls decorating their arms.

Icebreakers

Sometimes girls were like soft jazz music in an elevator: part of the background. Like when Santos took his girls to dinner in Miami with Jonas and a client named Ezra, a wealthy middle-aged commercial real estate developer in New York. Santos had described Ezra as one of his "best friends"; since Ezra had a taste for the company of tall blondes, he regularly invited Santos and his girls to join him and his male business partners at dinners.

Dinner was at Mr. Chow, an upscale bistro with rows of luxury cars, Rolls-Royce Phantoms and Ferraris, in the valet parking area. The girls were excited about the "amazing" food that Mr. Chow is known for, but Santos was stressed about arriving on time and described the event as something we "had" to do. He told the girls beforehand: "We have to go to dinner with Ezra tonight. He's a very powerful man and likes to have things looking nice, so put the high heels on, okay?" The girls didn't question these dining arrangements, since they followed Santos pretty much everywhere he went in Miami and mostly relied on him for meals, transportation, housing, and entertainment.

At the restaurant, Ezra sat with other men to his left and right, a row of girls and Santos across from him. He engaged in quiet conversation with a gentleman to one side the whole evening and barely spoke to anyone else, including Santos; in fact, his back was practically turned to the rest of the table for most of the dinner.

The other men occasionally flirted with the girls, but they mostly talked among themselves about business, politics, mutual friends in Gulf States, and redevelopment projects. By the end of the dinner, all of the girls were silent on their side of the table. Santos himself was unusually quiet. He was clearly bored throughout the dinner, watching a conversation about business that he could not join, and frequently checking his phone, unlike the other men. When the food came, plates of fusion cuisine to be shared family-style, he whispered, "It's not my kind of food. I want the crispy beef," closer to his taste for fried street food.

At the end of the dinner, Santos joked out loud, "Well, Ezra really paid attention to his friends tonight," but Ezra ignored him; he just settled the bill and continued his deep conversation. Tanya wanted to leave when the plates were cleared. She whispered, "I hate when they talk about money and extend the dinners, blah blah blah."

Outside, as the guests found their Phantoms and Ferraris and bid each other good night, Jonas embraced each of the girls in a goodbye hug. As he hugged me tightly, he added, just loud enough for the others to hear: "Maybe you'll surprise me later tonight in my bed!"

The other men expressed little interest in talking with the girls. While barely discernible as individuals, as a collective the girls played an important role in helping the men talk with each other about their worlds of business. One client described girls as "furniture women," because "they would be there making us look good, like furnishing the house." Most clients and promoters simply believe that a room full of men is less comfortable than a room with women. Rudik, a Russian promoter working in Hong Kong and occasionally in New York City, explained that company managers entertaining clients hire him to bring girls to the after-hours entertainment. "Because it's five guys, with a fucking magnum of champagne, and they look like fucking faggots. You don't wanna look bad. You wanna look good. 'So please,' they'll say, 'get us the girls.'" Sometimes, Rudik observed, the businessmen barely talk with the girls. Girls break the ice and help everyone to get comfortable in a homosocial world of business, where most of the power holders are men.

That women often grease the wheels of commerce in male-dominated settings has been well documented, especially in the context of business deals, be it hostesses in Asian financial markets or cocktail waitresses in Western gentlemen's clubs. Of course, the women in those settings are all remunerated for their efforts.[5]

In the course of researching this book I interviewed eleven men working in finance; nine said that they used bottle service to entertain clients. They explained that in finance, relationships are paramount. Max, the thirty-three-year-old hedge fund manager, described how in his business, concerned with energy commodities, the potential returns to entertaining clients could be compelling enough to warrant expensive bar tabs in VIP clubs: "In a lot of financial sectors, and I'm guessing other industries too, it works on the strength of relationships. . . . So it comes down to who you like, who you trust, and who you enjoy dealing with. Who wants you to succeed by giving you their business?"

Wade, a twenty-nine-year-old bottle client who had partied with his finance brokers in New York, explained: "In commodities businesses, I can go to anyone to push paper," meaning he can use one broker or another, because "I'm doing the deal, they're just executing. So short of being totally incompetent, all they're doing is processing papers, and they get commission for that." Whether he chooses one broker or another comes down to their personal relationship.

Of course, businessmen like Wade also build relationships with brokers and investors at other venues, like golf clubs. But you can't golf at night. And besides, said Wade, "*Everything* is better with models, and people hold up the presence of models to be like the pinnacle. So, they feel better about themselves, they're spending more, everyone loves taking pictures with models." As he spoke he scrolled through pictures on his iPhone of parties featuring lots of models and bottles.

Men may have more fun and find more pleasure in being around beautiful girls than not, but it would be hard for a client like Wade to account for this pleasure as deriving purely from deliberate status-driven pursuits. High-status places are surely pleasurable in themselves, in part because being high status feels good.[6] A beautiful woman communicates this, irrespective of her own status or class background: "I'd still rather be around beautiful people even if their lives are on derailment and they're college dropouts," insisted Wade.

Even if clients did not necessarily go out seeking economically enriching connections, the VIP scene gave them a place where they could build valuable social ties with other men like them. There was a law firm partner who met prospective clients at clubs. A cosmetic dentist met his celebrity patients. There was an Italian entrepreneur who worked in fashion and now in politics who was such a regular at one New York club that he had his own table reserved nightly for entertaining guests. He told me, "I never met a billionaire in a Starbucks. I've never met someone who could change my life in Starbucks." But look around, the club was full of such people.

Even if rich men didn't particularly care for the party scene in Saint-Tropez or in the Hamptons, they felt it was important to be there, if nothing else, to collect the stories and the credit to show colleagues and would-be partners that they too belong in an international circuit of VIPs. This is how Rhys, a white thirty-five-year-old financial manager from Paris explained it:

> I've been to all these places. Would I want to do that year after year after year? No. But definitely having the fact that I've been to the major spots, the right places, I guess it helps on the margin, in relating to business contacts or people that—just because for some of those people that you might deal with in a business setting, they say, "Oh I've been to St. Barts, have you been?" Or, "I've been to Saint-Tropez, it's so great." If you haven't been and you don't know, they'll feel you're not in the same circle, not as accomplished.[7]

Beyond just fitting in, some clients aspired to attract the attention of other VIPs. Girls were a quick and reliable tool to do this. "When these guys go out, they bring like fifteen girls," observed one client, Luc, the forty-eight-year-old French restauranteur from a wealthy background, who had been a part of the party scene in New York, the Hamptons, Saint-Tropez, and Ibiza.

> It's just decoration to show off. Even if they don't sleep with them they have them to show off: "Oh, who is this guy? Look at all those girls, wow! He must be rich; he must be famous." It's just superficial.

However superficial, this strategy of flashing girls works. Luc admitted that his head turns at the sight of fifteen beautiful girls, in part to take the measure of the man with them.

Catch a Whale

Sampson, the twenty-seven-year-old promoter, had never expected to join the upper class. Recall that this Queens native didn't finish community college, and that before promoting, he was selling cell phones. But with girls, he saw a pathway to meet valuable contacts in exclusive spaces in which he otherwise had little chance of belonging. He was promoting at Club X, he explained, because the owners noticed the girls around him: "You walk into a place with a couple of good girls, they're like, 'Who are you?' If you make an impression, they'll ask. And all you have to do is just walk around with girls."

Two years into his career as a promoter, Sampson was trying to build relationships with clients to organize their private parties independently of club managers. His end goal was to open a lounge or bar one day, and he knew that the wealthy men he befriended now could become investors later.

And so at a rooftop pool party one summer afternoon at a Manhattan hotel, Sampson shared drinks with George, the owner of a California software company, whom Sampson described as "one of the biggest ballers in LA." Talks were underway for Sampson to organize George's house parties in LA and St. Barts. Standing poolside and clinking glasses of rosé wine, Sampson showed George Instagram photos of a girl named Krissy, who both men agreed was very hot.

"See, I said George will love her. She's the hottest girl I know right now."

"She's definitely my type," said George. "Bring out some girls like that to LA."

Sampson beamed with a pride, "Yeah, she's one of mine. Look at this"—Krissy in a bikini; Krissy in a sports car. "The girl is crazy. though. She can drink so much."

"Bring her out to LA. That's the kind of girl we need to have out to party," said George. The rest was details: the party season George wanted was the month of August, in LA, and of January, in St. Barts, just where Sampson wanted to be.

Meanwhile, Dre was sure that within five years, he would be a multimillionaire.

It's not an exaggeration to say that every time I saw Dre, he boasted about his impending entrepreneurial greatness. Every night out with him at his table, every lunch, even a chance encounter on the street, brought fortuitous news of his business deals, the limousine company, a film production, a TV show, and, of course, his music career, which was always just about to blow up. One month he claimed he was raising capital for a tech firm because of his nightlife access to so many billionaires and investors. The next month, he was in discussions about a deal to expand a Serbian telecommunications company's coverage into Europe.

Dre could see the opportunities around him; he was in fact sitting shoulder to shoulder with multimillionaires, and even a few billionaires. Despite being a black man from a middle-class family, he had all it took to catch their attention. When these very rich men walked into an upscale place like Club X, "They see the sexiest table. They come in, and they see me, [and] they say, 'Who is that black guy with all the girls around him?' They come and talk to me. . . . They start buying bottles. That's how to catch a whale. We don't have to find them. They find us, because we have lots of hot girls."

Dre regularly received invitations to dine with whales, who were intrigued by his access to such high-quality girls and exclusive clubs. It was just this scenario that prompted a dinner invitation to get to know a potential billionaire investor. He wrote to me one afternoon, the excitement palpable even for a guy who regularly abused the exclamation point:

> Have to attend a dinner! A rich African billionaire new to NY!!! I am his guide. You should join us for dinner! I am gonna see if I can be his contact here in NY! His liaison! Introduce him to nightlife, the girls and capitalize.
>
> You know the game.

Dre was usually hesitant to take on the role of a guide to clients new to the city, which meant introducing them to the right people and taking them out to the right places to be seen around town. First, because clients could be demanding of his time without any guarantee they would pay it back. Perhaps the client might spend money at a club and then Dre could get a percentage of the bottle sales, but this was chump change compared to what he wanted—that is, an investor willing to put down serious money to back one of his many business ideas. Second, and most importantly, it was a role close to being a pimp. Too often clients mistook Dre's friendships with girls as sexual access, and they often asked him to arrange dates, sometimes even paid dates with particular models. He couldn't cross those lines without damage to his reputation among other clients, managers, and, especially, the girls he relied on.

This time, however, a girlfriend assured him the African billionaire was very classy and polite, and he would never solicit his friends for sex. "And that if I take good care of him! He can invest in all my wildest projects. Million times," he texted.

So Dre arranged a dinner on the Upper East Side with the billionaire, bankers, a few of their girlfriends, and a few of his trusted girls, to which he rode in the front seat of the cab with three pretty women in the backseat, who made a lot of jokes about the situation ahead:

"I heard you're a billionaire. That's great because I need some money," laughed Sasha, a twenty-eight-year-old model.

"Guys, do you think I can order the steak? Can I order a side of my rent with that?" joked another. And so on.

When his girls walked into the expensive restaurant, it was as if the space suddenly grew hushed so that everyone could take in the sight: three white girls in party dresses leading the way for Dre, one of the only black men in the room. The girls took their seats at a table; four older ladies in designer suits at the table next to them stared hard. Finally, one of them leaned over to ask, "Do you girls work for a company?"

The sense of humor from the cab ride faded; no one laughed. Sasha muttered under her breath, "They're like, 'Oh, a whore table just walked in.'" But after that initial embarrassment, the dinner was a jovial affair, with the African billionaire sitting at one end of the table, Dre sitting at the other, and the girls enjoying plates of expensive entrées and wine.

Dre didn't get paid for that night. He and his girls were dinner guests; they got to order whatever they wanted off of the menu. It was an investment of his time. "I look at the big picture," he said. "I want this guy to invest in my next project, my movie, my reality shows, my app, all that stuff" he was scheming and constantly talking about. "I want him to invest in *that*. As soon as he asks me, 'Dre, how can we make money—and *then*,'" he said, then he would capitalize.

Just as girls helped Dre to court the billionaire, they helped Santos get to know New York real estate tycoons and wealthy Arabian families.

Santos was from a poor family in Colombia and one of his partners in Europe, Luca, was from a working-class Italian family. Neither man had a yacht, substantial wealth, family connections, or a college degree. But with girls, they could feel like kings in the French Riviera. On their annual promoter gig in Cannes, during the month of June, Luca glanced at the row of yachts lining the harbor—million-dollar vessels flying flags of Bermuda and Cayman Islands—and he sneered at their claims to success:

> If the clients are cool, we hang out, or we do, like, their after-party. If they're not cool, I don't waste my time. Some of them, they have no pussy. Ninety percent of them, they have big yachts and no girls. So, fuck them.

Thus, girls did more than help promoters to build ties; they helped to level the unequal playing field shaped by the considerable social distances between clients and themselves.[8] Moving through New York, the Hamptons, and Cannes, promoters from uneducated and poor backgrounds shared dinners, dance floors, and swimming pools with rich men. With girls, men like Luca, Santos, Sampson, and Dre could find a legitimate claim as "very important" men.

Networking with the superrich in Cannes and the Hamptons, these men had come a long way, but they were painfully aware that they could go a lot farther still. They knew of promoters who had transformed successes in nightlife into bona fide hospitality businesses and brands. Perhaps the most renowned are former promoters Jason Strauss and Noah Tepperberg, cofounders of Strategic Hospitality Group and Tao Group, and widely described as pioneers in the "models and bottles" business formula. With a portfolio of hotels and clubs spanning New York and Vegas to Sydney, Australia, they are multimillionaires and celebrities in their own right.[9]

Strauss and Tepperberg are the stuff of legend in nightlife. They went from being nightclub promoters to heads of a major corporate enterprise, pushing the limits of what success in nightlife looks like. They had been the subject of two case studies by the Harvard Business School, where they were regularly invited as guest lecturers to discuss their business success.

Never mentioned in all of their publicity, however, are the gendered conditions of their path to success. Promoters who were men were far better positioned than women to capitalize on girls' beauty. Of the seventeen clubs I regularly attended in New York, just one was owned by a woman. Girls could generate enormous returns, but the profits were almost entirely concentrated in men's hands.

Party Girls and Good Girls

At the age of thirty-two, I found myself regularly referred to as a "girl," though I stood out as ten years older at promoters' tables. What is a girl, if any woman from her teens to her thirties can be one?

The term "girl" came into popular usage in England in the 1880s to describe working-class unmarried women who occupied an emerging social space between childhood and adulthood. Not quite a child, she was childlike in that she had yet to become a wife or mother, the type of modern urbanite who engaged in "frivolous" pursuits like consumption, leisure, romance, and fashion.[10] The idea and imagery of the girl spread from England to the rest of the world through popular figures like the "shopgirl" in newly opening department stores, the flapper—the original "It Girl" in America—and "chorus girls," those young female stage performers who danced in unison on stage. In these display roles, women found little longevity. One news report about a successful New York dancer in 1929 noted, "At twenty-one, she is through, as far as Broadway in concerned."[11]

Around this time, another kind of "girl" rose to prominence in popular culture: the fashion model. The first modern models appeared in the Paris salon of English courtier Charles Frederic Worth in the late 1850s, when the famous dressmaker pulled young women from his workshop floor to be mannequins for his wealthy clientele.[12] It was quite a scandalous scenario from the start, raising curiosities about what, exactly, was for sale: the dress or the young woman wearing it?

Models, chorus girls, flappers, and shopgirls all publicly displayed their bodies for profit. They were young and beautiful, and praiseworthy for it, but they also tainted their reputations by showing their bodies in public.[13] People both admired and despised them. A predatory man could assume their sexual availability, as the sort of girls who were "ripe for seduction but not for marriage."[14]

In the VIP club, "girl" was the dominant term for any woman, but over time I became aware of a typology of girls according to their perceived moral qualities. *Party girls*, of high value to clubs and promoters, are beautiful, young, and carefree enough to be out late and often. In contrast, a *good girl* was a rare gem: both beautiful and serious, and hence, rarely out late at night. Men imagined good girls to be relatively privileged and educated, and unlike the party girl, a good girl had sexual virtue.[15]

Party girls were generic and easily interchangeable from one to the next, and often models and party girls were considered one and the same. One club owner described them as "buffers." He elaborated: "Yeah, buffers, you know, the girls that are on the yacht in Saint-Tropez and they're on the sides in the picture with everybody. The party girls."

While valuable in clubs, party girls were spoken of with deep disdain by the men I interviewed. They talked about them as brainless, empty vessels who were uncultured, sexually loose, and, it sometimes seemed, worthless as humans though priceless as image. This is Ricardo, the twenty-three-year-old hedge fund associate:

> Most girls out there, I expect to be sluts or dumb bitches . . . You just recognize when you talk with them, they're just *empty*, no [other] word to describe [it], just empty . . . I might hook up with them but won't date them. Like I take them out and they don't know what sushi is. They say, "Oh, what is this? I never tried it before!" No, I can't deal with that.

In fact, I met quite a variety of girls, with diverse professional backgrounds and goals, at promoters' tables. There were plenty of underage and uneducated models, it's true, but there were also university students with majors ranging from fashion to law, business, sociology, and international relations. I frequently also sat beside young professional women who were developing careers as, for instance, entrepreneurs, real estate brokers, financiers, and doctors.[16] But by virtue of being regular visitors to clubs, all of these women were assumed by men to be party girls and thus to have unstable work lives.

Considering how much effort promoters spent to bring models to their tables, clients' denigration of models was surprising. Men mocked and pitied models in particular for having *only* beauty, the main asset they needed to enter a VIP space in the first place. It was as if models' exceptional beauty blinded men to their other possible qualities. As Marco, a thirty-five-year-old client and fitness club owner, put it: "I hate models. You can usually tell by talking to them who's a model and who isn't."

Or Aldo a thirty-three-year-old finance associate from Italy:

I've definitely dated some models but there's few of them that I find interesting. Like a lot of them are just like very young, and don't know what the fuck they're doing in their life. . . . You can generally tell whether a girl has something more to her or is a party girl.

Because party girls accept promoter's free treats, clients assumed that they must be lacking resources to pay their own way. They are probably broke, if they drink the free sparkling wine at a promoter's table. They are probably uneducated, especially if they are models, a career that peaks during the typical college-age years of eighteen to twenty-five. They are probably not ambitious or serious, if they are going out night after night until the early morning hours. Max, the thirty-three-year-old hedge fund manager who graduated from MIT, explained:

Well, every man would be lying if he said he doesn't like to be around a bunch of beautiful girls. But it's not the place I look to find a relationship. I just think, a woman who works as a model, she poses and walks the catwalk, I imagine . . . we would have trouble relating. So I would think I'd have more in common and could talk more with a girl that studies, or a girl that has a career, or is at NYU, for example, than one that is brought into the club by a promoter, and just stands there, and—that's not fun, I don't think, to talk to someone who's there because she's paid. Or, if not paid, then compensated in some way. I mean, call me crazy!

Even the promoters who made such handsome careers from models looked down on them, like Loïc, a promoter for twenty years who now hosted branding events for luxury brands:

> I meet a lot of women. They're all beautiful. But I need someone who is smart, intelligent. These girls, they travel around, go to these parties, flash their bodies. I'm not gonna find a serious woman there. Models are just "me, me, me."

Clients scoffed when I asked them if they were looking for a long-term partner among the girls in VIP clubs. Said Chris, a wealthy forty-year-old entrepreneur and long-time club patron: "I've pulled my fair share of girls but no one I'd take home to meet my mother." He scanned the room in Club X and added, "These girls, no way."

Indeed, demographers find that matches across different class positions are increasingly rare, as upper-class people tend toward homogamous unions, that is, partnering within their own socioeconomic strata. In other words, "like marries like," as women tend to marry men with similar education and income.[17]

To find girlfriends and long-term partners, clients said that they were more likely to rely on friends, work, and family ties. Ricardo, the twenty-three-year-old hedge fund associate, expected his future girlfriend would be a "serious girl," and he doubted he would meet her in a club. "I definitely don't think I'll meet a serious girl there. Someone will introduce me to her or she'll be the daughter of someone I know, or in the family of someone I know."

Wade, a wealthy twenty-nine-year-old client who partied often in New York, Miami, and the Hamptons, dismissed the possibility that he would ever find a wife at one of those parties. "They're playthings.

Like no self-respecting person would actually, like, marry one of those girls . . . Most of the guys that I know who are going out and spending $5,000–10,000 a week are constantly making fun of those girls, for just being little whores."

Wade's rich friends even shared notes and pictures of the girls that spent the night with them, sharing laughs about their drunkenness and promiscuity. "I get pictures of girls sleeping more than I should," he said. To Wade, the worst girls were the ones who don't care when their photographs get shared between men. That's how denigrated the party girl is, that someone like Wade assumes she doesn't mind when men disrespect her.

Luc, the forty-year-old restauranteur from an old moneyed French family, had had many relationships with models, but they rarely lasted more than one night. "Because when you wake up in the morning, it's like, 'Hello.' 'Oh, hello.' 'Uh, what do you do?'"—Luc here took on a high-pitched voice and pretended to be the imaginary girl in bed next to him—"'*I'm a model!*' . . . I have nothing to tell them and they have nothing to say to me."

Luc saw the irony in this. "It's sad. But everyone wants to be there, because the girls are there." But like Luc, no one seemed to want them outside of the club in the daylight hours. "It's contradictory, because you want easy girls, but then on the other side you want good girls. It's like, it's confusing." He struggled, himself caught in the contradictory value of girls: the very qualities that made party girls appealing in the VIP world—youth, beauty, and the capacity to go out often and stay out late, with few daytime commitments—made them totally unsuitable for serious relationships.

Yet he met his own girlfriend, the mother of his new baby, at a club in the Meatpacking District. "But she's not like that," he quickly clarified, noting that she had come with a friend, not a promoter, and she didn't stay long. She was a model but not a party girl, he assured me, because "she rarely goes out."

For clients and promoters alike, then, the real finds were not "party girls," no matter how physically attractive, but "good girls." What the good girl has the party girl lacks: sexual respectability and self-restraint, and a promising future in which she herself might fit in among the upper class. Good girls were candidates for relationships but unlikely to be found in the company of promoters; party girls were suitable for hookups, and clubs were overflowing with them.[18]

This very tension plagued the introduction of Melania Trump to the national stage during Donald Trump's presidential campaign. Melania Knavs, the Slovenian fashion model, met future husband and real estate mogul Donald Trump at the Kit Kat Club, in 1998, at a party organized by former model agency owner Paolo Zampolli, a man known for bringing together models and economically powerful men at exclusive parties.[19] But, Zampolli assured the press, Melania was *not* a party girl: "She was very determined. Melania was not a party girl. She came to do a job."[20]

The good girl and the party girl are both tropes, imagined archetypes that serve to anchor perceptions of a woman's sexual virtue and, closely linked, her class position, to one end or the other of a spectrum.[21] There were indeed some girls who were committed partiers with promoters, and there were others who had demanding careers and so came out rarely. Most fell in between the binary of good girls and party girls: most girls went out for months at a time between jobs or on summer break or during a period in their lives when they just felt like it and had the time. But by going out regularly and accepting freebies like drinks and comped meals, any girl could become a party girl, taking on a tainted reputation much like the first girls to appear in shop windows and fashion displays that came a century before.

Soft Hookers

The Port of Saint-Tropez connects the quaint old French Riviera town, with its artisanal shops and narrow cobblestone streets, to the clear blue sea of the Côte d'Azur. Every year from June to August, the port becomes a seafront parking lot for some of the world's megayachts, with Cayman Islands flags blowing in the Mediterranean breeze against a backdrop of small cafés and quiet restaurants.[22] By nightfall, the waterfront transforms into a catwalk of sorts, as yacht speakers blast loud dance music from their decks, on which owners and their guests dine, dance, and invite girls strutting below to come aboard. Girls pace back and forth on the promenade in high heels and dresses awaiting invitations, sometimes waving to the yacht occupants as they pass. If invited, the girls come aboard for a glass of champagne and perhaps a little dancing, always barefoot; they must take off their shoes before climbing on deck because the heels might scuff the wood floors.

I was here after a week in Cannes with Santos, joining some European friends of Enrico, the wealthy Spanish promoter, who put us in touch; they agreed to let me aboard their yacht for the weekend. At sundown Friday night, the promenade pulsed with small groups of women pacing. Some girls are university students on a European tour during summer holidays. Other girls are models here with friends. Some girls are what the yachting men call "real professionals."

On board a 120-foot yacht owned by an Italian banker, Giovanni, one such pair of girls climbed the stairs to join him and his Italian friends for a drink amid the pop music blaring from their deck speakers. Giovanni has one of the smallest yachts at the port. It's been docking here since he was a teenager on visits with his wealthy family. Now he comes once a year with his friends, a mix of men and women, young professionals in law and finance, all from upper-class backgrounds.

Giovanni hesitated when he saw the girls step aboard his yacht. They were tall, dressed in skintight Herve Leger dresses, with heavy fake eyelashes, plumped-up lips, and hair so blonde and coiffed it seemed like replica wigs of Paris Hilton. Giovanni warned his friends: watch your phones and wallets. But still, the men danced with them, talked with them, and drank with them for half an hour, staging an open-air dance party aboard the deck in the middle of the port.

In between toasts and dancing, Giovanni and his friends made joking asides out of earshot of the girls. "She's a student. Yeah, I'm *sure*."

"I'm gonna take her home to meet my mother." That got a lot of laughs.

When I met Giovanni in Milan before he set sail for Saint-Tropez, he explained that he and his friends have to be alert to these kinds of girls in VIP clubs, to tell if a girl is "a whore or if she's normal." If a girl is by herself at a bar in Saint-Tropez, especially if she is dressed overly sexily, she is probably working as a prostitute, he said.

Like promoters back in New York, Giovanni and his friends aboard the yacht shared a sense of women organized into moral categories by their perceived sexual virtue: the *good girl*, the *party girl*, and, most dangerous and despised of all, the *paid girl*. Based on a few loose cues, men thought they could identify the paid girl, who was a type of party girl they assumed to be for hire. Paid girls included bottle waitresses as well as any girl that was perceived as breaking gendered norms of sexual conduct by strategically seeking payment for her company.

The most obvious of paid girls were those that worked for pay by the club. The bottle girls, also called bottles waitresses, were cocktail waitresses who took orders from clients, brought them sparkler-lit bottles, and sometimes, if invited, joined their tables to entertain clients. In addition to waiting on clients, bottle girls are expected to bring male clients out to tables; that is, they try to mobilize their connections to wealthy men and former clients to get them to come out and spend money. They are the female counterpart of the promoter who brings girls out to tables. Once there, bottle girls are expected to hold clients' attention by any means, usually flirtation. It could be lucrative work. A bottle girl could expect a 20 percent tip at the end of the night ranging from $200 to $800, but clients often paid them extra cash on top of that. This could add up to thousands of dollars for a single night's work.

It was well-paid, but it was described as a "dirty job" by women who did it.

"You have to be [a] little bit of a whore to handle it," explained Olga, Enrico's girlfriend, who worked as a bottle girl in a small club. She typically took home $1,000 in tips each night, but the work was emotionally draining: "You have [to] bring the clients, you have to connect to the clients, it's kind of like, is kind of, a bit like dirty. Not like you have to sleep with them, but if you wanna have as many clients as you can . . . There is maybe a few girls is like super, super, um, successful girls in bottle service."[23]

Bottle girls were physically marked as more sexually available than girls at promoters' tables. They were tall (required to wear five-inch heels at one VIP club's outpost in Miami), and voluptuous, typically wearing tight and revealing dresses. They were also more racially diverse than promoters' girls. Physically and symbolically, bottle girls represented sexiness, and clients and promoters presumed they were for sale as much as the bottles they carry.[24]

One client claimed that he was regularly offered bottle girls with his purchases: "Our Club X host will tell us that for every $5,000 we spend, we get a girl. Like a bottle girl. To have sex with. Like blow jobs in the DJ booth, while Tiesto is spinning." I could not confirm this client's account, but he shared the widespread assumption that bottle girls were sexually available. They were commonly described as "slutty" and "dirty."

The term "bottle girl" even has associations with sex work and criminality in popular and legal discourse. In an FBI investigation of theft in Miami in 2014, agents called a ring of con women "bottle girls" (and "b-girls" for short) for targeting men at bars and aggressively upselling them alcohol, in exchange for a share of 20 percent of the bar's profits.[25]

In short, bottle girls were not to be trusted, clients told me. One investment banker, Thomas, forty-three, whom I met at Felipe and Thibault's table one night, said:

> All these waitresses, you know, pour themselves a glass of champagne. And your giant bottle of champagne that was full when they brought it over is now three quarters gone. And the girls drink their champagne, and they disappear. Or they'll hang out and flirt with you. But those girls are very aware that you're spending a shitload of money, so.

Another category of paid girls is the "table girls," pretty young women paid to wait around the bar for an invitation to sit at the tables of clients requesting female company. I saw table girls at only one club, Club X; a cocktail waitress was in charge of recruiting them and managers oversaw which clients' tables they visited. Table girls were viewed with distaste by promoters. Toni, a thirty-four-year-old white male promoter from Italy, described such girls as suspiciously close to sex workers:

> Because if you are sitting at a client's table and people see you doing it all the time, you might be a prostitute. If you are with me at my table with all the girls, you are a model. . . . I don't like them [table girls]. They can be slutty.

"Table girls" and the models at Toni's table are engaging in very similar practices—looking good and drinking free champagne at tables—but they occupy very different positions. The positions are maintained as distinct through the boundary work performed; in this case, through particular exchange media and discourses: the table girl is paid in cash and is "slutty" while the model is compensated in drinks and is comparatively high status. Because they are commodifying their looks for explicit payment, table girls and bottle girls are seen as akin to sex workers.

The stigma of prostitution threatened to pollute all party girls in the scene. While the VIP club space extracted value from women's beauty, women suspected of using their looks for their own economic gain were shunned. Club owners, promoters, and wealthy clients all shared suspicions around women who seemed to have economic motivations. They called such women "users," "hookers," and "whores." The specter of the paid girl loomed over all girls who, by virtue of being in the VIP space, had entered into a disreputable exchange, prostitute-like in that they capitalized on their looks for free champagne and vacations.

I too worried that I might be perceived as being on the wrong side of this moral boundary. By the time I made it to Saint-Tropez in the summer of 2013, I had acquired another Chanel bag, which I bought for $300 from a girlfriend, a former model who would otherwise have sold it on eBay while clearing out her sizable collection of designer purses, gifts from her wealthy husband. It was a black canvas quilted "2.55" bag, a recognizable rectangular box in the fashion world, though this one had started to lose its shape and it took a little massaging on the corners to make it look right. Still, it had the trademark gold-and-black chain and was better than my sister's bag with the leather patches. I thought the bag would help me fit in among the elite men and successful models around me. But the longer I carried it, the more uncomfortable I became: people could be wondering, What was a sociology professor doing with a thousand-dollar Chanel handbag? Perhaps, they might surmise, it was a gift from a wealthy benefactor.

This would have been consistent with a common suspicion among clients, who were wary of girls using them for their money and the material goods they could afford.[26] One client, Rhys, a financial advisor, described such girls as trying to "harpoon a whale." Another client, a thirty-five-year-old private-equity investor who regularly went out to clubs in New York and St. Barts with his financial clients, rebuffed the idea that serious women could be found out at night. "These girls will tell you stories that being at the club at two o'clock in the morning is an amazing way to network," he said. "No way, that's bullshit. You don't do any business at two a.m. except one business! I'm not expecting anything from the women I meet in the club. For me, it's a red flag. C'mon, who on a Wednesday or Thursday night is out at 2 a.m.? What do they do for a living?"

"They could be students?" I suggested.

"Students?!" He was incredulous. "They should be studying in the library, what the fuck! The education inflation rate is seven percent, and their parents are paying that," he said.

Another client, Wade, thought that girls who sought gifts from wealthy sex partners were not quite hookers, but he described them as engaging in what he called "soft hooking":[27]

> The girls don't even know they're soft hooking. They're just enamored by the trips and the clothes and the shoes. They actually never take money. Every now and again someone will pay their rent, but they don't actually think they're whores. I don't think they are. I think they're just girls.

Thus, clients could conflate all girls with sex workers, or *potential* sex workers, because the girls exchanged bodily capital for men's economic capital—the two assets that formed the very foundation of VIP nightlife. As the owner of Club X remarked dismissively, when

I pitched to him my research on nightlife, "You should do a story on how many girls going out become hookers," because, he implied, it happens frequently.

The distinctions between *paid girls*, *party girls*, and *good girls* mostly hinged on perceptions of women's sexual morality, meaning how well she abides by the gendered rules of sexual conduct.[28] As moral categories, these tropes classify women as virtuous and sexually unavailable, or as available and strategic about it.[29]

Perhaps sensing their potential, in the eyes of men in the VIP scene, to be seen as paid girls, most of the girls I met policed the boundaries separating themselves from sex workers. Girls were quick to put down others they saw as too interested in looking for wealthy men. They described such women as "sluts" or "bitches," the latter a term I heard among Eastern Europeans in Cannes.

For instance, Anna, a twenty-three-year-old Czech model I roomed with in Cannes, was concerned that I not confuse the two categories of party girl and paid girl. "Don't write [that] Czech girls are bitches," she told me. Normal people don't know about this free VIP world, Anna explained. "I didn't know. My friend in Milan, when I came she was telling me there is free lunch, dinner, party. I was like, 'Why? How can it be?' If I tell people from back home, they think you have to do something more, you know, you have to do a lot, like bitches." "Bitches" perform sex for money and gifts, as opposed to girls who just want to have fun.

In interviews and informal conversations, girls downplayed their interests in meeting men. Romance was conspicuously absent among the girls' stated motivations for going out. All but one of the girls made clear their belief that, as one Lithuanian in Cannes put it, "This is not the place to meet a boyfriend!"

Yet while girls usually described themselves as not primarily motivated by the prospect of meeting men, and many were adamant that they were not seeking a long-term or fortune-securing relationship in the VIP scene, almost half of the girls I interviewed had dated a man they met there. Reba, the twenty-eight-year-old girl in New York, for instance, didn't expect to meet a boyfriend out at a club: "I think somebody that shows up in those places is probably not a good candidate for a lot of reasons." She also drew a sharp line between herself, an educated professional, and girls who were seeking a rich husband:

> I definitely draw a line between myself and these particular girls, the girls who say, "I'm here to find a husband so I can get a green card." Or, "I'm here so that I don't have to work." . . . That's disturbing to me because I actually go out to have fun. I'm not going out to find somebody to pay for my rent, because I'm actually doing that. And I sort of feel bad for these girls if they think that. Because the truth is, and I'm going to say this as frankly as I can but it sounds terrible, but a lot of them are young, nineteen, twenty, twenty-one. By the time they're thirty, none of them are going to be very attractive. In fact most of them won't. They won't have anything left. . . . That's not to say all of them, of course, but definitely for a subset out there, looking for somebody who's gonna pay their way through life, I think that's a different kind of girl.

I met only one woman who spoke openly about seeking relationships with rich men. Jenny, thirty-one and the oldest party girl I met, was coming to the end of her modeling career and looking for a transition to a fashion design job. She was open about her "benefit boyfriend," a Saudi man who in the past had flown her first-class from New York to Singapore, "drinking Dom Pérignon the whole way." She met him through a girlfriend who was also involved with the man. She told me: "You have to get something from a relationship. Why not? They're all gonna screw you in end, anyway. Love is, like, for when you are a virgin."

In her frankness and her age, Jenny was very much an exception among the girls I met on the VIP circuit. Most were careful to present themselves within appropriate boundaries separating them from transactional sex.

But the party girl herself had entered into a dubious exchange by virtue of getting freebies for her good looks. If a girl was present at parties too frequently, if she accepted the free things offered to her, if she had sex with whomever she wanted (all of the things that clubs wanted and enticed girls to do), she was at risk of being seen as a user and a whore. All girls exist on the thin edge of a moral boundary separating them from sex workers. While promoters excelled at crafting strategic intimacies—the pursuit of intimate relations in order to achieve economic goals—this was a mark of shame for women.

Beauty, many people believe, can function as a form of capital for women, something women can trade for upward mobility. Perhaps, some argue, beauty is women's special power to subvert traditional hierarchies.[30] Hence the term "fatal attraction," Pierre Bourdieu once noted, aptly describes how beauty, an accident of birth, holds the potential to circumvent and destabilize traditional class hierarchies by allowing lower-class women to penetrate high society, whose members typically marry exclusively among themselves.[31]

The notion of beauty as women's "erotic capital" is popular but thinly supported by data. Hypergamy, or "marrying up," might look like a way in which women can use their erotic capital, but most of the research on assortative mating shows that homogamy is actually more common, and, since the 1980s, men are increasingly marrying women with similar education and income.[32] The VIP world brings together beautiful girls and rich men, but their relationships are expected to be for short-term pleasure; the men I spoke to certainly did not see girls as real potential partners for long-term romantic or business relationships. Quite the opposite: "strategic" women were exactly what they did not want.

Sexuality has always had asymmetrical consequences for men and women. Men gain status and respect with their sexual conquests, while promiscuity ruins a woman's respectability. Girls may have abundant riches in the form of bodily capital, but their capacity to spend it is limited by gendered rules of sexual conduct.

Women

Girls were centrally important to the VIP scene, but women seemed practically invisible, except as sad reminders of what happened to girls when they aged out.

As girls grow up, they lose their value. Especially the party girls, according to Ricardo:

You know girls especially, girls go bad earlier than guys go. They get wrinkles, they grow older faster than men. If they party every night that makes it even worst. It's the nature of girls. They just tend to wrinkle more than guys, they get used up, they get older faster than guys. It's confirmed. I read studies about it. It's true. They mature faster, wrinkle faster.

Another client, a thirty-five-year-old private-equity investor, similarly explained, "Men grow into their looks and peak later in life. For women they fall off around thirty-five or something like that." These clients' ideas are widespread, and demographic research on marriage and aging has found that, indeed, compared to men, women are judged more harshly and regarded as comparatively less attractive as they grow older. Starting at age thirty-five, the probability of being single is greater for women than men, and the gap grows each year. Men who marry in their thirties and older consistently marry women younger than themselves, and that age difference grows as men age, too.[33]

I never lied about my age, and the question came up often in casual conversation, especially when I mentioned my job at a university. Clients, promoters, and girls alike stared with a mix of shock and admiration when I told them my age. It was as if thirty-two were an unfortunate disease I was managing well, for now. One client congratulated me on making it past thirty and "still looking good. I mean, congratulations," he said, studying my face. On another night, I spoke with a celebrated musician, himself forty years old with a gorgeous twenty-year-old blonde girlfriend. Surprised to learn that I was thirty-two, he offered: "It's because you are brunette. Blondes, they break quite soon."

Blondes "break." Girls "get used up." Women "fall off" and "lose their looks." All terms of destruction and loss to describe the process of girls growing up. That age "progressively destroys" women, but not men, is the crux of what Susan Sontag termed the double standard of aging, back in 1972.[34] It is a pernicious standard of the VIP club, and of any other arena in which women are valued for their beauty.

There was another layer of injustice to men's disgust for aging women. If a girl were still partying into her thirties, clients and promoters tended to see her as losing not only her physical value but also her perceived virtue. When girls grow up, so it seemed to men in the VIP scene, they grow "desperate" and try to "cash in" on their fading capital with a wealthy boyfriend. In short, an older girl in the VIP club is a "loser," said Luc, the wealthy forty-eight-year-old Frenchman. "I mean, a thirty-year-old girl, she does this, she's sad actually. You're thirty and you're with one of the promoters and go out every night—that's really sad. It means you're a bit of a loser, no? No job, no family. You should have a boyfriend by now and be more steady," he said, describing a hypothetically older woman at the club, and perhaps not realizing that I myself was over thirty.

Dre thought that once girls reach thirty, they enter "the age of desperation in nightlife." This is when they realize that beauty, once their ticket to elite socializing, is fading, and so:

> They will do anything to capitalize. Meeting a celebrity or a guy with money, make a baby so they can get the alimony . . . They don't really wanna have fun, [these] girls that hang out are running after celebrities or billionaires . . . Those models, you have to remember, they didn't really get to finish school, they were taken out of school at an early age . . . So for them, when they realize they reach a certain age and they [are] not going to have anything, they start panicking. And they want to capitalize.

I wasn't likely to find women in VIP clubs as clients, either, because women seldom buy bottles. I often saw wives and girlfriends join their men at tables, but rarely did they appear to be older than thirty-five or so, and all were clearly in the company of economically or socially significant men. Everyone used male pronouns to describe clients. Promoters explained that while women occasionally buy bottles, these women are strange or silly exceptions, like the ex-wife of a wealthy Saudi Arabian man upon receiving hundreds of millions from a divorce settlement. Such women are always assumed to have derived their wealth from rich men.

Everyone explained the distinction in gendered terms: women show off by consuming other status goods, like clothes and handbags, while men, said one promoter, "They want to be looked up to. They want that feeling of 'Yeah, I'm a man. I'm having this much fun, surrounded by this.'"

During fieldwork, I noticed older women at tables on only a few occasions. The first time, in Miami, a woman who appeared to be in her fifties, wearing a conservative and expensive-looking dress, sat at a table with a group of wealthy older gentlemen flanked by models. She was clearly uncomfortable and soon left. In fact, after a week of parties with a promoter in Miami, I caught a 7 a.m. flight directly from an after-party, and was struck while boarding the plane by the sight of so many older women, whose presence had been near absent from my eyes for the past five days—despite Miami being a longtime retirement haven.

On the second occasion, I was out at a club in New York, when Penny, a twenty-five-year-old model, and I were asked to move from the table because, the promoter explained, a famous jewelry designer was coming and they needed to sit there. He said he would introduce us to the designer. "Hell yeah, I want some jewelry!" Penny said to me. But when the clients arrived at the table, effectively kicking us to the dance floor, Penny was incensed: the client was a heavyset middle-aged woman.

"Nuh-uh!," Penny shouted in my ear over the music. "I mean, *seriously*," she continued, "Who is that fat old bitch in the club? It's disturbing. That's someone's mother!" Penny looked with disgust at the table and shook her head. As Penny made clear, it is problematic for a woman to be old (and "fat") and included in the VIP space. Older gentlemen with white hair were hardly the norm, as most clients in the scene appear younger than fifty, but never did their presence elicit such hostility.

A third time, Anna, a thirty-year-old ex-model and herself the mother of a young child, noticed a group of older women dancing nearby our table. "Gross! Those forty-year-olds are wearing totally age-inappropriate clothing," she said to me, eyeing the group. "When

I'm forty, I hope I'm not in a fucking club, unless I rent that mother-fucker out, like, for myself!" She laughed, and added, "I just hope I'm not in a club at the age of forty. And that's just, like, as a rule of thumb."

Girls themselves could be critical of the double standard of aging, even as they were complicit in it. Eleanor, the twenty-year-old fashion intern, thought it unfair that that in ten years, she wouldn't be welcome in the New York scene she so enjoyed now:

> It's beyond, like, natural to see forty-year-old, fifty-year-old guys in a club. You're never gonna see a fifty-year-old girl. You're never gonna see a thirty-year-old girl come inside! . . . It amazes me that older guys are allowed to do all this shit, but older girls aren't . . . I think a lot of guys take advantage of their money. They take advantage of their status in nightlife and everything, and they get the young girls that they probably always wanted when they were younger. It's fucked up. It's not normal.

Aware of the harsh judgment facing women, girls didn't expect to be hanging out in the scene for long. Eleanor and others suggested that, by their thirties, they would no longer be going out to these places. They didn't want to end up looking like failed women, like "someone's mother" or a desperate "loser."

Even with money to buy a table, social connections, and cultural capital, women could still be rejected at the door if they didn't have the right bodily capital. This was frustrating to several men clients I interviewed who could not go to clubs with women "civilian" friends and work associates.

As Max, the thirty-three-year-old hedge fund associate, recounted about going to a club in a group with a woman from his finance network: She was the only woman among a few guys, and their group wanted to buy a table. But the door person didn't want to let her in, despite being pretty and relatively young, because she was not tall enough to meet the club's standards. Max explained, "You know, she had really tall heels but they gave us a hard time at the door. We were getting a table and they said, 'Sorry she can't come in.' And it became this back-and-forth, and I felt so bad for her, because this is a girl that's very pretty and nothing like that had happened to her in her life, you know. Anyway, we all got in, but it was just so awkward."

The consequences for women are obvious: they are effectively excluded from the spaces in which their male colleagues' careers can be strengthened. Max, for instance, used nightclubbing as a way to foster ties with investors, as he explained:

> A good way to build relationships is in, like, flirting with girls. Like older men bond over golf, younger men bond over this. . . . If you go out with someone who's a business contact, and meet women and party with girls—one of the things we can enjoy talking about is women, like in following-up with the clients . . . A lot of business is won through experiences like this. I've seen it be a problem for some women in my business.

Located near the bottom in a gendered hierarchy that prizes youth and beauty, women face exclusions not just from the party, but potentially from business circles.[35] Women generally have little recognizable capital in the VIP scene, where value is defined by the beauty of girls.

Girl Capital

One might expect that girls, in the face of a closing window of opportunity, would try to capitalize on their assets before they become women. This familiar cultural logic is captured well in the lyrics of "Diamonds Are a Girl's Best Friend," a song that playfully describes the painfully short-lived exchange of women's beauty for male-derived economic security, two assets with mismatched time frames:

> Men grow cold as women grow old,
> And we all lose our charms in the end.
> But square-cut or pear-shaped,
> These rocks don't lose their shape.
> Diamonds are a girl's best friend.

> Shouldn't girls also be strategic?

I met a few girls who did strategically cultivate social ties through nightlife to the same extent that promoters and clients did. For instance, one twenty-five-year-old model described finding an internship in finance through the connections she made at clubs. Another, a good civilian working in fashion, built a network of valuable social connections through the brunch parties held by clubs in the Meatpacking District, which she was mobilizing to start a concierge company. "All my connections came from those parties," she said. Finally, I met a former model who was launching a beauty and lifestyle website, and she strategically sought business opportunities that could come her way just from being in these kinds of places. She explained that when she went out, she was looking to meet people relevant for her business. "As a beautiful girl, I know I get more opportunities for my business," she told me. "I know what the game is and how to play it," echoing words I heard so many times out with Dre.

Most girls, though, didn't strategically cultivate social capital to the same extent as men, nor did they typically have a plan for how to monetize their ties. A few expressed doubts that any concrete opportunities could be found in the VIP club, at least not beyond their free meals and fun experiences.[36] Twenty-six-year-old Beatrice had graduated from art college in London and was a part-time model who also worked freelance in public relations during the day. She didn't think she would find leads for jobs in a club, at least not the type of jobs that she would want, anyway. And it was certain that she would not meet a long-term boyfriend there, she said:

> It's more about just having fun with friends. Like, it's certainly—that is where my goal begins and ends. It's certainly not about, like, I could never see myself meeting someone that I, like, really want to be with at a nightclub. And I could never see myself actually networking to find a job at a nightclub. . . . I don't feel like people I meet in that context are the kinds of people I would call, "So, do you know anyone that is hiring a PR assistant?" Like, no.

Beatrice had an intuitive sense of what girls were valued for in the VIP club, and it wasn't their business potential. While girls did meet important people out at night, they were in a weaker position to leverage their social capital compared to clients and even promoters.

There were, however, plenty of opportunities in the VIP scene for girls to acquire cultural capital that could benefit them in the future. For girls (as well as promoters) who lacked formal educational credentials or who didn't have upper-class upbringings, VIP nightlife opened up a back door for them to learn the cosmopolitan tastes of global elites.[37] Girls became familiar with elite culture by, for example, holding conversations with MBA graduates, hearing their book and media recommendations, traveling on private planes, and recognizing high-end brands, foods, and wines. By traveling to exotic destinations and elite enclaves, girls learned the importance of being globally connected and at ease with people from different parts of the world. You could see this transmission of cultural capital at the dinners, when Dre routinely replayed conversations about technology and politics he had been privy to among various industry moguls, inviting the girls at his table to discuss complex topics. Once Jane, twenty-eight, understood the significance of holding her fork with her left hand when dining with Europeans, she adopted that style of eating. Reba adopted upper-class makeup styles, since "everything is built around the model culture, and you notice models don't wear a lot of makeup; they're praised for their natural beauty." Such familiarity with elite consumer culture could potentially benefit girls later in life in their romantic and professional lives. As the twenty-five-year-old model Petra put it, "If you have a head on your shoulders, it's a great way to meet people who work a lot and have money."

This is what Reba believed. The Columbia University graduate worked in advertising, and she had met many highly successful men going out with promoters over the years, including politicians, hedge fund managers, and venture capitalists:

Like the people that I've met, it's unbelievable, where else would I get that? It's such a cool opportunity . . . You have great conversations with them about what they do and you learn about venture capital or politics or about these sorts of things, so for me it's sort of an educational thing. . . . How else would I get to talk to a guy who started a venture capital firm or whatever else? I'm not gonna meet him out at a bar on the Lower East Side. I'm just not.

Reba wasn't thinking about how to monetize those connections to the same extent as were promoters and clients, but she did see their potential value to her career down the road: "Maybe one day, as I'm more senior, it will come in as far as connections are concerned, and I can't imagine that it wouldn't. I think most people at senior levels end up in these circles somehow. Maybe not in a club but maybe at the dinner. It's a small societal circle."

Mostly, however, when girls claimed they could benefit from these social ties, they tended to echo vague allusions to the value of meeting successful men. When I asked the twenty-one-year-old model Renee about any networking opportunities she had found, she replied, "Oh, absolutely, absolutely. Because you meet people, who knows, other people or whatever else, you know, even just, like, little things"—and she began discussing times she and her friends met celebrities, though the encounters she described were brief or sexually charged.

Similarly, Penny was a model and film actress from London who went out regularly in New York, who explained, "Yeah, I've met like movie directors [and] stuff like that. And if you know them and keep in contact with them, it's a beneficial thing for you."

"Does that actually work?" I asked.

"You never know."

It's not that Penny was wrong. Indeed, you never knew where the night could take you, or with whom. But it rarely seemed to amount to anything beyond brief romantic liaisons. Girls may have been at the center of the action, but they remained on the margins of men's powerful networks.

Thus girls had a powerful asset in the form of bodily capital that gave them access to the VIP world, but it was worth far more to men, for whom girls functioned as a valuable currency, a resource we might call *girl capital*.[38] With girl capital, the real estate broker Jonas could party with chief executives and Dre could dine with billionaires. Clients like Donald leveraged girl capital to get coveted invitations to parties that might lead to financially enriching deals. With girl capital, Santos could level the playing field of Cannes, where uneducated promoters from poor backgrounds comfortably shared dance floors with rich men. For the most part, girls were cut out of these benefits. Girls who demanded a share of profits, in the form of financial support or gifts, were deemed users, schemers, and whores. And while their own bodily capital depreciated in value with age, men could always refresh their supply of girl capital, easily recruiting the city's newly arrived young women into this glamorous and deeply unequal world. Beauty may look like a route to get ahead for women, but, in fact, beauty is worth more in men's hands than in women's own.[39]

The unequal ability of one person to capitalize on another is a classic measure of exploitation in Marx's terms. Men's surplus value from *girl capital* goes largely unseen, since girls' participation in the clubs is assumed to be fun, leisure, and *not work*—much like other forms of women's labor, like care work and reproductive labors in the household.[40] Women's labors are so well disguised that it's hard to recognize their leisure in the clubs as work.[41] Further obfuscating their labors were the many pleasures women experienced from their position as girls.

Traffic and Its Pleasures

It could be powerfully seductive and pleasurable to become the object of men's desire and to be on display night after night. To Katia, it was fun.

I caught up with the twenty-year-old Ukrainian model, after our time with Santos in Miami, when we were both back in New York. At a sidewalk café in SoHo, we drank cappuccinos and talked about our various nights out together, and about what she thought of those promoters who now regularly texted her with invitations to hang out, take her to lunch, share their pot with her, and, they hoped, take her out at night. Even club owners were calling her now. Her phone buzzed constantly with their messages during our hour-long talk.

(And rather predictably, a male passerby interrupted us to praise her beauty.) Katia was going out almost every night in New York, which she explained in very simple terms:

> I wanna have fun, you know. I don't care about other people, like who is the client, or whatever. I just wanna go out and see my friends, you know.

Katia didn't feel pressured to have sex with anyone, and when men grabbed her and tried to kiss her—as happened with a prominent club owner a few nights earlier—she pushed them away and kept on partying. If a guy she liked grabbed her, "it's fine, you know," and she freely had sex with men she found attractive, including promoters. She especially liked hooking up with male models; in fact, she stopped going out with Sampson because he didn't have enough "model boys" around to hold her interest: "It's not fun at all to be with a lot of girls which you don't know."

Whereas I struggled in Miami to keep up with Santos and his demand for a beautiful entourage, to Katia, going out never felt like work. As she put it, "I don't care. If I wanna leave, I'm gonna leave, if I don't like the club or the people."

In practice, this wasn't exactly true. In Miami, for example, Santos insisted she wear her high heels inside the club. "When I went out, he never let me go with the sneakers. It's the high heels. I don't like to dance with the high heels. And I don't have so much fun 'cause I'm always thinking like, 'Oh my feet' or 'I'm gonna fall.'" While in Miami, Katia couldn't so easily leave the club when it wasn't fun anymore. She kept a credit card tucked in the back of her phone for emergencies, but she didn't have much money, so she relied on promoters to get around. In the face of these constraints, she took what she could from the scene, including sex with Santos, smoking his pot on the beach, dining in upscale restaurants, and the excitement of seeing where the night would take you. In the end, her assessment of those weeks spent partying in Miami: "It was amazing, no?"

It's hard to say if Katia didn't notice or didn't mind the constraints on her time and mobility. It's possible she just liked partying, plain and simple, and this was the best way to get what she wanted.[42]

By consenting to these terms, Katia upheld a deeply unequal system in which girls circulated between men on men's terms, while generating surplus value for them in the form of money, social ties, and status. This system is what anthropologist Gayle Rubin referred to, in her now famous 1975 essay, as "the traffic in women." Rubin had sought to address the puzzle of gender inequality that consumed feminist debates in the late twentieth century: Why were women subordinate to men in nearly every society on earth?[43] To find an answer, Rubin revisited the classic anthropology of tribal kinship, leading her to observe that at the heart of men's power is a circulation of women. Men give their daughters and sisters to other men to marry to forge alliances between male-led kin groups, as a way to amass wealth and power.[44] Women were conduits of men's power, Rubin argued, because men control the exchange systems through which women circulate as gifts. Women are largely cut out from the value that their exchange generates.

While Rubin wrote about sexual slavery and systems of trafficking in which women had zero agency or freedom of mobility, her analysis usefully describes systems of consensual traffic today. Women's beauty offers returns to men in a range of industries that men control. In financial industries in the States and across Asia, the bodies of sex workers help financiers to forge business deals.[45] In the hip-hop music industry in Atlanta, new tracks are often played in strip clubs, where the energy of the women dancers for a new song can launch it into stardom and further enrich the male-controlled industry.[46] And across service industries, from hotels in China to the Hooters restaurants in middle America, women's bodies are strategically deployed to attract male customers. Women, sociologist Amy Hanser writes, perform "recognition work" in the service industry; they stroke customers' egos, helping them see themselves as special.[47] The resulting profits disproportionately accumulate to men.[48] Women's beauty work can even lift the profile of fraternity houses on college campuses. The best frat houses are those with the wealthiest, most powerful, and most successful brothers. To recruit new brothers, fraternities aim to have the best-looking girls at their parties, sometimes called "little sisters" or "rush girls." With girls, frat houses accumulate institutionalized power and prestige; the girls get free beer.[49]

Rubin never thought that trafficking women was a relic of premodern societies, nor that it would be likely to disappear in advanced capitalism. On the contrary, she predicted, "Far from being confined to the 'primitive' world, these practices seem only to become more pronounced and commercialized in more 'civilized' societies."[50] The exchange of women will flourish wherever there are resources that can be disproportionately accumulated in men's hands. The pressing question is, Why do women consent to being exploited?

In the VIP world that I examined, there were plenty of practical benefits girls gained from circulating among men, like comped meals, rides, and housing. There were relational benefits as well, like the chance to belong among a network of friends in a new city. There were also powerfully seductive sensual pleasures girls could experience.

Some pleasures are straightforward, like Katia's enjoyment of getting high and having sex with good-looking men. Some girls loved to dance, like the girl I met who was so into dancing that she wore "dance pants," little shorts under her dresses, for when she started swinging on the dance floor. For some, the club provided a sensual break from the rest of their lives. When I met with Reba, she was wearing a business suit on her lunch break in the middle of a typically long work day, and she explained, "I'm at work all day, so it's nice to be able to get dressed up and go out, and I can play a completely different role." Petra went out three nights a week for a short while after a breakup, and she found solace in clubbing: "I had a really bad heartbreak . . . and that was like a party life for me, because you kind of wanna go and be yourself, and the club gives you that."

Other thrills of the VIP world are harder to explain, as they involve taking pleasure in things that initially seem to be conceptually at odds with women's empowerment. Consider Leila, the French twenty-six-year-old MBA graduate who started going out in Manhattan with Trevor, Santos, and Malcolm. She was pleasantly surprised that all of these doors were open to her just on account of her looks. Getting all of those free dinners and drinks and the VIP treatment was some-thing of a compromise of her "deep moral principles," namely, her belief in women's financial independence. She was not what she would call a "*feminist* feminist," but she believed in equal rights and opportunities for women and men, and she thought that women should be valued for qualities beyond their bodies.

And yet, Leila felt seduced by the VIP scene even while she was critical of it. As she put it, this exclusive world invites women to be an object of desire, not necessarily a subject.[51] "And it's flattering," she said of that invitation. "It's fucking flattering." She said to herself, "Okay, I can take advantage of it." Leila was not playing a game of trading her looks for maximum benefit—she too was not a paid girl, she wanted to be clear about that. But the VIP scene opened up a world of fun and exciting experiences to her, while making her feel flattered to be included.

What should we make of all of this fun that girls and men are having?

In a *Buzzfeed* article mocking media coverage of New York's "hot-test nightclub," 1 OAK, the women seeking entry to the VIP club sound like clueless semi-naked sycophants eager to get into the club to prove they are pretty enough.[52] They do all kinds of silly things, like wear impractical shoes and dance with their arms up in the air to make their bodies appear thinner. By the end of the article, the author sums up that women should remember that the club is about men's enjoyment and women's objectification.

Herein lies the theoretical discomfort with girls' good times. Much popular and academic thinking about gender relies upon a concep-tual distinction between women's structural objectification and their own subjective pleasure, as though only men experience power and enjoyment in the male gaze. This misses how objectification itself may be pleasurable and empowering for women—especially when being objectified by the rich.

There was something incredibly enticing about being invited to become the object of *rich* men's desires. Girls put this into words obliquely by telling stories of how struck they were by displays of wealth around them. In New York, for example, Katia had been to a successful club owner's apartment, which she described with awe:

> I went to his place, in the daytime. *Ohmygod* he's got the most beautiful place I [have] ever seen in New York. . . . It's so huge, it had to be expensive. And it's like on the fiftieth-something floor so you get *amazing* view. *Amazing.* I was like, whoaaaaa.

Similar stories of being struck by shows of riches were told by other girls, like Reba, who mentioned that, on the way to her twenty-fifth birthday party, a promoter picked her up for the night in his Porsche. Girls got access to refined foods and wines and exclusive destinations; they met celebrities and went to high-profile events. They got what women who are usually excluded from social and economic power cannot get on their own.[53]

Nora, a twenty-five-year-old ex-model who went out with Dre, explained these seductions and their contradictions:

> I guess it is that whole thing where, in a sense, I don't want to be judged by how I look, but in a sense I am happy to have—to see all this stuff, and to have this opportunity that other people wouldn't normally have. You do end up feeling like one of the elite. I know it sounds so stupid, but . . . it's being able to hang out with friends and having someone tell you, "You're beautiful," so you don't have to pay for anything.

Part of the thrill of joining the VIP scene was in accessing an exclusive world that "other people wouldn't normally have," as Nora phrased it. Eleanor, the fashion intern, put it this way: "I just—I love the whole, like, aura in New York. I love the vibe. I love the exclusivity." Exclusivity is central to pleasure here; that is, girls liked that they were valued more than women who couldn't get so close to elite men.

I finally made sense of the mutual constitution of women's pleasure, objectification, and hierarchy one night out with Enrico. I joined Enrico and his wealthy Spanish clients with Anna, an old friend of mine and a former model. After rounds of drinks and dancing on top of the sofas, one of Enrico's clients approached Anna to speak into her ear over the loud music. While reaching over, he spilled his drink all down my dress, not noticing; indeed, I had met these clients of Enrico's many times in clubs and restaurants, and they rarely noticed me. Now, cupping his hand onto Anna's face and pressing his thumb onto her near ear, his face close to hers, the client told her, "You're pretty enough to be my friend."

I know this because Anna told me soon afterward, such an arrogant remark sending us into fits of laughter. But we didn't discuss the division that his comment necessarily marked between Anna, valuable enough to be included in the company of those rich men, and myself—implicitly excluded and devalued.

Being on the receiving end of a wealthy and powerful male gaze could feel thrilling and seductive, especially as the VIP men's gaze produces status distinctions among women. One powerful pull for women to join the VIP scene is precisely the knowledge that other women are not allowed in. Part of the fun is getting to join a world that excludes and devalues others. Women thus strike a patriarchal bargain by gaining access in exchange for their own subordination as girls in the VIP world.[54]

In a supposedly post-feminist world, equality is talked about as a matter of individual rights and access. But empowerment is never an individual project, and the pleasures that empower girls as objects of men's desire produce hierarchies among women who are ranked in a value system according to men's perceptions of their worth. For every woman empowered to embrace the privilege of her beauty, there are many more who are marked as devalued, and inequalities grow, both among women and "girls," and between women and men. Those girls deemed pretty enough to be at the center of the most exclusive parties in the world were still outsiders, always adjacent to the real power concentrated in men's hands.

The organizational trick, mastered by promoters and orchestrated by club managers, was to get girls to consent to these terms, without seeing it as exploitation.

5

Who Runs the Girls?

Tuesday, 2:30 a.m., New York

By 2:30 a.m., Thibault, Felipe, and Nicolas were ready to head to the next club, two blocks over in the Meatpacking District. They rounded up their ten girls, dressed in heels, tight dresses, and skinny jeans, still dancing and drinking the free champagne at the Lux hotel's rooftop club. Giddy from the party, the girls bounced out of the dark club as its strobe lights splashed color into the elevator's white fluorescent box. Beyoncé's hit single "Run the World (Girls)" boomed. The music shook the elevator walls, and the girls continued to shake and dance to the song's refrain, "Who run the world? Girls, Girls!" Felipe joined in the chorus, adding a line at the end, "Who run the girls? *Boys, Boys*!" Everyone laughed.

I squeezed into the backseat of Thibault's black Escalade alongside six girls, headed to the next club, hip-hop blaring. En route, Felipe's Escalade sped by, lots of thin arms waving out the windows, girls inside shouting. Felipe pumped the brakes to make the car hop like it had hydraulics, eliciting more laughter and shouts from both cars. Another Tuesday night out in New York with Thibault.

Thibault and his team brought a razor-sharp focus to the goal of amassing as many models as they possibly could each night, five nights a week, every week. What made them so effective as promoters was the way they fused the VIP club imperative for quality with quantity.

"People think we get paid per head, like per girl. It's not like that," said Thibault. "We've been doing this a long time, and it's the image we bring to the club. We bring the quantity of the quality."

"Quantity and quality?" I asked.

"No. Quantity *of* quality. We bring the most and the best-quality girls, and we don't stop. It's not like we have a set number and we're satisfied. We want more, always more of the best-quality girls."

As a recruitment strategy, their pursuit of the "quantity of quality" was a numbers game they played from within the fashion world. The team had fine-tuned the aggressive recruitment of models from the reserves of the New York fashion industry. At night, they were exceptionally attentive to each girl's needs and serious about showing everyone a good time. During the day, they also showered models with attention. Their schedules revolved around social activities with girls, like treating them to generous lunches and driving them to their castings in big SUVs. There was even an ongoing competition among the team to see who could bring out the best or the most girls each night. The competition was in the spirit of fun, and sometimes one promoter's count could run as high as fifteen models.

"The most important thing is bringing the girls," explained Felipe. Each member of the team had distinct, specialized strengths. Thibault was really good at meeting new people and inviting them to come out. Once there, Thibault and Felipe were good entertainers and dancers, but Felipe especially was good at keeping relationships going: "I have better social skills, like to relate to people," Felipe said, "and making it like a friendship to get the girls coming out again." Meanwhile, Nicolas had a strong business network and he brought out clients who spent on bottles.

If one of them made a consistently poor showing, the game would turn serious with a rebuke: "What's going on, man? You're slipping."

To achieve the quantity of quality, they preferred real fashion models, because even if a girl looked almost as good as a model, that "almost" meant that she wouldn't fit in with the group. She might feel intimidated and bring down the energy of everyone, or her presence could insult the real models, who might resent being lumped in with the good civilians. So Thibault, Felipe, and Nicolas built their personal networks primarily out of models and people who either had access to models, like models' agents and boyfriends, or people who had access to things that could make them more attractive to models, namely, rich men who could pay for lavish dinners, plane tickets, and villas in jet-set destinations like St. Barts and Cannes. This put the promoters at the center of a global network of VIPs and made clubs beholden to their rising fees. "They know that we're bringing not just the girls but we're bringing the whole party for the night. They know they're nothing without us," Thibault boasted.

At the same time, Thibault relied on girls for prestige and profit. Promoters told me often that they were nothing without their girls. Girls may run the VIP world, but promoters must figure out how to run the girls.

For Thibault, this meant the dedicated organization of his daily habits and lifestyle toward the goal of befriending as many pretty girls as possible. After a full day of chauffeuring models around the city, his team called up their apartments starting around 5 p.m., picked them up for dinner around 9 p.m., held conversations with them over dinner, and kept them entertained in the clubs from midnight into the early morning hours. Finally, they drove them home around 3:30 a.m. Those arduous hours required extensive physical and emotional labor, and much of it was subtle, in terms of how they learned to interact with girls and rich men. "There's so many little things that you can't see from the outside; you have to be on the inside," Thibault said.

Key to their success was the promoters' closeness to the world of fashion modeling. Thibault didn't bother with street scouting—though if a pretty girl walked by, he would surely chase after her to introduce himself; mostly, he inserted himself as close as he could to the modeling industry, and his team illustrated the striking inter-dependence between the fashion and nightlife economies. Thibault and his team knew a lot about the fashion industry: which castings were going on, what models' seasonal labor patterns were, and the exact dates when dozens of international models arrived and departed. They knew which model agents, called "bookers," were switching jobs, and which bookers had birthdays coming up. I met models who told me that they found their agencies through Thibault, who was friendly with a number of bookers and offered to scout new faces for them. They were deeply embedded in New York's Brazilian model community, since, beginning in the 2000s, a large number of Brazilians had been recruited to the industry, and the promoters often traveled to Rio and São Paulo with groups of models for Fashion Weeks and holidays.[1] On some nights out with them, Brazilian models made up as much as two-thirds of their group. One of their competitors told me that Thibault was such a pro that he taught himself Portuguese, to be a more effective promoter.

"It's more like he picked up Portuguese," clarified Thibault's girlfriend, Nina, by virtue of spending so much time with so many Brazilian friends. Nina cautioned me against believing in too many rumors about promoters. But, she agreed, Thibault's team represented the best in the business. From Nina's perspective, when I interviewed her in 2012, what made them different from the rest was their level of dedication to the girls around them, whom they always and without exception described as "friends."

Nina was a gorgeous and vivacious twenty-three-year-old model from Croatia, and an incredible dancer, especially with Thibault. Their bodies rarely separated once they started dancing. She met Thibault in 2009, when she first arrived to model in New York. A girlfriend introduced them in a club, and Nina was immediately impressed with how friendly his team was, and how affectionate they were with the girls—like dear old friends. She started to go out with them regularly, and the nights were endlessly fun, especially when she danced "like crazy" with Thibault. He tried to kiss her on the dance floor a few times in those early days, but she refused. She didn't think of him like that until a year later, one afternoon in SoHo, when she fell ill with a terrible stomachache while out to lunch with her girlfriend. Her friend could only think to call Thibault, who arrived promptly in his big SUV and drove her to a doctor. He spent the day nursing her through a case of stomach flu, and she fell for him shortly after.

That was a year and a half ago. In the time since, there had been an exclusive romance, holidays in Spain and Greece, and trips to the Balkans and the Caribbean to meet each other's families. Some of their time together was rough, marked by jealousies, fighting, and breakups. She had to share her time with him with a lot of other beautiful girls. She had to watch him flirt with them. She went out most nights with him, even when she didn't feel like it, and also when she was trying not to drink after signing with a new modeling agency that ordered her to keep her weight down. One afternoon I asked her where she was going out that night, and she laughed sarcastically, "Do I have a choice?," meaning that she would be going out wherever Thibault would be.

Still, she described Thibault, his team of promoters, and their networks of models as "family." They were people that you could count on for help when you really needed it. They were also a lot of fun. She had met amazing people through these promoters, traveled to jet-set destinations with them, and had fallen in love with one of them.

She also made them a lot of money. She was their friend, and eventually even Thibault's fiancée, but she was also their economic asset. Promoters are in the business of extracting value from girls, work which is most effectively done by forming relationships with them. This potential source of tension between friendship and economic utility, between intimacy and money, looms over the relationships of all promoters.

At the time, Nina did not feel any tension. When she heard that I was doing a study on promoters, she hugged Thibault tightly and said, "You see, promoters can be the cutest, sweetest, most amazing people ever!"

However, other women felt nothing except the insult of promoters' crude economic interest.

"They are clowns," said Sasha, a twenty-eight-year-old model from Russia who used to live in an agency-owned apartment uptown when she arrived in New York, in 2006. One evening the apartment phone rang. It was Thibault, clearly not calling for anyone in the apartment in particular; rather, he was looking for models in general. She told him not to call back and hung up, and he called back right away, demanding to know why she was so rude. "What did I do to you?" he asked her.

"You aren't respecting my privacy," she told him. "This is my home and I don't know you, so don't call here." She hung up on him again. To women like Sasha, the problem with promoters was that they aspired to treat her like a commodity, a good they could trade at the clubs for their own profit. This rendered all promoters' expressions of friendship disingenuous: "If we didn't look the way we do," Sasha said, "they wouldn't talk to us. They wouldn't even hold open the door for us."

Between Nina's devotion and Sasha's contempt, there is a range of sentiment that motivates girls to head out to promoters' tables each night: intimacy, desire, fun, and belonging, and sometimes just the material need for a free meal. Promoters try to shape girls' feelings through relational work: strategies by which they try to redefine their economic transactions as part of a personal connection. They have to work around the entrenched cultural incompatibility between the realms of sentiment and friendship on the one hand, and markets and commercial exchange on the other hand.[2] You can see relational work in all kinds of contexts where people match money and intimacy—in sex work; in organ, egg, and sperm donation; and in care work for children and the elderly. Anywhere moral questions arise about *if* and *what* should be exchanged on the market, there ends up being an elaborate set of social practices around *how* to do the exchange.[3]

Promoters face a specific problem stemming from the hazards of mixing intimacy and money—or, to put it another way, of capitalizing on their friends. Their job is to appropriate economic surplus from girls, something that to outsiders resembles pimping, while appearing to be girls' genuine friend. Men like Thibault invest plenty of time and energy into *strategic intimacies* with girls, interpersonal relationships that are economically based.[4] Promoters therefore have two jobs: to capitalize on the economic value of girls and to make it look and *feel* like they are just hanging out with friends.

Thibault expertly balanced a delicate mix of friendship and money, the personal and the economic, in the ways he took care of his "friends." A good promoter like himself had a number of tricks at his disposal. From gifting goods and services to flirting and even having sex with girls, promoters strived to make sure that their relationships became socially meaningful, that is, understood as just friends hanging out or hooking up, rather than merely economic. They didn't want girls to see them as brokers or employers compensating girls for labor. But promoters do indeed manage girls' labor. They recruit, compensate, control, and discipline them like a manager oversees his workforce. It is a highly gendered form of management and there are few women who work as promoters. During my fieldwork, I found only five of them in New York to interview and observe. Male promoters said that women were not cut out for such a tough job, but, in fact, women were disadvantaged by their sexuality. They lacked masculine domination and heterosexual flirtation as tools to mobilize girls to come to their tables and stay there. Because relational work between promoters and girls was so heavily sexualized, there emerged a distinct set of practices that men and women employed to perform the work.

When promoters got it right, however, girls could feel closely connected to them. Ties among "dear friends" solidified through months of sharing experiences together, as they did on the many nights when Thibault and Nina danced in perfect harmony with dozens of girls around them. But other nights were terrible. Sometimes the energy was low, like when girls sat with arms folded across their laps for most of the night, or when Thibault was tired or fighting with a jealous Nina. Some girls left the table when it got dull. On some occasions, a promoter yelled at them if they tried to leave. When that happened, the instrumental terms of their relationships became clear, and their friendships were likely ruined. It would be too easy to say that promoters and clubs exploit girls for monetary gain; we would miss a crucial insight into how relations of exploitation operate. In short, promoters show us that exploitation works best when it feels good.

Promoters worked to build relationships with girls by treating them to lunch, driving them to their castings, taking them to the movies, even helping them move apartments. Thibault helped me, too: when my car got towed, he and Jack drove me to the pound on the Far West Side of Manhattan. It was a kind gesture. But after a few months of watching how they work, I came to see these gestures as part of their craft. After all, Thibault said that as a promoter, "Everything that you do, you are working."

Recruitment

"*Hello*! Hey! This is Ashley! I'm friends with people in nightclubs, and we're organizing a *big* dinner and a party tonight. Do you girls wanna come?"

After a few tries calling up the model apartments with Thibault, these were the best opening lines I had. I was 6:00 p.m., and I was sitting on the floor of Thibault's bedroom, mobilizing models to join his table that night.

"Who is this?" demanded a tiny Eastern European–accented voice on the other end of the line. I stumbled and offered a rapid series of explanations that sounded more like excuses for intruding on this young woman's landline. "Umm, I'm Ashley, and uh, I'm friends with Thibault, and we're trying to get cool people to our party tonight." Silence. I offered lamely, "We'll send you a driver?" The young woman said something about being tired, and hung up without further discussion. I exhaled a deep breath.

"Yeah, that's okay. You did okay," said Thibault, sitting on the floor next to me with his mobile phone in hand, adroitly texting invitations. Even better, he suggested, would be to use key words like *big party* or *cool party*, and *sushi*. Models love sushi. And I shouldn't use words like *organize*.

"These are models. They don't understand academic words, you know; models don't have the attention for that. Just say we're throwing a big party."

Here we were in Thibault's "office," his modestly decorated one-bedroom apartment in Harlem, which was rent-controlled at $815 a month. We could do this work anywhere, but he thought it better to do it in one place and be systematic about it. Earlier in the day we drove to castings and hung around Union Square for lunch with models. During this "free time," from 2:00 to 4:30 p.m, Thibault mass-messaged the 2,500 people in his phone contacts to let them know about his evening plans. By 5:00 p.m. each day, he headed uptown to begin organizing the night. Now he was sending specialized texts and calling the fifty or so people he knew were in town and were most likely to come out.

His invitations were colorful, flirtatious, sometimes outright silly:

A model is someone who will tell u 2 go to hell and u will still look forward to the trip . . . Are u shaking it with us at CLUB X 2nite? Dinner b4 at Lux Hotel. Thibault

Normally he copied and pasted lists of numbers in his phone into a single invitation, but this function on his phone wasn't working. He had to send them one by one and this was slowing him down.

Thibault had me make calls on a small laptop computer connected to a phone with a cord, which enabled him use a free Internet phone service. He handed me a list of phone numbers of model agency apartments, Nina's copy of *War and Peace* to place under the paper, and a pen to strike out the numbers I called.

Thibault's own approach on the phone was to be silly or wild, and he said funny things in a deep growl of a voice like, "Whassssup! Girrrllls it's gonna be CRAAAAZEEEE tonight." Because, he said, models are young and they like to have fun.

Another strategy was outright trickery. For instance, I could call and pretend to be a model's work acquaintance: "Hey, this is Ashley, we met at a casting a while ago." Thibault assumed gender should work to my advantage here, since girls would be more open to my voice than to that of a strange man calling their home. Once I hooked her attention, I was to tell her that we were throwing a big party with sushi, and that we would send a driver—this was Nicolas, Felipe, or Thibault—to pick her up. I could always add that a celebrity was going to be at the club, like Leonardo DiCaprio or Kanye West. This was not entirely a lie, Thibault noted, since celebrities went out sometimes.

Another trick of his: when the girl said she couldn't go out at night because she was tired, ask her what she was doing during the daytime. Then, Thibault would work around her schedule to hang out during the day. If you got to know them during the daytime, then the night was easy.

When someone answered the phone I could also pretend to be a booker, as in, "Hey, I'm with the agency. You girls ready to go out tonight like we talked about?" This seemed like an egregious privacy violation, but Thibault reassured me, "Yes, you can talk like the bookers." I must have looked doubtful, because he added, "Listen, this is what we do."

Thibault got the phone numbers to these agency-run apartments from various girls he hung out with, girls that once lived there or had friends living there. Most model agencies in New York have at least one apartment that they rent out to new recruits to the industry. The apartments are scattered throughout Manhattan and, increasingly, New Jersey and Brooklyn. They are usually sparsely furnished units outfitted to house as many transitory models as possible, girls coming from around the world to New York with no other place to stay. During busy seasons like Fashion Week, as many as nine models will share a two-bedroom apartment, four per room sleeping on two sets of bunk beds, and one on the sofa bed in the living room. The cost per model is fixed, regardless of how many or how few roommates she has. One 2016 report found that models in New York were charged $1,850 per month to stay in a packed two-bedroom model apartment.[5]

Agencies charge the rent against the model's future earnings. The rent per bed is so high for each girl because agencies try in this way to offset their losses from those models who won't be able to pay their debts to the agency from their earnings. The rental bill goes onto her account, along with the costs of her plane ticket to get to New York, her visas, the pictures in her portfolio—in short, all of the start-up costs that models, as independent contractors, must pay for themselves. But since so many models have so little money at the start of their careers, agencies will front these costs at inflated rates, typically putting models in the red up to several thousand dollars even before she books her first modeling job. When models need pocket money to get around the city, agencies advance cash to models with a five percent fee.[6] Modeling is an expensive job, and paychecks come slowly, if at all, after expenses are paid.

During New York's Fashion Week, the population of models in town swells to the thousands, but they are largely doing the unpaid work of castings and the underpaid work of runway shows.[7] Some of the most celebrated shows of Fashion Week don't pay their models, at least not in money. As model Sara Ziff, founder of the trade organization the Model Alliance, has noted, "Models lack minimum wage protection—many shows at Fashion Week pay in clothes."[8]

Few agencies sue models for lost rent money, since failed models are unlikely to be able to pay back debts or the legal fees involved to collect from them. Rather, modeling agencies play a different sort of numbers game: they recruit a lot of potential top models knowing that most of them won't make any money, but hope that one or two might strike it big. Because modeling is a "winner-take-all" market, a few lucky breaks can reap significant payments to offset the losses from all of the wannabes who left behind unpaid debts as they cycled in and out of the agency.

Since the 1990s, model scouts have tapped into previously closed labor reserves of women in the former Soviet bloc of Russia and Eastern Europe. As a relatively weak economy with few opportunities for fashion work, the former USSR offers scouts fertile recruiting ground, especially with the liberalization of trade and travel in Europe since the 1990s gave Western modeling agencies new access to young white girls. Likewise, Brazil, because of its relative economic weakness and large white population, has been prime scouting ground since the 1990s.[9] Model scouts thus exploit global economic inequalities as they reproduce a colonial structure of extracting raw commodities from economically marginalized parts of the world like Eastern Europe and Brazil to profit from them in more developed markets in metropoles like New York and Paris.[10] Hence Thibault's nightly company of a dozen Brazilian models and a Croatian girlfriend.

There are a lot of underpaid and indebted models at agencies in New York, many of them staying in cramped housing, most of whom are newcomers to the city with few friends. Model apartments are thus fertile recruitment grounds for promoters offering free dinners and fun nights out with new friends. One promoter, now a club owner, went so far as to disguise himself as a pizza deliveryman to elude the doorman. Once inside the building, he would ditch the pizzeria uniform, knock on the door, and invite the girls to his party.

Competition among promoters has encouraged them to develop other ways to recruit models, even from within agencies. When the promoter Ethan studied Thibault's team, his role models, he figured he needed his own way into the modeling industry. So he made a dummy résumé saying he was a fashion student and secured an unpaid internship at one of New York's top modeling agencies.

"I was the first person in there and the last person to leave every day. I put in, like, ten-hour days, for free, five days a week." After a full day in the agency, Ethan went to the gym, showered, and then headed out to the clubs where he was promoting that night.

"So I was sleeping, like, three or four hours a day, just going super hard. And I did this for two months. Like, just dedication to meeting these models and figuring out how to become, like, the Thibaults and Felipes of the industry."

He was such a hard worker that the agency offered him a full-time position with benefits, even after learning of the lie, that he was really fronting for nightclubs. He would have to quit nightlife, they said, to work full-time for the agency.

He quit the agency. "The only reason I was there was to become a better promoter," he said.

Today, Ethan continues to work with modeling agencies, but in a different capacity. He brokers housing and other necessities to ease models' transitions to New York. When we met in 2012, he was planning the arrival of three models from Slovenia, whom he would pick up from the airport and take to accommodations he had arranged at a deeply discounted hotel run by one of his many acquaintances. He would be handling their dinner reservations and, of course, their nightlife outings.

Three promoters I met used this strategy of providing concierge services to agencies. They spent their days running models to and from airports, carrying their luggage up flights of stairs to their apartments, and bringing them to their agencies to start working. At night they reaped the benefits of their labors: a steady supply of high-quality girls at their tables.

By 2012, Thibault's competition was fierce. A lot of promoters had followed his lead in aggressively recruiting from the modeling industry. Some of the girls living in the apartments were loyal to other promoters and disliked Thibault just for his reputation. Some of them knew about Thibault's team and loathed the promoters simply for calling them at their price-inflated temporary homes. Felipe had warned me of this. In at least one model apartment in New York, a girl had spread the rumor that Thibault was sixty years old. (About this rumor, Felipe said, "I'm like, 'Do you know what a sixty-year-old looks like? He's not sixty years old!'") In other apartments, girls had written up on the wall that Thibault and Felipe were bad people, drug dealers even.

"Never have or would I ever touch drugs!" insisted Felipe. He and Thibault didn't even drink alcohol. "But then, like, she leaves the apartment," he continued, "and you can get in with the others, and eventually they'll see you're really cool to go out with."

Sitting on the floor of Thibault's bedroom, I dialed all thirty-four numbers on the list. A lot of the lines were dead, or no one answered. When the weather was nice, like this spring afternoon, girls went outside to the parks or they went shopping, Thibault explained. I would have to call back in a little bit.

"You doing good talking, but just relax," he said. "Don't worry if they hang up on you. It's gonna happen."

Compensation

"All freeeeeeee," read the caption to a girl's Facebook picture of a lavish dinner table she sat at with a promoter in an upscale restaurant. Meals were one of the biggest tools at the promoter's disposal for tempting out girls, who often took delight in explaining to outsiders that their lavish dining experiences were completely free.

There are no free gifts. We always pay them back, and usually with interest.[11] Whereas squandering yields status through the display of magnanimity—the big-man is made at the moment when everyone sees his expenditures cannot be reciprocated—gifts build up expectations of repayment over time. All gifts necessitate a countergift, even if this only in the form of goodwill. Giving and receiving gifts thus enrolls people into webs of obligation with one another. This, argued anthropologist Marcel Mauss, is how gifts forge the building blocks of any community.[12]

Gifts are so interesting because the ideal type of exchange circuit of "gift and countergift" is rarely so straightforward. There is an aura of secrecy around the exchange, hinging upon our willful misrecognition of repayment.[13] The uncertainty over exactly how or when repayment happens can make a gift *more* burdensome than a clearly delineated market transaction.[14] Girls and promoters dance around this silence: By accepting the invitation to dinner, she is in a social debt to the promoter, but what, exactly, is expected of her?

This ambiguity has been with young women since they began to consume the city's nightly entertainments, when, over a century ago in America, courtship moved outside of the home and into commercial realms. Modern, early twentieth-century dating was originally called "treating": unmarried young working-class women accepted men's invitations for entertainment and consumer goods in exchange for implied sexual favors.[15] Known as "charity girls," they worked in low-paid jobs like factories and lived at home, often in tenement flats too cramped to host gentlemen callers. They were also expected to contribute most or all of their earnings to the household finances. This left working-class women little money with which to consume the urban delights all around them, a deficit they boldly bridged by accepting men's treats.

Unsupervised dating in public places offered new freedoms but also new risks to women's reputations.[16] Women could gain status among each other by bragging about the men they dated and the treats they got, but they lost status in public, where they were disparaged as "near whores."[17] Women went to great lengths to explain the difference between treating and prostitution: money rarely changed hands, they insisted, and was instead earmarked for things like movie tickets and arcade games; when a woman expected more than entertainment, it was most commonly clothing and shoes, which she needed for the outings. Historian Elizabeth Clemens found a case of one young New York woman in 1916 whose date only had cash on hand to give her; rather than accept it, thus crossing the line into prostitution, she insisted he accompany her to the butcher shop to pay her bill.[18] Girls policed the moral boundaries around appropriate forms of compensation for the sexual debts they incurred in order to distinguish their dating lives from pure market transactions.[19]

Treating girls is the basis of the VIP economy. In exchange for dinner, girls are implicitly expected to spend time at the club with a promoter. These are the terms of "the deal," as many promoters called it. Dinner is a good way to round up all the girls at once, delivering a striking visual impact when the promoter walks into the club surrounded by models.

Restaurants also like to appear busy, and busy with good-looking customers, so many restauranteurs partnered with promoters and the owners of nearby clubs to give away a fixed number of comped tables per night. At these dinners, the promoter is expected to pay a cash tip to the wait staff, typically 10–20 percent of the bill, a sum that runs about $100 to $200.

At such dinners, weird dining experiences were common. Waiters might have brought out only a few plates of salad and cold appetizers if the kitchen was closing soon and unwilling to prepare fresh dishes. On those nights, girls complained and a few even left in protest instead of going to the club. Sometimes the food might be good but the service could be lousy, with missing utensils and inattentive waiters. I learned to eat beforehand just in case. Otherwise, as one promoter cautioned, dinner might end up being french fries at 11 p.m.

Usually at comped promoter dinners, dishes were served family-style and without regard to anyone's preferences, and the kitchen often sent out the cheaper food, or what hadn't been ordered much that evening. If sushi came out, it was rarely sashimi, but rather cucumber rolls. Girls dined on the "stuff in the middle," said Jill, a nineteen-year-old model who went out with Sampson.

"Because they don't really give us a menu . . . It's like the leftover stuff they're making," she said. "The alcohol is, like, we only get the cheap champagne and wine." In fact, they were almost never served champagne at dinner, but sparkling white wine.

"It's shit wine," her friend Hannah, also a model, added.

"Yeah, but it's good food," said Jill. "And it's free." Girls may not have gotten the chance to choose their free dishes or their fellow dinner guests, but their free evenings out were typically acceptable, if not always completely enjoyable.

There were times when the girls went out primarily for the food: "There was a time when I didn't wanna spend any money for dinner but I didn't wanna go out to the club," said Hannah. "So I was like, it's just free dinner, I'll just leave early." This strategy could work once or twice, but it could also lead to a fight with the promoter, who expected girls' support in exchange for dinner.

Sometimes promoters footed the entire bill themselves at restaurants as a special treat for the girls. Enrico, the wealthy Spanish promoter, did this often, and one night he took me, two other friends, and his model girlfriend, Olga, to an expensive Italian restaurant in Chelsea. But, over the course of the meal, he grew annoyed that Olga was constantly texting on her phone.

"It's not a promoter dinner, Olga, please don't text during it," he finally reprimanded her. Enrico considered this a special dinner, a gift to her and his friends, though surely he would be paid at least twice the dinner bill at the party we were all expected to attend afterward. Annoyed, she eventually put the phone away.[20]

In contrast, promoters also arranged "client dinners," in which a promoter's wealthy "friend" wanted the company of beautiful girls and was willing to take a whole group out to dinner. At a client dinner, girls could order off the menu. Going out with clients meant better food and better drinks; or, as Sampson said, it wouldn't be "shit champagne." Sampson texted me such an invitation:

Going to dinner then a drink at Club X with a multi billionaire friend. You should come. Order whatever you like :D

Such a dinner was a real treat, as few of the girls that went out with promoters—students, fashion models, even the occasional sociology professor—could afford to order whatever they wanted from the menus of upscale restaurants in Manhattan. These dinners were especially welcomed by newcomers to the city living on fixed budgets in cramped apartments. An NYU undergraduate student seated next to me said it was either dinner with a promoter or fried eggs that night, the only thing she could cook in her dorm. As Petra, the twenty-five-year-old model who began her career in Italy, told me, a lot of girls "don't have enough money for food, literally; that's why promoters know that they have to bring food if they bring girls."

In fact, girls had mixed class resources. The family backgrounds of the twenty girls I interviewed ranged from working class to upper class. No girl identified herself as coming from a poor family background; I also met very few wealthy girls, for whom price was no issue. Promoters' tables, such as Enrico's and Dre's, featured a mix of girls in different stages of their careers, from students to young professionals. Only three of the girls I interviewed had economically precarious situations, like twenty-year-old Katia, the unemployed model from Ukraine who was hanging out with Santos in Miami.

Beatrice, the twenty-six-year-old model who also worked in public relations, had plenty of friends in the art world, including writers and designers. She would hang out with them at warehouse parties in Bushwick, Brooklyn, but they couldn't come out with her to the Meatpacking District for free champagne: "They're not dressed appropriately, they're not tall enough, they're not thin enough, things that I wouldn't even think about in terms of what makes somebody a valuable person," she explained. When she was busy with freelance work, she rarely went out with promoters, she explained, but when she was in between gigs, she joined the VIP scene often:

> I'm way more willing to go out when I can't afford to do other things, which is something that no one likes to say, but it's very much true. Um, I don't need to go through the awkwardness of not being able to invite certain people to dinner if we can all pay for our dinner.

Similarly, Jane, the twenty-eight-year-old actress and philosophy student, lived alone in a small apartment but went out regularly, at least twice a week, often to Club Jewel with a promoter named Celia. She did so partly to show her support for Celia, and partly, she added,

> to drink for free. You have to have a social life, right, in the city? You can't just stay in your apartment and live alone. So you might as well socialize in a place, in a beautiful place, where maybe you'll meet interesting people. I definitely, you know, being in grad school, I can't afford to go to Club Jewel every week, you know? So it's like a trade-off. An everybody wins kind of situation.

In addition to dinners, gifts that girls might receive from promoters included lunches, favors, attention, experiences, and services. Promoters took girls on group outings to Disneyland and Six Flags, to go bowling, to the movies, on picnics. Sampson offered to bring girls to mixed martial arts classes with him. Luca, the promoter from Milan, gave his most loyal girls 200 euros each for shopping sprees when he had a windfall of cash. Dre sometimes brought girls to the spa for nails and massage treatments. Malcolm knew that models were fond of a juice bar on East Tenth street, so he would sit on the bench outside on sunny afternoons and when a model walked in, he would offer to buy her a juice, and the owners would laughingly say to him, "That's the fourth you ordered today!" Or, if it was cold outside, he treated girls to warm coffees in Starbucks: "See, so they know I'm gonna take care of them." Malcolm's language of "care" was typical in promoters' talk; in return they expected girls to be "loyal" in their "support." The circulation of gifts was highly gendered, such that whenever I interviewed promoters over lunch or coffee, they refused to let me pay. Men pay. Girls never pay.[21] Girls repay treats with their time.

Promoters also offer lots of rides. Either they drove models to and from clubs like Thibault and Sampson did in their big SUVs, or they gave girls $20 to take a taxi home. If a girl couldn't go out because she had a flight to catch early in the morning, the promoter would take her to the airport straight from the club. In fact, promoters gave rides to girls for almost any occasion. Sampson responded to a model's distressed call one afternoon, when no taxi would stop for her and her midsize dog. Sampson gave her a lift to her apartment uptown, clearly unhappy while the dog shook himself off in his backseat, but also glad to help out a model.

A few promoters also provide free drugs, but these were exceptions. Santos didn't like to provide hard drugs to girls—he wasn't a dealer, he insisted—but he offered to share his marijuana with anyone in his company. Rather, about half of the promoters I went out with prided themselves on keeping drugs away from their girls, another expression of care for them. As Mustafa, thirty-two, explained:

> People think we are into drugs and we corrupt the girls. But it's just that we go out, and some girls are already like that and they go out with us. In reality, to these girls, I'm like a father to them. People think we mess them up but we are the safest for them. We want them to be safe. It's bad for us if they are too wild. For example, I know what they are up to, I even know who they sleep with. I know their mothers! Some of their parents come and stay with me when they are in town!

Dre, Thibault, and Felipe also rejected drugs at their tables, and Felipe especially saw himself as a guardian, which was part of what he offered to the girls who came out with him:

> We don't do drugs. We don't drink. We drive the models. If you're a model, you don't have money for a cab. Okay, I'll drive you home and pick you up to take you out. Nobody gets into trouble with us, nobody gets left behind with us or sick from drinking or drugs. We take care of them. So nobody gets into trouble with the cops, which is why we can have underage girls with us.[22]

It was thus not unusual for promoters to see themselves as protectors, even father figures, who watched over girls in nightlife. Many claimed to genuinely help girls navigate and enjoy city life. All of these forms of care, of course, came with a price, that of "support." Support had its owns gradations—from standing for hours late into the night at a club to just popping in for a drink—and promoters could be pretty explicit about what they needed from girls and when. For instance, Trevor texted me with a typically personal appeal to go out with him on a night that he thought was especially important to his career:

> Ashley, My clients tonight play for a professional soccer team in Europe. I bring them to Club X tonight. Can you come out?

> . . . Def come to Club X babes. Have the clients with me now and would like the support :)

Promoters sometimes offered girls one of the scarcest resources in New York: housing. About a quarter of the promoters I interviewed arranged girls' housing in their own version of a model apartment; Santos claimed that he was the first to come up with this idea, by offering his apartment to house models in Milan. Vanna and Pablo, two promoters who teamed up together in New York, operated a model apartment in Union Square, a spacious four-bedroom, two-bathroom apartment, with an open-concept living room and a back patio. One room had bunk beds and could accommodate up to four girls. When I first met Vanna and Pablo, ages twenty-five and twenty-nine, there were seven girls living in their apartment. They were models or retail workers who aspired to be models.

The apartment required a hefty deposit of $50,000, but within six months, Vanna said, they had already made it back. Girls living there were required to go out at least four nights a week with them between Monday and Saturday, for a minimum of three hours, from 12:00 to 3:00 a.m. Clubs paid Pablo, Vanna, and their sub about $1,000 total each night for the six nights a week they went out. Promoters could make serious money with a model apartment, which guaranteed a reliable quantity of high-quality girls at their tables every night.[23] Though the spacious apartment in a terrific downtown location sounded great on paper, the apartment soon deteriorated into a mess. Vanna and Pablo hired a housekeeper to come once a week, but in the meantime, trash piled up everywhere: garbage bags near the front door, cans of Four Loko energy drinks and full ashtrays in the living room, dried-out contact lenses stuck to the kitchen counter. Food didn't stay long in the pantry. One girl hid a set of clean dishes, since her roommates were always leaving their dirty dishes in the sink for days.

Over half of the promoters I interviewed in New York also paid for girls to join them at seasonal parties in places like Miami, Cannes, the Hamptons, Saint-Tropez, and Ibiza. Girls in these promoters' networks got expenses-paid trips, basic and precarious though they might be, with promoters booking their plane tickets and arranging their accommodations, meals, and transportation. It was common for clients to invite girls to party at faraway destinations such as Ibiza, Israel, and St. Barts, and to events like the Coachella festival and Formula One races. "Because it's all foreign guys who have just stupid amounts of money," explained twenty-one-year-old Renee, who was working retail while searching for a new model agency. "I met someone from Dubai the other night. He's like, 'Do you wanna come to Dubai?' I'm like, 'I just met you and you're asking me to come to *Dubai*?'" Renee declined the invitation, but plenty of other girls accepted similar offers. Petra had a great time traveling to Haiti with a promoter; Laura, an ex-model turned jewelry designer, had been to Saint-Tropez all-expenses paid; and Katia lived in Miami for free for almost a month.

There was one gift that promoters rarely gave to girls: money. Cash payment was notably absent from promoters' strategies for recruiting girls. Promoters frequently offered to pay models' cab fare to and from the club (about $20), but this money was always explicitly earmarked for cabs, lest there be any confusion about what she is doing out. Sometimes a promoter might share a windfall of cash with his favorite girls, but it was expected this would be used for shopping sprees and not considered payment.

Only rarely did promoters offer girls payment to come out, about $40 to $80, which girls considered an act of desperation. About two years into his career, Sampson broketies with Trevor and Malcolm, which left him low on girls. At this low point, he offered Hannah $40 a night if she could come out a regular basis. Hannah rebuffed it: "I don't wanna get paid, because then it's like work, you know?" Payment changes the explicit nature of the relationship between girl and promoter from friendship to economic exchange, and the meaning of her experience transforms from leisure to labor.[24]

When I asked a club owner why he doesn't just pay girls directly to attend his club, he told me, "That would ruin the fun," a testament to the transformative power of money. Malcolm, likewise, would never pay girls to party with him; he didn't want to have such a "depressing table." Promoters didn't want girls to be their employees. Mostly they wanted their relationships with girls to feel authentic.

Girls, likewise, did not want to become *paid girls*, a morally disreputable category and one that threatened to redefine their leisure as labor. One night in the Meatpacking District, I stood with two young models before we entered a club with a promoter. A third model, their friend, walked by and stopped to say hello, but she had to quickly get moving. "I have to go to a different club with my promoter," she explained. I asked which promoter. "George. He pays us. It's $80." She shrugged her shoulders in resignation. "So, it's work."

After she left, her two friends said: "*Thank God* we don't have to do that!" In fact, all four of us would do the same things on this night—attend a club, drink for free, and dance at a promoter's table—but only one of us would be paid, and looked at with some pity for it.

Like "charity girls" a century earlier, most models can't afford to take part in New York's famed dining and nightlife scenes, but they also don't want to enter into an explicit paid arrangement to gain access. VIP treating has expanded as a system to subsidize the fashion industry's low wages and to capitalize on models' unusual position as, on the one hand, a precarious labor force and, on the other, a highly valuable commodity.

Sex Work

While promoters use gifts to conceal their economic interests in girls, clubs use promoters to obscure clients' purchases of status and girls. In VIP clubs, rich men implicitly pay for the company of beautiful—and for the most part, broke—women. It's an arrangement that looks like sex work. But it *feels* qualitatively different than sex work, because the club does not sell the company of girls directly. Rather, clubs sell marked-up bottles of alcohol that usually result in the presence of models, typically brought there by promoters or arranged by the club managers who ensure clients are surrounded by beautiful women. Paying for women outright is stigmatized, but there is nothing wrong with paying for drinks. By bundling expensive bottles with beautiful girls, clients get the illusion of authentic company with girls.[25]

Hiring a broker is a common means of obfuscating a stigmatized exchange. A broker is a third party who does the dirty work of connecting two parties that do not want to transact directly: clubs do not want to hire girls directly because it moves them out of the business of nightlife and into the business of brothels.[26] The broker alleviates this stigma, but then he bears the moral burden of the suspicious transaction.

Most people, when they hear about the work of a promoter, associate him with a pimp. The strategic tricks promoters use—gifts, flirtations, touches—do in fact resemble the work of pimps.[27] Promoters were painfully aware of how their job looked, and they tried very hard to distinguish themselves from pimps. They were adamant, even without a sociologist asking, that they did not pimp their girls. Almost all of them said they were not interested in setting up clients with girls, in any form, because this could potentially damage their reputations.

In one of my first conversations with Sampson, he exclaimed he wasn't a pimp and didn't want anything to do with clients that had the wrong idea. He described a typical "bad client" as unfit for his company, quite unlike his "friends" with money:

> Saudis are exactly what I don't want. Because they're the clients that just want to get laid . . . When it comes to clients like those, and I've seen them, I know the difference, I just don't like dealing with those guys . . . I would want a client who I'm comfortable with, who sees me as a friend. And gain a bond instead of me sucking up, but sees me as a friend, as an equal. Instead of, "It's a promoter bringing girls to me."

One year later, I went out with Sampson again. He was no longer scouting for girls on the street; he now hired subs to do the grunt work of bringing in high-quality bodies. His new focus was on hospitality; that is, bringing clients to clubs and hosting girls at their tables, earning commissions on their bottle purchases, and organizing their private parties. His stance on transactional sex had taken a noticeable turn, and now he admitted that paid sex was an economic opportunity:

> One time, or a few times, I made like three grand one night. A client gave me a grand just for gathering together the party. And at the end of the night he actually got laid by two of the girls and he gave me another two grand, and then the club paid me [20 percent commission from the bottle sales].

Sampson didn't tell me if the girls themselves got paid in this arrangement, and he was careful to frame his own payment as a tip or a bonus, rather than outright payment for the labor of procuring a client sex. I came across only one other promoter who disclosed doing anything that fit loose definitions of pimping. Trevor, the nineteen-year-old newcomer who worked with Sampson and Malcolm, hosted girls in a weekend Hamptons home during the summer season, and everyone stayed overnight for free as guests of a wealthy client. He described the arrangement like this: "As a promoter I will tell you, because we are staying in the client's house for free, I will make sure I introduce the girls to the client to establish a connection, not a hookup but, but, a *connection* as a payback to the favor."

Even Trevor was careful in his wording—he establishes a connection, not a transaction. Sampson and Trevor were outliers among promoters, who mostly downplayed their role in brokering sex between clients and girls. If and when sex between clients and their girls occurred, it wasn't their business, and they didn't want to directly profit from it.

But if anything looks like sex work in the VIP world, it's not the sex between clients and the girls. It's the sex between the promoter and his girls.[28] That is, promoters have sex with a lot of girls. All male promoters continually touched, kissed, hugged, and leaned in close for selfies with girls. Their small flirtatious gestures ranged from chivalrous to creepy. Dre always greeted a girl with a kiss on each of her cheeks. He also regularly kept one hand on a girl's lower back to signal that he was listening to what she was saying. Other promoters, like Thibault and Felipe, would pull girls in for close dancing and grinding. Initially unnerved by this when I entered the field, I came to see such gestures of physical closeness as routine efforts to produce social closeness.

Then there were their text messages, loaded with sexual innuendo. Promoters texted plenty of emoticons, sex jokes, pet names like "baby," "babe," "hon," and compliments. Thibault's texts were the most outrageous. Take this invitation to his Tuesday night party:

> I only wanna have sex on days that begin with T: Tuesday, Thursday, Taturday, Tunday, Tonight . . . Best Tuesday night u can't miss. Thibault

While I interviewed twenty-six-year-old Beatrice, whom I had met at Toby's table the night before, she received this from him:

> What a wonderful evening you looked great last night.

"See, that's just unnecessary from Toby," she said, laughing at how corny he was and how he probably sent that message out to all of the girls at his table the previous night. Beatrice was fond of Toby, but not when he did obvious things like this. "Even if you look at last night, you see that, like, a lot of Toby's job is having all of those girls want him and think that they've got a shot, because that keeps them out."

A few minutes later, my phone buzzed with a message from Toby too:

> Ps I had an amazing time last night you looked beautiful i hope you had as much fun as the rest of us

It's not that Toby's affections were completely disingenuous, but they were strategically motivated. When I interviewed him, Toby described the fun of hooking up with girls at his table; in fact he could make out with two or even three girls in a single night, usually without provoking jealousies, he explained, because he and his girls shared an understanding that "We're young. We're just having fun." He believed that he was fairly close to most of his female guests; he said, "My girls aren't random people. It's not like I take out ten girls and I met them all yesterday, you know? It's people that have been going out with me every day for the last year. Which is why I feel so comfortable out." Still, it was his job to bring girls out, and like a lot of promoters, he used his sex appeal to get girls to his table.[29]

"At one point I had the most models at my parties," boasted Duke, a forty-five-year-old black man who promoted in the early 2000s, right when clubs began selling bottles and recruiting models. He refined a practice of recruiting models based on strategic sex, judging that having sex with a girl ensured that she would reliably show up to his events:

> How do you get the most models? You have to convince them to come out. How can you convince a whole models' apartment to come out with you at night? I'll tell you, you find the popular girl—the most exciting popular girl in the apartment—and you fuck her. Pardon my French. You find the popular one and you fuck her. It's that simple. Not the quiet girl, not the dull girl, you go for the popular energetic girl, because she will motivate everyone in the apartment to come out.

Another ideal kind of girl to have sex with was one who works with good fashion clients and agencies, because other models want to be around her, and the promoter can tap into her network. Explained Dre, "If you sleep with one at IMG"—a top modeling agency in New York—"you get all the girls in the model apartment to come out. 'Come out and support Dre tonight girls.' They'll all come."[30]

It might seem that girls were naive to fall for promoters, who were so clearly motivated to both profit from and cheat within their sexual relationships. Most girls that I met were strikingly self-aware of promoters' intimacy strategies, and some of them played along in pursuit of their own pleasure. Katia had romances with Sampson and Santos, both of whom, she knew, were sleeping with other women, but, she said simply, she liked them and felt like being with them at the time. She viewed sex with them as her own decision, regardless of the structural inequalities in her relationship with both men, and she embraced sex as individual pleasure with "no strings attached."[31]

It could be thrilling to be the object of a promoter's affections, especially since he was surrounded by so many other beautiful women. Leila, for instance, was attracted to Santos because of his looks, but in addition, she explained, she was excited by the very fact that Santos chose her among many other potential sex partners. This made her feel so special that she went out with him regularly for a few weeks just to be around him. "He made me feel so beautiful," she said, without a whiff of regret or disappointment that the relationship didn't last.

In another case, Eleanor never expected that she would sleep with a certain promoter, because, she explained, "Like, when I first met him, I was like, '[He's] so unattractive.' But," she said, "there's something about him, like, meeting him, interacting with him. And I think he knows it, too. I mean, these promoters, the good ones, they know exactly how to work it. They know exactly how to communicate with girls. It's like, because it's their job. You know, when you become a salesperson, each year you get better and better. And that's what the promoters do." Both Eleanor and Leila were aware that promoters were doing a job, yet they chose to accept their flattery for the pleasures that it brought them.

Most promoters were open about their promiscuity, having as many as one new partner per week. Joe, a promoter of five years, seemed embarrassed when explaining this:

> But I have gone through phases. Like, there's been weeks that is, like, every night a different girl. Like, every night . . . I mean, if she's, like, a real free, free person, it won't affect her. But, you know, if it's the kind of person that's very emotional, then, you know, it'll mess it up. But, like I said, at the same time, I'm constantly getting so many new ones [girls], it doesn't really matter, you know? But, yeah, promoters, we're, we're, we're male sluts. 'Cause you hit on them, and then, you know.

Malcolm put it this way, "I read in a book the average woman sleeps with five guys in her lifetime. And a man sleeps with fifteen in his lifetime. I'm like, you put those two together, I've lived a few lifetimes."

He added, "If I had to say who got more, the guys who buy the bottles or the promoters, it's the promoters every time. Every time."

Putting it more bluntly, a promoter named Brooks, twenty-three, warned me: "If any promoter tries to tell you that fucking isn't part of his business plan, he's a liar."

In the event that girls are not attracted to the promoter, he typically arranges a surrogate object of attraction by inviting one or two men, such as male models, to join dinner. As Malcolm explained, "Like, we figured out that not every girl's gonna want to hang with us. Not every girl is attracted to us, and whatever. So what we do is we have other model boys, or just cool people, hanging around the table to keep everybody there."

Dre's own strategy of getting top models to fall for him was to ignore them, and he talked explicitly about his psychological tactics to reel in a girl:

> I was out with a group of ten girls, and the one I want, I ignore her. I don't talk to her. I don't look at her. Just pay attention to the other nine girls, and I ignore the one I want. What does this do? It has the psychological effect of making her doubt herself. She thinks, "I'm beautiful, I'm making millions." But when I ignore her, it breaks the girl's confidence.

However cold his strategies, they seemed to work. Girls frequently stayed the night at his apartment, a studio apartment in a luxury Tribeca high-rise. He kept it immaculately clean, like a hotel room, in anticipation of female guests coming over for hookups. In fact, girls slept at Dre's place so often that he stocked his bathroom cabinets with tampons, hair brushes, and little samples of French soaps and face creams from the boutiques on Prince Street. Though his own head was mostly shaved, he kept a hair dryer in the cabinet. He explained that when girls said to him, "Dre, I can't stay at your place tonight, I don't have any of my things. You don't have any hair, how will I fix mine in the morning?" he would hold up the hair dryer and smile: it even had a big diffuser attachment.

Promoters were strategic, even predatory, in targeting models for relationships that were personally enriching. But for the most part, girls didn't seem to experience these relationships as exploitative or transactional. Sometimes they even talked about guys like Dre with affection.

We Are Your Friends

Promoters were at the center of various webs of intimate—both sexual and nonsexual—relationships they forged through clubbing. Girls formed strong ties within promoter-girl dyads, among multiple girls, and also within whole promoter crews that could function as extended family.

Among all the promoters that Nora, the twenty-five-year-old ex-model, could go out with, she only went out with Dre. "I've known him for forever, but we're just friends," she said. "He's a great guy."

Nora had modeled for a year and a half in New York City before she decided she was ready to experience its famed nightlife. She had heard about the clubs and the free champagne, but she also heard "the horror stories," mostly from her conservative Midwestern parents who warned her about the risks of drinking with strangers. Once she quit modeling and was looking for her next career move, she said to herself: "I'm twenty, what am I doing? I need to be going out. All these people are having fun . . . All these models tell me you can go out for free and have a good time. I wanted to experience what that would be like."

So she took the unusual route of looking up promoters on Facebook and contacting them herself. Soon she was in touch with Dre and they were having "actual, real conversations." Dre naturally invited her out. "Of course, I was very unsure," said Nora. "Here's this guy that I don't know how old he is. I just know his first name, his last name, or what he says his last name is." Cautiously, Nora went with a girlfriend to meet Dre at the Downtown for dinner before the karaoke party.

That was five years ago. In the time since, she began a new career as a spa aesthetician, and while she has gone out with other promoters, she prefers going out with Dre. She considered him a real friend, and they hung out in "real life," beyond the club. Their thing was to watch camp horror movies at the cinema. He insisted on paying for the tickets, so she rushed ahead to buy the popcorn and soda. She never felt pressure to sleep with Dre, and from her vantage point, sex was not very central to his networks:

> For whatever reason with Dre I felt like he's an actual friend. I feel really protected when I went out with him. Everyone that you talk to at his table is like, "I've known Dre for ten years, or, I've known him for seven years."

Other promoters may have offered her access to different clubs, but Nora didn't like how they operated. She went out for a short while with Sampson, until one embarrassing night she brought two girl-friends, not models but still pretty, who Sampson turned away from the dinner because of their looks. "He kept trying to text me after and be like, 'Let's go out tonight.' I wouldn't respond. I just got so over it."

In fact, most girls would only go out with promoters who, as Hannah put it, they "actually like hanging out with." Beatrice described her daytime rule: she won't go out with a promoter if she hasn't also hung out with him during the day. She also would never go out with a promoter she felt was trying to sleep with her. It was clear that, among a share of their girls, promoters developed meaningful and mutually beneficial friendships without sex.

With some girls, like Nora, promoters established deep and durable feelings of connection. Another example was Petra, who was familiar with promoters from her time in Milan and Hong Kong, where they were also closely intertwined with the local modeling industry. But when a friend introduced her to Thibault's partner Nicolas upon her arrival in New York, she felt that they shared a unique mutual respect.

"We are friends, like, really friends," Petra said. "Nicolas, I can count on." He helped her get set up in the city when she didn't have an agency yet, letting her stay at his spacious apartment in New York with no explicit obligation except that she occasionally walk his dog. They shared information, too, about events and opportunities, and he helped her find an apartment in Paris: "I get information from him and I give information, because we know a lot of the same people and are interested to do the same things." She didn't see their relationship as transactional exactly, but it was mutually beneficial, like when Nicolas took her out to events for political elites, which was helpful to him and exciting to her. When Nicolas transitioned out of party promotions and into fundraising events, Petra seemed genuinely proud of him:

> He's always wanted to do more. And he succeeded. He has a huge apartment now. He's living the jet-set. He doesn't do promoting anymore; he got into some business deals and he does something even with [top politicians] . . . So that's really cool and that's what he was always aspiring to.

Girls also valued the relationships they formed with each other through the VIP scene. Clubs gave newcomers to the city an instant social network where they could find long-term friends. The best part was, the scene has a global reach, so when a model traveled from one city to another, as Petra explained, "The scene is there and you just have to go out and find it. Yeah, because sometimes it's hard especially to meet new girlfriends in a new city."

Among Dre's network of girls, Nora had met two models around her age with whom she became close friends. The three girls went out for dinner and dancing every Tuesday night, comped by Dre. Her day job at the spa consumed so much of her time, six days a week, sometimes up to twelve hours, that going out was a welcome release from her work life. It helped that it was free. At the time I interviewed her, Nora could barely cover her monthly $1,300 rent, which was her share of a small two-bedroom apartment. Nora came from an upper-middle-class family and aspired to open her own spa one day, but for the time being, Dre helped her afford what little leisure she had time for.

With the right mix of intimacy, gifts, and strategy, promoters could forge close personal bonds with girls and overcome suspicions about their motives. Girls gained several considerable benefits from their promoter "friends," who helped them feel rooted in the city. "I'm not a bad guy," one promoter told me out at a club. Girls' moms bought him birthday presents. Most of his business was about relationships, after all.[32]

And, sometimes, girls could feel so close to promoters and their networks that they viewed them as like family.

Such was the case for the crew that went out with Pablo and Vanna, the promoter team that operated the model apartment in Union Square. The apartment was a moneymaker for them. But for Catherine and Renee, both part-time models who lived there, it was also where they called home. Catherine was nineteen and had been living in the apartment for six months. Renee, twenty-one, had been working at Abercrombie & Fitch when coworkers introduced her to Pablo. She had lived in the apartment for an entire year, still working at the retailer while she was searching for a modeling agency to represent her. The girls adored Pablo and Vanna, and they looked up to Vanna in particular, who had a successful modeling career. They described the promoters as their "brother and sister," because they really cared about their well-being, even though their relationship—and their housing—was predicated on their agreement to go out with the promoters four nights a week until 3 a.m. Though all of this partying could be physically taxing, and on some nights they would rather stay home, the girls didn't think about going out as a job; but they did recognize it as a form of labor.

"I don't look at it as a burden but I look at it as work," Renee explained. "Because I know that—"

"We're, like, representing them," offered Catherine. "Like, we understand that we're there to make them look good—"

"Exactly," said Renee.

"We understand that we're friends but we're supporting them; we don't mind—" began Catherine.

"—It's just really important, for me at least, to like make sure that we're representing them well, then more girls are gonna wanna come with us, and more girls will make them look better," finished Renee. Wanting to reciprocate the same generosity they had received, the girls made an extra effort to help make these promoters look good when they went out.

They even called their Saturday night at Club Jewel "family night," for they had "ridiculous" amounts of fun and felt so connected to each other. Explained Renee:

> I've never seen another group, like, no matter where we are, [like us]. It doesn't matter, we just go and have fun. That's what we wanna do. If you have to go out, what's the point of sitting there hating your life?

It's not that they *weren't* aware of their economic worth in VIP clubs. Though they didn't exactly know how much, it was obvious that they generated a lot of money for Vanna and Pablo. But they didn't see their economic value as being at odds with their friendships. On the contrary, at many times during the nights, the girls reveled in their capacity to generate promoters' profits by encouraging clients to purchase expensive bottles of alcohol, like jumbo-sized bottles of champagne, a practice known as "upselling."[33]

One night when Pablo had a big client at his table, Renee approached him to say hello, and when he offered her a glass of champagne, she gladly accepted, even though she had no intention of drinking it. This way the client would quickly empty his bottle and buy another one, which meant a higher commission for Pablo. "Because he has a client, and he knows that I know what he's doing. Like we're all kind of supporting each other," she said.

Sometimes the girls subtly pushed men into ordering more expensive bottles. "So a lot of the times at the club, none of us will be drinking that night, but we'll all take a glass," and here Renee raises her hand up in a toast, "and be like *Yeah*! And we'll just take it and set it down behind us, or busboys come and pick it up anyway."

Or they did "dump-outs," their term for furtively pouring out a glass of champagne into the ice bucket when no one is looking. "You pick up on these things," Catherine said. "Like the first time, Vanna probably gave me a drink and I was like, no, I don't want it, [and] she probably was like, 'No, no, no, just hold onto it.'" Encouraged to refill everyone's glasses, clients then bought more champagne, and Pablo would register his delight about his increasing commissions by telling the girls, "Oh, they're spending so much money, fuck!"

Catherine and Renee even began to cultivate their own networks of girls to invite out with Pablo and Vanna. In a trick out of Dre's playbook, Renee would get on her phone during the day and text to her model friends, "Oh I miss you," to urge them to come out. Catherine did this too, she explained: "Like you make it a point to connect with the girls. It always becomes a friendship. But in all honesty, the initial motive is, 'We need to be friends with this girl so she'll come back.' Like, *always*, that's the motive." Thus the girls were informally working as subs for Pablo and Vanna.

Given all of their hard work, shouldn't they get paid? I asked them. The pleasures of the fun and friendship they experienced were so at odds with what they imagined wage labor to be—burdensome, unenjoyable, and uncaring—that they steadfastly refused to accept their time out as meeting the definition of work. "It's like work that's not work, though," answered Catherine, "because you meet *amazing* friends, and we're all just hanging out and it's never work because we're all friends."

Renee added, "Like we've said, this is our family. Like, I would do anything for them. Anything." As it turned out, Renee had been steadily falling in love with one of Pablo's sub promoters over the past year. Catherine, meanwhile, was far away from her home in Oregon and she was eager to be a part of any social network. Vanna and Pablo were some of the first people she encountered who made her feel like she belonged in the city. From Pablo and Vanna's point of view, they invited only girls that they genuinely liked into their network; both promoters saw themselves as cultivating authentic friendships with the girls. But it is also the case that the girls' weaker structural positions inclined them to join the crew and view it as family.

"Family night" was on Saturday, when the vibe was thrilling and the group had the most fun. But by Wednesday night, the girls were facing the middle of a week usually marked by missed model castings and failed goals from sleeping late and waking up with hangovers. By 2:30 a.m. on a Wednesday night out with Toby, Pablo's sub, Catherine was tired and ready to go home. Toby simply told her no. She had to stay at the club until three, per the condition of her free housing agreement. "I love her," Toby shouted to me over the loud music in between shots of tequila, "but that bitch has to stay till three. That's the rules! Blame it on the game!"

In these moments, the model apartment looked a lot less like a gift and more like a wage. So Catherine remained at the table for the duration of Toby's required time, with her temporary family in the nightclub, under conditions dictated by her friends' profit motive.

Promoters' own families were not typically based on stable unions. The same tactics that made promoters successful in the job made their private romantic lives suffer. Most promoters formed romantic unions with models or good civilians, but it was difficult to maintain them so long as they were perfecting the craft of charming girls for a living. Only one promoter in my sample, Ethan, was monogamous. He had been dating his girlfriend for over a year, and their relationship was additionally unusual because she was a civilian, not a model.

Some promoters tried to be in monogamous relationships. Sampson was married at the time of our first interview to a thirty-one-year-old ex-model who expected his fidelity. She regularly came out with him and she looked young enough to be a girl at his table. They had been married for two years and had a small child. Sampson was proud that he could afford to rent a big house in Brooklyn, plus pay for childcare and a big car, all on his promoter earnings. However, part of his success in mobilizing girls was his ability to attract and flirt with them. He was handsome and charming, and that posed a dilemma, especially when his wife came out with him:

> Like the girls will start creeping up on me, trying to touch me and dance on me. I'm like I need water or I have to pour shots. I basically just have to keep moving to avoid it. [My wife] gets jealous. When she comes out with me it's hard because I can't flirt as much.

Within a year, Sampson was divorced from his wife; she caught him sleeping with one of the girls at his table.

While Thibault and Felipe's success in VIP clubs was celebrated, their personal lives were less enviable. When I met them, they each had young children growing up with ex-girlfriends—former girls, whom they had once brought to their tables, some of whom now harbored resentments toward the fathers of their children. Felipe had three children, each from a different woman. Thibault had fathered one child with a woman still working as a model, and that family now lived in Miami.

So perhaps it wasn't a surprise that soon after I got to know them, Thibault's girlfriend Nina got pregnant.

Nina wanted to be a mom, she said, though she thought it sounded crazy at the age of twenty-three. She was in love with Thibault and was ready to start a family with him, so she stopped taking the pill. "This is an amazing person," she said, "really the most beautiful person that I ever met in my life. Nobody in my life did so many good things for me."

People who knew Thibault were doubtful that Nina's dream of a family with him would turn out well. Nina herself knew that it looked bad. Recently at a casting, someone was conducting survey research with models about their risk behaviors, like their frequency of drinking, smoking, and taking drugs. There was a question asking how frequently models hooked up with promoters. "I was so offended," she said. "I was like, well, I'm gonna marry a promoter, what does that mean?"

But Nina was insistent: "I tell this to everybody. Thibault is the most beautiful person ever. We got so close, I said that's gonna be my husband." He gave her a tiny ring with a white stone for the engagement. She wore it for a little over a year, twirling it on her finger at his table in the club when she was bored.

Control

An economy of intimacy bound models and promoters together. But these bonds sometimes needed reinforcement to keep girls at the tables during the crucial hours of 12 to 3 a.m., when club managers cruised by to take head counts and assess quality. To ensure their tables maintained a high quantity of quality girls, promoters managed girls' time, bodies, and movements ever so subtly, to avoid damaging the intimacies they had painstakingly constructed.

Promoters first had to control the space of their table, policing who could join and sometimes physically blocking people they deemed undesirable, such as unattractive girls and fillers. They had to keep other men, including other promoters, from poaching girls away from their tables. And they had to keep their own girls from leaving early, to go to another club or even just to wander around to other tables.

Girls who wanted to leave early, like Catherine, were discouraged from doing so. Some promoters checked girls' coats or put their handbags inside discreet drawers within the same banquette sofas upon which girls would end up dancing later in the night. This made collecting one's belongings to leave without the promoters' help rather difficult; promoters were likely to be slow and unhelpful getting girls' coats and handbags much before 3 a.m.

One of the biggest threats to the table were unattractive friends of girls. Promoters were on constant alert that girls might try to bring friends with them to the free party. Sampson tried to resolve this problem quickly at dinner. If a girl brought an unattractive girlfriend, he would tell her:

> "I'm sorry, your friend can't come. She can't have dinner." . . . But I'm up front and I'm fast with it. I don't waste time, 'cause it would hurt my image. And then girls will start saying, "Hey, if she can bring a friend, I can bring mine," . . . and then my sub will start doing it, and bring a bunch of midgets. So before they even start, I say no.

When I tried to bring my own friends out, promoters requested their full names in order to check their Facebook and Instagram pictures to ensure their good looks.[34] They often reminded me that beauty is the price of admission to party with them. When I texted Enrico to ask if I could bring two girlfriends one night, he replied:

> Of course!!!! Beautiful like you impossible, but still good looking right? Lol.

Promoters also controlled girls' bodies, ensuring they look good. Santos kept his girls' high heels in his car, making them change from their sandals before entering a club or restaurant. Sampson kept a simple tight black American Apparel dress and high heels in his SUV, and he was ready to tell a girl to change into this outfit or go home. His wife explained matter-of-factly, "Some girls can't dress."

Failure to look the part could lead to public humiliation. Hannah recounted a yacht party in Miami organized by Santos, where a girl had an unshaved bikini area. Santos ordered her to the bathroom to "fix it," meaning, to shave. This was embarrassing for the girl, but, thought Hannah, quite justified: "I mean, if you're on a yacht in a bikini, you should shave." Girls had to look good for their promoter, whose status was reflected in their bodies.

Girls perform emotional and physical labors that mirror what sociologists have termed "aesthetic labor," common in the service industries. Flight attendants, retail workers, waiters—pretty much anyone in service has to "look good and sound right" according to their company's brand identity.[35] Workers must pull this off even when they don't feel like it; it's part of their job. Girls, too, perform valuable aesthetic labor, not just by showing up and looking good, but by participating in the party vibe. These labors happen within worklike arrangements that promoters must manage. When it looks like work, the party suffers.

For instance, in Milan one early-summer night, I met up with Santos at the Dolce club, a fixture on the high-fashion circuit and a place he regularly worked when he was in town. It was a mostly outdoor space, and there was an unseasonable chill in the air, such that within two hours, Santos's girls were freezing. My feet were aching in high heels, but there was no place to sit at the standing-only tables. Some of Santos's girls were coming out five nights a week, as required by a formal agreement with him to live for free in his Milan apartment while they were looking for work as models. Some of them had runny noses from colds. It was clear that they were simply waiting for their shift to end.

When girls refuse to accept the implicit terms of their work and become difficult to control, promoters frequently resort to disciplinary actions. They can discipline gently, by reminding them of their obligations to stay with them. This looks like a scolding, a rebuke, like the one I received from Malcolm when he found out I was headed to another party with a different promoter: "You met him through me. Your loyalty is messed up. I'm insulted," he told me.

At one client dinner hosted by a club owner, I tried to leave after the entrée to make it to another party. The club owner, himself a former promoter, stopped me and scolded my manners in front of everyone:

> Whoa, whoa, whoa. Are you doing a dine-and-dash? . . . You can't just leave. You at least have to stay for dessert and coffee, not run out on the bill. Now, because you're girls you don't have to pay, of course, but you have to stay to the end. And it's New York, you know, so then you have to go downstairs [to the club], have a drink, stay a little.

Embarrassed, I apologized, sat down, and stayed another hour. Malcolm called this promoter etiquette, that a girl should uphold her end of the implicit bargain. "We pay for that shit, you know what I'm saying?" he complained after an expensive dinner. "Know promoter etiquette. If you drink and go to dinner, then you gotta go to the club for an hour or two, at least."

Discipline is a delicate act. Girls cannot be treated as workers, because they are not there to work, but to have fun. The promoter should not act too much like their boss, yet he needs them to do the job of being girls. One client, who hosts girls and promoters in his weekend Hamptons home, explained: "I say when you are a pro-moter, it's like herding kittens. You have to do two things: make them purr and hit them with a spray bottle." Dominance and intimacy must both be maintained.

This balancing act doesn't always work. When a promoter tried to keep Reba from leaving his table to talk with her ex-boyfriend across the room, she broke off contact with him. "They think they have ownership of you. And I haven't been out with him since, because that's not fun to me. I want to talk to whoever I want."

Similarly, promoters dismiss girls who are too difficult to control. "I've done that before," said Malcolm. "I gave a girl $20 to get home and told her to leave dinner. She was being a pain in the ass. I said, 'You will not ruin my dinner. Go get a cab.'" This effectively ended their relationship.

As both girls and promoters reach their limits, fights can break out. Sometimes promoters yell at a girl, and insult her, or kick her out of the group. This happened to Nina when she first arrived in New York. Before she ever met Thibault, she began hanging out with Brian, a good-looking black American promoter, also well established in the upper echelons of the VIP club world. They went out a few times, and eager for a change of scene, Nina and three girlfriends asked him to take them to a strip club, just for fun. At the strip club, Brian paid for their drinks, and then they headed to the VIP club where Brian worked. By 1 a.m., Nina was ready to go home, but on her way out, Brian grabbed her by the arm and shook her while he shouted, "'No, I'm making money! You're not gonna leave here, because you went to [the] strip bar, and I paid for your drink, so now you stay here at least until three.'"

And then it was clear: Brian saw her as a source of profit and not as a friend, and money was at the heart of their relationship. In that instant, their relationship transformed from a lateral to a hierarchical relation, from friendship to employment. Nina was so shocked when it happened that she broke off all contact with Brian.

Nina told Thibault this story when they met, and she was glad to see that Thibault and Felipe were different.[36] Indeed Felipe prided himself on how his team cared for the well-being of their girls: "We're not like other promoters. We don't try to control the girls. If you want to go out with another promoter, you can." Nonetheless, Felipe was sure that girls would notice the difference in their level of care and friendship and choose to hang with their team.

But Felipe constructed, I think knowingly, a false distinction between care and control, as though those two practices could not coexist in a single relationship. Their crew was successful because they appeared to fuse these two modes together so seamlessly. They exerted control over girls through their care for them.

Vacation

Going on "vacation" with a promoter quickly exposed the amount of control he exerted over his girls. "You basically get paid to go on vacation," that was how Sampson described his trips to the Hamptons and Miami, when the New York clubs opened seasonal outposts to cater to their jet-setting clientele. The clubs hired Sampson, Santos, and Thibault, among others, to bring girls for long weekends and special events. The promoters were paid per night, and the club managers or clients helped to pay for all of their crews' accommodations. Sampson had talked up these trips as one of the amazing perks of his job.

And so I went with him, Malcolm, and Trevor for Memorial Day weekend in the Hamptons, the kickoff weekend of the summer season. Fifteen people shared a two-bedroom, two-bathroom home rented by one of Sampson's "good friends," an investment banker who rents a house every summer in South Hampton. He let promoters and girls stay there for free, as Sampson explained:

> It's just a favor from the guys who have houses out there for the season. Because they want to party in the company of pretty girls. It's all anybody wants. You know, who doesn't want that? Rolling in with all these models in the club, everybody looking like, "Who's that motherfucker?" They want that vibe, you know, that appearance. I would too if I had a lot of money.

For two nights during the weekend, we put in long hours at the clubs until closing time, then attended after-parties at the owners' mansions, where girls were so exhausted that one of them fell asleep sitting upright at the kitchen table. At 7 a.m. on Sunday morning, we finally left the last after-party of the weekend. I drove Sampson's SUV packed with nine intoxicated and sleeping people—including himself, his wife, and girls—through Southampton in the early morning sun. When we reached the Southampton house, Sampson threw up in the bathtub.

Night after night of going out felt more like work than vacation. According to the unspoken terms of the deal, girls' time was not their own; it belonged to the promoter. This became especially apparent on trips because promoters controlled all girls' movements all of the time, due the simple fact that girls did not have their own keys to the borrowed villas nor easy access to transportation should they want to go somewhere else.

Such was the case in Cannes, where I stayed with Santos for five nights in a four-bedroom villa, filled that week in June with ten girls, mostly models, and one of Santos's subs. Santos and his partner were on contract at Club Holla, one of Cannes's celebrated VIP clubs and a fixture on the high-end party circuit. They were obliged to bring at least twenty-five girls to the club during the hours of 12 a.m. to 4 a.m. For a two-week stretch, however, they had fifty-six girls, an oversupply that enhanced their reputations but caused logistical problems like the need to find enough beds for all of those valuable bodies.

Santos and his partner each occupied a villa housing a rotation of girls. During my trip, Santos's villa was home to three Swedes for a weekend, three Lithuanian girls for two weeks, five Czech models for two weeks, and one Russian model from Brooklyn, who shared Santos's bed and claimed to be his girlfriend. She became aggressive with him over the course of her stay, accusing him of infidelities and flirtations with the other girls. Santos recruited Eastern European models from his part-time home of Milan, where he kept an apartment and opened it to models. It was cheap to fly girls to Cannes from Poland, Lithuania, and the Czech Republic, and if he knew one girl at a local agency in a city like Prague, he could ask her to recruit models from her agency. Such girls were likely to be beautiful and available, given the limited modeling jobs in Prague, and, it being summer time, they were probably out of school and eager for a seaside holiday they couldn't afford on their own. You could see the global reach of Santos's fashion model network in the national cliques formed at the dinner table each night: the Lithuanian models sat on one side speaking Lithuanian, the Poles and Czech girls sat conversing on the other side, the Swedes clustered together in a corner.

Each evening at 8:30 p.m., the girls got dressed and ready, then headed to dinner by 10:30, usually at the same restaurant (owned by Club Holla and offering comped meals). They stayed at Club Holla from 12 until at least 4 a.m., sometimes as late as closing, 5 a.m. Typically, nobody in the villa woke up before 1 p.m. This gave them a six-hour window, from 2 to 8 p.m., to enjoy the day in Cannes.

During that window, Santos would sometimes take the girls to a beachfront restaurant, also owned by the club, where they could eat a comped meal and have free access to the lounge chairs. The girls had hopes of tanning, but they could never catch enough sunlight by the time they made it to the beach. They wanted to explore the Riviera, but there wasn't enough time in the day, the rhythms of which they did not control. They would have liked to eat someplace new, but Santos wouldn't let them stray from the group. Their free villa was a fifteen-minute ride from the city center, but the cost of a taxi in the summer season was about 50 euros, too steep for most of them.

The girls from Lithuania, Sweden, Poland, and the Czech Republic had, in short, come to Cannes expecting a vacation, and instead they found themselves carefully controlled and put to work in the service of Santos and Club Holla.

That work could be exhilaratingly fun, or it could be miserable.

Santos could be the life of the party. Some nights he danced on top of the sofas with the girls, took occasional sips of MDMA-spiked cocktails, and stayed out late chasing after-parties. But all of this fun took a toll on him and his girls. He often slept until two o'clock in the afternoon and had unpredictable mood swings that set off loud arguments. Even if they were tired, moody, sleep-deprived, and hungover, Santos and his girls still had to be at the club the following day.

One night, the club got unpredictably exciting in the best way. Club Holla put on a show with a famous rapper, and the vibe was infectious. Santos and his business partner Luca danced for hours on the sofas, surrounded by over four dozen girls, including even Santos's suddenly cheerful self-proclaimed girlfriend, all dancing, shouting, and taking pictures as sparkler-lit bottles floated by. The party ended around 7 a.m. at the villa, with Santos finishing the last drop of alcohol in the house—a shot of vanilla Stoli vodka—as girls danced in their pajamas in the early morning sunshine. It was in this moment that Santos repeated to me his accomplishments: he was at the very top of the VIP club world, spending time with multimillionaires and beautiful models at glamorous parties across the jet-set scene.

The next afternoon, around 2 p.m., I awoke on a deflating air mattress I shared with a twenty-four-year-old Czech model, next to another three Lithuanian models sharing the other bed in our cramped room.

That day, everyone was hungover and sluggish, and by the time we got to the beach club, the girls were grumbling. They couldn't catch any sun, which was by now low in the sky, they were sick of eating the same food at the same places each day, and they were exhausted from this free vacation. In six hours, it would be time to get ready for the club again. That night, the club was nearly empty. As house music pounded, the girls sat with arms crossed on the sofas, some of them falling asleep, and no one was drinking or dancing. Santos disappeared from his own table for two hours. He took a nap in his car.

The Madam

At first glance, Celia looks like a good civilian. At twenty-eight, she is tall, stylish, and slightly curvier than a model. She's out with similarly pretty women most nights in the Meatpacking District and every summer in the Hamptons, always dancing at a table. Watch her for a little while, though, and you'll see that she is not drinking, but pouring drinks. She stands at the table perpetually shaking her shoulders as though she loves to dance, but in fact her body never aligns with the beat, because her attention is always fixed on her girls and her table. When I first encountered Celia, two of her clients were rich business partners whom she had met at Club Jewel through the club managers. They liked her fun crowd of good civilians and they bought bottles regularly at her table, which earned her lucrative commissions, though they jokingly called her "the madam" behind her back, since "she's around all the girls all the time."

Few women do the job of promoter. I met male promoters nightly in New York, but only after some effort did I learn about ten women promoters in New York. I interviewed and went out with five of them.

"It's a tough game for women," said Dre when I asked him why there were so few women doing the job of promoter. "Women can't handle it," said a club owner. "Nightlife is a boy's club," one girl told me, and so on.

Whereas most male promoters relied on their flirtatious charm to attract women to come out with them, women became promoters if they were well positioned within valuable social networks of girls. All five women promoters I interviewed had ready access to pretty girls. Four of them had direct ties to modeling. Two were models themselves who frequented clubs with female model friends enough to be noticed by managers or promoters and invited to work for them. One owned a small modeling agency, the start-up costs of which she subsidized by bringing her newly signed models to clubs. One was a former booker with numerous ties to models.

Lastly, there was Celia, who was recruited into promotions because she had easy access to girls through a bakery and café in SoHo that she co-owned. It sold expensive French-style pastries and espresso, exactly the kind of place where the promoter Enrico liked to spend his afternoons. He became friendly with Celia, both of them being from upper-class European families, and he immediately saw that she had connections with a lot of young women who frequented the bakery. It was a popular spot with students from NYU and the Fashion Institute of Technology as well as models. Celia was outgoing; Enrico saw "good energy" connecting her to a veritable treasure trove of girls that could fill his table. He invited her to work with him as a sub-promoter, and eventually, she branched out on her own.

After clubbing from 12 a.m. to 3 a.m. each night, Celia managed the bakery during the day. Her family back in France had suffered financial losses after 2008, and they were no longer willing investors in her business. She wanted to prove that she didn't need her family's money anyway, and, eager to strike out on her own, Celia poured everything she had into co-owning the chic café. She loved the work but it was stressful, and after a year, it became clear that she would not make any money with the café. In fact, it was draining her savings. So when Enrico befriended her and explained that she could make a few hundred dollars each night working with him, she gladly accepted.

She was a fan of electronic dance music and familiar with high-end nightclubs, which she frequented back home in Paris. In Europe, she said, nobody cared about models; they came for the music. But in New York, she adjusted to clubs' insistence on girls' images, and she made it her job to bring out the best civilians she could mobilize from her network. She aimed for a dozen girls at her table each night, five nights a week.

Celia faced two major disadvantages compared to her male competitors. As the vast majority of her girls were straight, she lacked flirtation as a tool to hold their interest, and she lacked the masculine authority to control her girls and deal with aggressive competitors and club managers. She tried to overcome both limitations with a particular feminine style of promoting that involved building strong ties with her girls and leaning on men for help.

"I don't sleep," she told me when I visited her basement studio on the Lower East Side one Sunday. It was her day off, and she was still wearing her pajamas in the afternoon. "I used to have insomnia, for like ten years I didn't sleep. Now when I see a bed I crash into it." Between her two jobs—at the bakery in the day, in the VIP clubs at night—Celia was always tired. She said she actually had a third job, which was the real source of exhaustion, and that was the work of cultivating friendships with girls in hopes that they would go out with her.

Being in the club itself was an easy three hours of playing host to girls. It wasn't fun, exactly—it was a job, and it required some emotional labor to produce what Celia called "sparkle," the energy that propelled the group's vibe for the night—but it wasn't anywhere near as difficult as the nonstop work of building relationships with girls. She was always calling them, texting, and trying to get them to keep their word that they would come to her table.

She couldn't flirt her way to a full table, she explained. "It's not a job for women. The sex is everywhere. Girls go out with a promoter to think something can happen," like sex and the flirtatious excitement around it.

Instead, all Celia had was friendship. "I would not survive without it. I know them, the girls, each of them. And when I text them, I text to say hello first." She would never send girls a mass text or one with sexual innuendo (like Thibault, who did both at the same time), and she couldn't sleep with them, as Dre and Sampson did. I never heard of a woman promoter scouting in the streets, either. Celia wouldn't dare; she thought such behavior would raise confusions that she is a lesbian. The other women promoters thought it unbecoming for a female promoter, straight or gay, to do street scouting.

"I can't do what they do," said Vanna, the promoter who partnered with Pablo and had been promoting for three years when we met. She thought male promoters were "creepy old men" who "prey on girls" by strategically picking them up at castings. As a fashion model, Vanna met a lot of models daily, but she was very cautious in how she approached them.

"I never, never, never *ever* went up to a girl in the street, or in my own castings. Like, randomly say 'Hey' and pretend I like you." Vanna, being a friendly and outgoing person, waited to see if she "clicked" with someone first; that is, if she genuinely felt a possibility for friendship with her, and then she invited her to "hang out." Of course, Vanna stood to make more money the more often she "clicked" with a girl, but the money shouldn't come first, she said.

Lacking flirtation, women promoters relied on friendships and reciprocity. From Celia's point of view, when girls went out with her, they went out *for* her. Ideally they didn't know or care about other promoters. They were there because they liked her and her group of friends. "My job is to put together a good group and make it fun, so when I'm with my friends, or sort of friends, we are there for the fun together."

All of the women promoters I met shared this belief: that a night out with them was more fun because their group was bound by a feeling of real friendship. The women promoters stressed how much fun and energy their crowd brought to the party, an energy produced not through sexualized ties but deep connection.

"Have you been to one of those tables where the girls just sit there?" asked Kia, a twenty-year-old black American promoter. "Yeah, I hate those, like why would you go out if it's gonna be like that? We have fun. I love to dance. I wear all kinds of crazy outfits, and it's just me and my friends all jumping around, dancing, having fun."

Celia's table was full of good civilians, for which she was paid $500, about half of what she would get with models. Like Enrico, she had a short fuse when dealing with models, because they were too aware of their beauty and its value. She gave a lot of herself to girls, but models demanded more than she had: "Okay, if you're so beautiful, then stay with your beautiful people," was her philosophy. Rather, she was known for having good-looking and *fun* girls. "Celia cultivates a look, and also an attitude," one of her girls said.

Celia tried to give a little bit of her attention to each girl each night, and she was sure to introduce everyone to each other, encouraging them to talk and dance together. In fact, Celia regularly hosted girls for dinner at her apartment before going to the club. At these dinners, between six and eight girls enjoyed her home cooking, and many brought a bottle of wine or a dessert. Afterward, they split the cost of cabs to the club, thus fostering a sense of camaraderie.

During the daytime, Celia continued to shower her girls with her attention, calling them, texting, listening to their endless stories about boyfriends and breakups. This is how she spent her rare days off work. "There are so many promoters, that the most important thing for me is to establish friendships. I know all these girls," she told me one night while shaking her shoulders at her table.

Indeed, girls at her table frequently talked about their fondness for Celia as the main reason they came out, to support her, to hang out with her, or to meet the other people in her orbit who they expected would also be interesting. Jane, the twenty-year-old actress pursuing an MA in philosophy, was a regular at Celia's table for the last two years and pretty much only went out with her, or sometimes with Enrico, who she knew supported Celia. She understood the VIP economy, that in order for men to "pay way more than they should for a bottle of alcohol, they need to feel like they're surrounded by beautiful women . . . If they're having a great time, they'll even buy a second or third bottle."

Jane wasn't a model; she didn't have the height or the slender-ness, and with a short pixie haircut, she didn't fit the image of "super-model-y beautiful," as she put it. But for the chance to go out with Celia and drink and eat for free on a grad student budget, she turned on the charm to be as valuable as possible:

> One of the reasons I get to go, because I'm not, like, model skinny or model tall, is because the men really like to talk to me. Like, I make people laugh. And with some of them I'm like, actually friends. So, um, I can keep the conversation going which a lot of the girls can't, and the men aren't gonna stay with a bunch of mean girls who aren't talking to them . . . So it's my job to make the party. Like, the drinks are free, but I don't go there and not work. Like, my job is to come in and Celia will be like, "You, get on the couch and dance," if I looked really good that night. Or, "You, get on the table and dance." If I look really bad, she won't want me to be seen. I had a jacket on once, and she was like, "Take that jacket off."

In short, Jane made sure Celia's table was fun. She saw her role as a type of work on behalf of Celia, making her both capital and friend.

It's safe to say that Celia could be so blunt with Jane because of their close friendship, underneath which was an understanding that they support each other, albeit in different ways. When asked why she doesn't seek payment for all of the work she put in at Celia's table, Jane paused: "Um, because of the friendship line. Because a lot of nights I don't want to go out, but I'm like, Celia's my friend, this is how she makes money. Like, I'll pop in—you know? Like, there's, like, a weird loyalty I have for Celia. I want to help her. She's helped me, in a lot of ways, outside of this scene."

There were limits to this friendship, though. In the beginning, Celia had her on a "screen list," which meant that Jane would have to come to Celia's apartment before dinner to check her looks, and sometimes she made Jane change outfits. Jane was sometimes made painfully aware of her relatively bigger body size. When she started going out with Celia two years ago, she dropped down to 128 pounds, the same weight she was in the eighth grade. "I actually think about it a lot," she said about her weight. "Because I worry that if I get too fat, Celia will stop inviting me. Or she'll only invite me to the lame things." Jane accepted these terms of their relationship, because, she said, it was also Celia's business.

Then there was the time when Jane and one of Celia's clients had a brief romance, and in the aftermath of their breakup, Celia continued to invite out the client but not Jane, even though he was soon moving away from New York. "I was like, I've been your friend for two years and he's leaving in two months? But she needs him more than me, because he pays." They had a fight that played out over text messages, with Jane claiming that she wasn't being treated as a friend, but as inventory, and threatening to go out with another promoter. Celia texted back, "How dare you call me a promoter, we are friends." The two made up, but the rift revealed the vulnerability at the core of Celia's business model: her closeness to the girls got them to come out with her, but then she couldn't so easily brush them off.

Even with her girls' friendship and loyalty, Celia still knew she was disadvantaged compared to flirtatious male promoters. She made up for it by keeping a proxy flirt around her. She always had at least one man at her table. Her men were good-looking professionals with money; girls found them attractive and this could draw them to come out and stay at Celia's table. The men she invited also paid the tip at the comped restaurant dinners and to the bottle waitresses, which meant she rarely footed the bill herself. She baited these men with titillating promises of the girls they might meet in her company that night. One of her clients showed me her text invitation:

> Johnny come to Club Jewel, have 4 real models with clothing line, so down to earth . . .

Such a promise of girls with the unlikely combination of beauty, entrepreneurial success, *and* nice personalities was intended to lure Johnny to come out and bankroll Celia's table.

Meanwhile, Celia texted her girls invitations that mentioned the successful and single men who would be in attendance that night. She sent a text to Jane one evening, for instance, claiming that a client named Max would be there and that he couldn't wait to see her since their last flirtatious encounter. Jane went out, she said, "And then I saw Max, and he was like, 'I didn't know you were gonna be here.' Well, there you go. Celia's so good at it, it's so classic."

Celia enlisted other men for help, too, to establish the kind of masculine authority she lacked when trying to control her girls, who tended to wander away to other men's tables or even to other clubs. To keep the girls near her at all times and keep other men away from her table, she sought help from the bouncers. When drunken men from other tables encroached on her space or tried to talk to her girls, she raised her arms and snapped her fingers, summoning security's attention to protect her space. She tipped them very well, as she did the waiters and the bottle girls, to ensure that she never ran out of alcohol at her table. "You have to take care of your people, and they take care of you," she said. She even paid the security guards a tip to let her girls illegally smoke at her table, rather than risk them having a cigarette outside where they might get picked up by another promoter. Even if she had a client foot the dinner tip, Celia could still spend up to $300 a night on tips and cabs.

Even with the help of men, women promoters faced the continual challenge of asserting their control over girls, starting from the moment they got in line at the door. When Eleanor, at age eighteen, worked briefly as a sub for two male promoters, she had difficulty keeping her group of ten girlfriends in line at the door with her when a competitor promoter walked up and invited them to follow him inside. She recounted, "I'm an eighteen-year-old girl. These girls aren't gonna listen to me. They just want to be getting fucked up in the club. They don't care who's getting them in. So I feel like maybe when you're a guy, it's just easier maybe for the girls to, like, listen to you." The male promoters who hired Eleanor reprimanded her for giving the girls away to a competitor, and that was the night she quit working as a sub. "It's very aggressive," she concluded.

While Celia worked to establish friendships with the girls—who were there, they mostly explained, because they genuinely liked her—homosocial bonds among women had limits in a heterosexually charged place. A client noted with some frustration that by 2:30 a.m., the girls seemed to have evaporated from Celia's table, heading to another club to join another (male) promoter. This client said to me, as we stood around her now empty table: "It's really not cool of her girls. I think they leave because she's a woman. If I was a promoter, I would make them stay."

Celia and other women promoters faced another challenge in dealing with club management. Because promoters were constantly undercutting each other and competing for clients and their commissions, disputes could erupt into aggressive arguments between promoters and managers over significant sums, sometimes thousands of dollars of commission fees. Men were always strong-arming each other for that money, and Vanna couldn't take it: "You have to go head to head" with club managers, she said. So she strategically teamed up with Pablo to let him negotiate with club managers and chase after payments.

And quite unlike Thibault, Sampson, and Dre, promoters like Celia and Vanna didn't seem to gain any status from being around beautiful women. They were simply mistaken for being girls themselves, and treated as sex objects. Explained Kia, "It's hard being a girl in promotion, because women in the club are just ass, basically. That's it. Selling girls as sex, and that's all that girls are there for."

In fact, rather than giving them status, being a promoter in charge of beautiful girls threatened to tarnish a woman's reputation with the stigma that she was profiting from her friends and brokering girls for money, like a madam. Three of the five women promoters were adamant that they did not want to be publicly identified as promoters; one of them wore wigs when she went out to avoid being recognized as a promoter during the day.

In the VIP clubs, women became girls, which were assets to be brokered. They could not very easily work as the brokers themselves.

The Costs of a Free Cocktail

With dinner, transportation, and possibly rent paid for by promoters, girls spent relatively small amounts of time and money to access the free parties. Models, especially, were considered so beautiful that they could wear a basic dress out and still be considered top quality.

Hannah, nineteen, claimed it took her five minutes to get ready, as she never fussed with her hair and she wore the same clothes to the club at night as to her castings during the day. Jane, twenty-eight, tried a little harder, because she was self-consciously not a model and, not long ago, Enrico had ridiculed her for wearing the same dress on Thursday and Sunday nights. She bought a new dress about once a week for roughly $70 from a store like Zara, got manicures weekly for $20, and paid about $40 in cab rides to and from the club each night she went out. The money she saved on dinners and entertainment was still greater than the amount she put into it.

But there were other costs that girls described in interviews: the emotional and embodied tolls of trying to fit within the hierarchy of valuable girls. Reba, for instance, noticed right away the luxury accessories other girls carried: "I think when I originally started doing this I felt really bad because you look around and you can tell somebody's carrying a $5,000 bag." Over time, she realized that models and other fashion workers get access to industry freebies, "so it's not that these people are really able to afford it most of the time. So I was really insecure about it at first, but then I realized people aren't all that impressed."

Maintaining a slim body was another challenge. Hannah and Jill, also a nineteen-year-old model, went out regularly with Sampson and accompanied him to the Hamptons on weekends. Sitting poolside at a Hamptons mansion with Sampson's wife, thirty-year-old Olivia, the girls looked at their own bodies and those of the young models around them, and they could not help but compare.

"It will make you feel fat, yes," said Jill, about being in the scene.

"It makes me feel really self-conscious," agreed Olivia.

"Yeah, me too," said Hannah. "But at the same time, I'm like, well, it can't be that bad, if I'm here with them." They laughed, but she continued. "It's like a confidence booster and killer at the same time. It's like, 'Fuck, this is cool!' But then like, '*She*'s really skinny,'" she said, gesturing to another model across the pool.

Olivia, especially, felt pressure to look good to hold the interest of her promoter husband. "I'm surrounded by hot bods all the time. I have to look my best. He can't come home to a toad." Inner beauty wouldn't cut it in this world: "Inner beauty is when you eat make-up," she concluded, and the girls laughed.

It didn't help that men frequently remarked on girls' clothes and bodies, usually with compliments but sometimes with breezy insults that could sting. One evening, a client at a promoter's table told Reba that she should lose weight. "It really hurt," she said. "Basically what he was saying is he prefers tits on a stick, he actually said that. I didn't go out with them again. I was just shocked he even said that to me." Another man at a dinner table in Cannes during the Film Festival told Beatrice, who was at that time an art student, "that I made up for my lack of, sort of, blonde sexiness by having a personality, and he compared me to this other girl who was sitting there and didn't speak English but who was blonde and sexy. And I felt really offended for her, so I felt like I had to spill champagne all over him. I don't think he realized it was deliberate, but I felt better." Perhaps because girls' inclusion in this scene was predicated on their beauty, men felt entitled to publicly discuss and critique their looks.[37]

Maintaining a girl's body grows increasingly difficult over time, because girls' beauty is defined as youth, and because drinking alcohol and staying out late can tire out any body eventually. The girls I spoke to were acutely aware that they got to enjoy free access to the party scene for a short period of time in their lives, a predicament that all models share given the fashion industry's pernicious standards for youthful looks in women. Some girls managed this by lying about their age, but that could come with another set of concerns. For instance, I interviewed one thirty-three-year-old regular at promoters' tables who told everyone in nightlife that she was twenty-eight. She was so worried about revealing her real age that she made me put in writing that I would conceal her name.

Beyond having to monitor their bodies to access the free parties, girls also questioned the authenticity of the relationships they made in the scene, especially relationships with men. Promoters were economically motivated to befriend girls, but along the way girls developed mutually caring connections, such as between Nina and Thibault, Jane and Celia, and Nora and Dre. Figuring out just how authentic these relationships were could pose a challenge.

"Do I consider promoters my friends? No," sighed Reba, who had been going out with some of same promoters for the past ten years. "I think it would be really hard to consider them friends. There are certain things I can't share with them," like her age of twenty-eight, for instance, and her last name, both of which she hid from promoters and on her social media accounts.

To cope with the potential inauthenticity of these relations, Beatrice "played dumb," to deliberately not know her economic value to promoters like Toby:

> I try not to know too much, because I don't want to feel like I'm going out—first of all, I don't want to feel like somebody's my friend because they can make, like, twenty-five dollars or whatever if I show up at something. That's really awkward to think that. And second, like I don't want to feel compelled to go out because of someone who's broke.

In fact, I found that girls and promoters rarely made instrumental motives explicit in their interactions, though most people acknowledged them in interviews. Most girls did not know exactly how much promoters made. Rarely did they ever inquire into the finances of their tables, and almost all girls I met estimated that promoters earned far less than they actually did.

Girls viewed other men they met in the scene, not just promoters, with suspicion as well. To Reba, being a woman in New York that someone deems to be attractive was a "double-edged sword. While you get a lot of privileges like free access in the nightlife, for example, you're only treated a certain way." She suspected that some of the men she dated used her for her looks, to show her off at professional and social events, for instance. Laura, the jewelry designer and former model, described such men distastefully as "modelizers," those who only hang out with models.

Similarly, Eleanor, the twenty-two-year-old fashion graduate, was critical about her social ties to men she met out. She began going out when she was just a freshman studying at Parsons School of Design. Her college friends introduced her to the world of promoters, and though not a model, she was thin and pretty and, at five feet six, tall enough. "I always wear heels," she said, pointing to her four-inch Jeffrey Campbell platforms. After partying with promoters almost every night of her freshman year, Eleanor got to know doormen, club and restaurant owners, and a number of older wealthy men. She described these men, who were often clients of promoters, as "guys that are nice and aren't promoters but are willing to buy tables, and are willing to go to four-star restaurants with my girlfriends and pay for everything." Now she rarely goes out with promoters, who were a stepping stone to her greater access to the exclusive nightlife scene.

Yet even as she independently navigated this scene, without a broker profiting off of her, Eleanor struggled to assess the authenticity of her friendships with wealthy men. Such was the case with Zach, a forty-two-year-old cosmetic dentist whom she initially described as "a good friend." Zach was rich and handsome, and he was also well connected to the city's top club and restaurant owners. Eleanor liked hanging out with him. He regularly treated Eleanor to dinner and drinks, but sometimes they just watched sports together at his apartment. Their relationship wasn't physical, but it was transactional in a way that always bothered her:

> But you have to say to yourself, like, okay, Zach's in his early forties, and he's hanging out with people half his age. There has to be something off, you know? But I love him. He's a good friend. He takes care of me and stuff. But I always wonder, if I wasn't, you know, skinny, if I wasn't attractive, would he really be friends with me? Probably not. And there's always that in the back of your mind.

This became more clear to Eleanor when she wanted to invite some of her plain-looking girlfriends from her New Jersey hometown to come out with them one night, and Zach refused. "It's like they don't even want to be seen with people that aren't attractive," she said. "It's—it's gross."

And yet, Eleanor continued to hang out with Zach and other rich men so that she could afford her taste for upscale entertainment:

> If I can be affording to buy everything, it would be a different story. But I know how to work it, you know? I know—I love going out.

I love nightlife. I love New York City and, like, all that. But, I feel like I'm just one of the luckier ones, where I've found people that don't expect anything, for the most part, from me. Except, I guess, my presence.

Maintaining the desirability of her presence meant dressing up, wearing the platform heels, and dieting. Girls felt a constant pressure to be attractive, she said, "or no one will want to take them out."

Still, Eleanor maintained, "I don't feel like I'm being used as much." She hesitated, and added, "Of course I'm being used, you know? Like, everyone uses each other."

I asked, "And you're using them?"

"Yeah, I mean, I can't afford to go to four-star restaurants. I can't even afford a cocktail at my favorite club."

Use and Abuse

Rocco put in his time to convince girls to come out with him through multiple text messages, lunches, and long strolls through the city. The thirty-one-year-old African man was likable, to be sure, but he also worked really hard to be liked by pretty girls, slowly building up his network by befriending modeling agencies; he dated a Russian model himself. His true passion was DJ'ing and music, but as a promoter, his focus had to be on the girls at his table, who always expected what was to him an unreasonable amount of attention.

When I made it to his party at Club M one Friday night, he gave too much of his attention to me, and a girl sitting to his side, feeling ignored and bored, got up and left without saying goodbye. He sighed and shook his head when he saw her text moments later:

I would appreciate next time a hug or high five instead of ignoring me all night. I feel stupid. But it's ok.

"They all want attention," Rocco said. "You see? I have to pay attention to everyone. What about the promoter? Nobody asks me how I am. Nobody cares about the promoter."

It was a rather laughable complaint coming from a man whose job was brokering his beautiful girlfriends to a nightclub from which he earned about $800 a night. But Rocco raised a concern shared by nearly every promoter I met: that girls were using him for the fun and attention in an asymmetrical relationship in which *he* was being exploited.

We can think of these webs of friendship, favors and gifts, intimacies, obligations, and reciprocities as a relational infrastructure that supports ties between promoters and their girls. If the infrastructure is sound, the exchange goes smoothly, and girls provide valuable labor for promoters that doesn't look like labor at all; it looks like fun with friends. But this infrastructure can break down when intimacy between girls and promoters feels lacking, when the promoter is perceived as being too strategic and the calculation behind their friendship feels too cold. We could then say there is a relational mismatch: the terms of the relationship, the exchanges, and the forms of compensation are not aligned, and usually then someone gets caught off guard.[38] Promoters and girls alike described those relationship failures as moments of abuse, and they could lead to a break in the ties between them.

"Everybody is using everyone," the promoter Malcolm once told me. Girls used promoters for any number of things as much as he used her for a paycheck. Perhaps she liked to party, maybe she needed friends, or maybe she just couldn't afford a nice dinner. Luca, Santos's associate based in Milan, saw it this way: "A lot of them [the girls], they just use me—for holiday, party, connection. It stinks. I know that. But I do same. I use them for work, they use me for connection, free holiday."

"But there's a difference between being used and getting taken advantage of," continued Malcolm. "The club is using the promoter, the promoter is using friends, [and the] friends want to party, so they're using the promoter." This, after all, was the deal, the unspoken terms of exchange between promoters and girls. The trouble was when either promoters or girls were perceived as not just using but abusing the other, as when, for instance, a girl did a dine-and-dash or brought unwelcome male friends to his table. "That's taking advantage," according to Malcolm, and it violated the terms of exchange.

Relational work isn't just a facade; it doesn't just mask intensions. Promoters can believe in these ties, and they too get hurt when the meanings don't align. Enrico, in particular, was sensitive to any behavior he perceived as strategic attempts to use him for his money or his time. For instance, it was vexing that girls asked him for cab money when they had expensive handbags and designer clothes. "What's with girls?" he asked me after a dinner in which a stripper, one of his guests, told him she would only go to the club if he took care of her cab ride home. "They have a Chanel bag, Louis Vuitton, but they still say, 'Give me ten dollars for the cab.' I don't get it." Ten dollars was a minuscule amount of money to him, so he didn't mind giving cab fare if someone asked for it. But it signaled to him that the girl was using him, which he could not stand. The dividing line between use and abuse of friends was thin for Enrico. And it was deeply unfair. While claiming to seek egalitarian terms of friendship, without instrumentality, he could profit handsomely from his girls, only to deride them for being inauthentic users when they demanded something in return.

Girls recognized this dividing line too, and their tolerance for abuse was also generally low. Their drinks, dinners, and holidays were hardly free, because they paid with embodied and emotional labors, including the general sense of weariness of being used by putative friends. In exchange, they expected a certain level of treatment. They regularly left outings if and when they lost their appeal or the girls felt too explicitly taken advantage of.

Leila, for example, said about the promoters Trevor and Malcolm, with whom she went out often, "We are friends, but I know they are working." At the core of that friendship was a mutual exchange of value: their income for her fun. If the night wasn't fun, she stopped participating. She recounted a story of when she got up and left Trevor's table. He had been constantly tapping on his phone throughout dinner, and so were all of the girls at the dinner table, such that no one was talking to anybody. She gave it a few minutes, then said to Trevor, "Okay I'm bored. I'm going to go."

Can you be "real friends" with a person who profits from your friendship? Does the fact of a profit motive make a genuine relationship impossible?

In contemporary market society, we draw sharp distinctions between interested and disinterested ties. But "pure" friendship is always an idealization, one that misleads us from seeing reciprocity and mutual obligation at the very foundation of all social relations. It would be naive to reduce all of these relations to cold calculation simply because they have an underlying economic value.[39] It would also ignore the widespread ways in which market and nonmarket settings are blurred in late capitalism. People in commercial settings, from salespeople to sex workers, routinely seek to make their business relations meaningful. Direct-selling organizations like the makeup company Mary Kay rely on the commercial value of friendship for its business model.[40] Lots of us use our friends for economic gain, but importantly, we follow social expectations for using—and being used—in ways that feel acceptable.

One reason we can't account for these kinds of relationships is because we are blindsided by their ambiguity. We tend to think a relationship is either exploitative or authentic and pure. But exploitation works best when it is enjoyable and when it feels like a relation of authentic friendship.

Hence the importance of relational work to promoters' efforts to build strategic intimacies. Through gifts, shared experiences, favors, sex, and the language of "my friend," promoters endow their relationships with meaning and obfuscate their economic motives. Promoters who are good at their jobs make going out fun among friends. They exploit girls in the classic Marxist sense in that they can extract surplus value from girls' bodies, because they have a structural advantage over girls, who are unable to broker girls or benefit as much from their own value.

Through the exercise of managerial control, the promoter extracts labor from girls under the guise of leisure. He manages her looks, time, and movements in a way that must not appear managerial. In fact, promoters' strategies for managing girls appear very similar to other managerial strategies employers use to extract the most productivity from their workers. Under industrial capitalism, employers bled surplus value out of their workers, with long hours and grueling conditions, leading to early deaths. Cruel force has long since been deemed inefficient; it rarely works for long before workers revolt, and most industrialized democracies now regulate labor abuses. In the 1970s, studying manufacturing plants, sociologist Michael Burawoy found that the best way to extract the most labor was to align workers with management's aims, to get workers to consent to their exploitation by changing their subjectivity.[41] Exploitation doesn't have to feel bad to get workers to do their jobs; in fact, productivity goes up when workers believe in the value of what they are doing.[42]

In the popular sense, exploitation is thought to be unjust and, therefore, painful. Yet, I saw how the more enjoyable a girl's relationship was with a promoter, the more she provided him with valuable labor that she experienced as the opposite: as friendship, leisure, and fun. Relational work is the promoter's tool for obfuscating and redefining unequal market exchanges. This doesn't mean that all promoters' relationships with girls are based on lies or somehow inauthentic, though all of them were structurally asymmetrical.[43]

Where I see a problem is in the construction of deliberate asymmetries, when one party extracts value from the other's misrecognition of an authentic relation.[44] Some promoters, like Malcolm and Enrico, used the ideal of friendship to demand loyalty and deference from their friends, and therefore, to extract more value from them. Other promoters deliberately constructed asymmetries in information, such that the relationship was more meaningful to the girl than it was to the promoter.

This was how Thibault operated.

Thibault repeated to me a couple of times that most people didn't realize how much money promoters could make, nor how much effort the job truly demanded. You have to take the work seriously and come at it hard, he said, not like those young guys that entered promotions for a short stint, mostly just to have fun. Those guys drank too much and did drugs, and that made them sloppy. "I don't put one leg in, one out. When I do something, I do it all the way," he said.

Nina had Thibault's baby. Late into her pregnancy, she discovered he was cheating on her with a substantially younger woman, one of the girls that had been going out with them. Nina left Thibault when their child was born. She became a single mom and continued to model in New York, but she was not on good terms with Thibault, who refused to recognize their child. After years of fighting him in court, Nina had not received any child support from Thibault. He spent most of his attention on his new girlfriend, a young model from Brazil.

Unfair as they could be to their girls, promoters were striving to join better-positioned men and their elite worlds of business. Like their girls, promoters found themselves cut out from relationships with the real power holders.

6

Started from the Bottom

Sunday, 6 a.m., Miami

It had been a long night in Miami, but Santos wasn't done yet. The clubs had closed hours ago and there were no more after-parties, so Santos wired up a portable speaker in his guesthouse bedroom and blasted hip-hop while he danced with Malcolm and the girls. The room was strewn with clothes and empty beer cans, and Tanya was coming down nervously from the last of her cocaine. Still, Santos kept the party going. He knew by heart the lyrics to his hip-hop playlist, which contained hits by Rick Ross and Drake with names like "Hustle Hard" and "Started from the Bottom." A song called "I'm a Boss," by Meek Mill, came on and Santos sang along with feeling:

> Thank God, all these bottles I popped
>> All this paper I been gettin', all these models I popped
>> I done sold a hundred thousand 'fore my album got dropped.
>>> And I'm only 23—

He stopped suddenly and turned to me to interject, "Well, I'm twenty-six," before continuing to sing:

I'm the shit, now look at me
>Look at me

By the song's end, Santos leaned close to me, still dancing, and said: "These are the songs that people all over the world listen to. They in every club. And what they all talkin' about, a little bit—it's incredible—it's me. No? Every one, it's about my life, what I do. Everybody wants to be me."

He shrugged and started to turn away to dance, but stopped himself to add: "You should do a psychology of me."

This was a common theme as Santos narrated his world. On our first night out in Miami together, he told me that I should write my book, "not about nightlife but about *my* life, because I have the biggest clients and friends with private jets! And you know where I came from."

Most promoters don't come from money, but they end up surrounded by it. Most of the promoters I interviewed, twenty-eight out of forty-four, didn't go to college or didn't finish it. Nineteen of them described their backgrounds as poor or lower-middle class, and only eight of them identified as from upper-middle-class or wealthy families.[1] The majority of them come from lower-middle- and middle-class backgrounds, yet they earn six figures, drink high-priced champagne, and share social space with the superrich. Given the limits to class mobility in the United States, this is a remarkable accomplishment. For a child born in the bottom fifth of the income distribution in the United States, the probability of reaching the top fifth is about 7.5 percent. By comparison, the odds are about 14 percent in Denmark.[2] Promoters experienced class mobility that was unlikely to happen in most Western countries, but it was especially unlikely in the United States.

For most promoters, nightlife opened an unexpected pathway into elite networks. One former promoter, Duke, who built a real estate business in part through his connections from his fifteen years of promoting, noted: "It's an easy business for the uneducated to get into and break into without college."

Because most promoters do not come from upper-class backgrounds, they must cross social distance to relate to their clients. The class differences between the two manifest themselves in the ways they present themselves: how they talk, style their bodies, and display their tastes. In sociological terms, promoters lagged behind clients in their "cultural capital," but they were as rich as them in social capital, or connections, which could be as valuable as things like education credentials or upbringing.[3] Taken together, cultural and social capital are resources that people marshal in the struggle to achieve status and mobility. Bourdieu noted that the capacity to build social capital "takes an unceasing effort" that is unequally distributed; in other words, people without initial privileges of money and status must work harder to accumulate social capital.[4] As "the life of the party," as one promoter described his role, promoters act as brokers trading in relationships with beautiful women and rich men in elite worlds largely unfamiliar from their own upbringings. How do these outsiders manage to build ties within elite networks? What is the conversion potential of their social capital, and what are its limits?

Most promoters believed they had found a way into elite society and had limitless potential to advance within it: "I'm gonna make it so big," Santos liked to say, echoing Dre, who also thought he was on the cusp of becoming a multimillionaire. Pablo and Vanna hoped to broker business deals for all of the rich men they partied with, and Thibault aspired to open an upscale hotel. Sampson and Malcolm, too, thought they'd be as rich as New York City's biggest club owners in due time. In fact, at twenty-nine, Malcolm had been in the business for eight years, having moved up from mass to image promotions. When I met him, he had recently begun to travel the world hosting exclusive parties in New York, the Hamptons, Miami, London, and Saint-Tropez. His climb correlated with the rising quality of his girls. He thought of himself at this point as part of a network of elites:

The reality is that the people we party with, whether it be New York, Miami, Saint-Tropez, Ibiza, it's the 1 percent. The same faces all the time. So you may not know them; you may not even know of them. But you recollect them. You acknowledge them, like, "Hey, what's up, man?"

Malcolm's goal was not to get rich, but to get superrich, like the clients with whom he toasted champagne in Saint-Tropez and the Hamptons.

Promoters' dreams of upward mobility highlight the perils of service work performed for superrich clients, whose absurd wealth skewed promoters' definitions of success and stoked their desires to be boundlessly rich as well. But for all of their extravagant dreams, few promoters found a path into the 1 percent, and they remained in their upscale service role frustratingly adjacent to the real money.

Funny Money

The promoter's job can be quite expensive. To reach the status of international VIP promoter, promoters have to invest a considerable amount of money out of their own pockets. Promoters pay for the "treats" that incentivize girls to come out with them each night, starting with the tip on comped meals at trendy restaurants. The dinner bill is almost always comped by the restaurant or paid for by the club, but promoters are expected to pay the tip, which can run as high as $200.

Inside the club, promoters' tables receive free bottles of champagne (or more likely a cheaper alternative, sparkling white wine), vodka, and mixers, for which they are expected to tip the bottle waitresses between $10 and $20 per bottle, to ensure speedy service; this also helps keep their girls at the table. Busboys should also be tipped well, because they bring ice and fresh glasses, and promoters need their attention, too.

The costs continue to add up outside the club. Promoters often pay several girls' cab fare ($20 each), or they offer to drive their girls home, almost always in large and expensive SUVs. They also pay for girls' daytime perks, such as trips to the movies, to lunch, to amusement parks, to play pool or go bowling—all of the little freebies whose aim is to make girls feel like they should reciprocate with their time out at night. In addition, promoters often employ sub-promoters, to outsource some of their work of recruiting and entertaining girls.

It adds up, as Malcolm explained. On paper he made $1,000 per night, but his take-home pay after taxes and expenses could be more like $200 per night. Promoter's earnings, he said, are a kind of "funny money."

"When you're looking at your tax returns, you're like, 'I made what? I got paid $200,000 where?' There were times I used to look at my tax returns, like, you got to be fucking kidding me. I'm like, I got a $70,000 BMW, okay, you can only take ninety-three [octane gasoline], gas is at five dollars a tank, $120 every time I fill my tank, which is every three days, because I'm always driving around. So it adds up. And then there's days you're not working, you still spending money, because you need to continue building these relationships."

Getting paid by clubs could be difficult, if not impossible. Because clubs turned over quickly, promoters' paychecks were frequently held up by changing management, and in cases where clubs went bankrupt, owners reneged on their owed paychecks entirely.[5] Meanwhile, as independent contractors, promoters didn't have health insurance unless they bought it privately or still qualified on their parents' plans. Given the high costs of health care in the United States, they shared vulnerabilities with other precarious workers, including fashion models. Like other workers with nonstandard employment, they had no retirement packages and no sick leave, with the exception of a handful of promoters who worked "in-house" exclusively for one club company on salary.

"If you are sick, you don't make money. If you can't come out, you don't make money. If you miss a night, you don't make money. It is always up to you to make money, every day," explained the promoter Celia.

There were other, less measurable costs of the job, like the considerable physical and emotional costs of going out every night, even if you felt tired or hungover. And the job seemed impossible to balance with a family life.

Joe, the thirty-one-year-old African American promoter, was so burnt out after five years in the job that he bluntly told me at our first meeting, "I can't *stand* being in the club. I look like I'm having fun, I'll be dancing just to entertain people, because I'm supposed to be the life of the party. I have to look it." He faked drinking by surreptitiously filling his shot glass with water, or pretending to throw back a drink and then hiding the full glass. While some promoters seemed genuinely energized by the excitement of nightlife, many also found it exhausting work that they simply could not enjoy every night.

But even with the awareness of the funny nature of their money and the precariousness of their income, most promoters thought the job was worth pursuing. First, the job paid these men a significant "lifestyle wage"; that is, it conferred on them contingent access to social status and its accompanying privileges that was otherwise only accessible to people with greater financial resources. Promoters got to take part in glamorous events and high-priced meals, and sometimes they traveled on yachts and private planes; they could be conspicuous consumers of a world they could not actually afford.[6] Second, promoters believed their access to elites was priceless. It was striking how frequently they described their wealth of social capital, in interviews and in their day-to-day talk. They believed that these ties would advance all kinds of career aspirations, from music and acting to restaurant and club ownership.

"At the end of the year, I'm not making crazy amounts of money," explained Ethan, the image promoter in New York. "But I'm meeting great people, you know, which I think is priceless. You can't really put a price on, you know, meeting amazing people and being able to befriend amazing people, you know."

Meeting such amazing and important people, however, was more than just an interesting experience for Ethan and the rest. The encounters shone a light onto a world of wealth, beckoned them in, and fueled unrealistic expectations that they too could be superrich.

Who Wants to Be a Billionaire?

Surrounded by wealth and power, promoters sensed the tremendous potential of their position. When Santos walked along the docks at the port of Cannes, he saw dozens of jumbo yachts flying flags from the Caribbean—a tax shelter for the superrich. To him, each ship represented a potential opportunity: "Here it's like all these contacts. I'm just gonna [stay here] for two months collecting numbers. And it goes all the way down." He pointed to the long line of yachts docked at the marina, an abundance of contacts that seemed to be just waiting for him.

Sometimes he got giddy at his prospects. "When I'm fifty I'm gonna own everything. I know all the rich people here; they don't even know each other!"

Promoters aimed to capitalize on their networks for both short- and long-term gain. In the short term, their ties had immediate practical value. They could eat for free or at a steep discount in cities around the world and they had a steady stream of invitations to events like concerts and art shows. Dre hardly ever paid full price for dental treatment, because he had a couple of dentist friends he was sure to always comp at the club. Dre's collaborator Errol, a former promoter, made a low-budget music video to promote his singing career by calling on his nightlife ties; he got insurance for the shoot for only one hundred dollars with the help of an insurance salesperson he knew from clubbing. Errol called nightlife a "trampoline for whatever you wanna do," from music to real estate.

Thinking about the long term, almost all promoters believed that the ties they formed in nightlife could further their careers in other fields. The twenty-three-year-old promoter Brooks, also an aspiring actor, thought his contacts would further his acting career:

> Part of the reason I still do this job is for the networking . . . I know that some of the friends that I have through this business will afford me a lot more chances.

None of the promoters imagined that they would promote until retirement; indeed, most men agreed that they envisioned serving only a short stint as a promoter, to build networks and transition into a better career. Nine of the promoters I interviewed had goals to be creative producers or artists such as DJs, club designers, actors, filmmakers, and musicians. Five wanted to make the transition into brand marketing and public relations, and five more were angling to be real estate agents. Almost half, nineteen, of them had some entrepreneurial goals of owning a club, lounge, bar, restaurant, or hotel. Seven were transitioning or had already become owners or operators of clubs or restaurants. This was the most visible path upward for promoters; three major nightlife conglomerates in New York (Strategic Group, EMM Group, and the Butter Group) are owned and operated by former promoters.

There were a handful of extraordinary success stories of promoters who made the transition from nightlife into other high-powered arenas. One of the most admired was Nicolas, the fifty-six-year-old Jamaican man who had previously worked with Thibault and Felipe. Over the previous few years, he had begun organizing fundraising events, tapping into his network of former bottle clients for various political causes. Promoters regularly invoked Nicolas's name as an example of someone who had landed a "golden ticket," as Malcolm put it, out of clubbing and into a distinct and important field where he commanded respect. Malcolm went on: "Nicolas got all his contacts through nightlife. He had one main guy [who] spent a million dollars in [the] club; now he introduces him to fundraisers."

That level of success was the goal for a handful of promoters, including Malcolm, Santos, and Dre, each of whom aspired to exit the nightlife and hospitality industries in order to set up business deals among their wealthy clientele. All promoters thought of themselves as people who could "connect the dots" across various social worlds. Michel, a forty-year-old black promoter from the Caribbean in the business for over twenty years, was transitioning into fashion photography when we met, and he explained, "I'm a photographer and I work with clients . . . Sometimes they say they want to get in touch with this advertiser, and I can say, 'Oh, that guy hangs out at Club X. I know him, I can introduce you.' And I met them all from nightlife."

This positional advantage is known in network science as "brokerage." In the social sciences, network theory predicts that brokers will capitalize on their network ties, because when brokers put people in touch with each other, they should reap some advantage or "rent."[7] Five of the promoters I interviewed were angling to do this in what is called "B2B," or business-to-business brokering, among their clients.

Their goal was not to get rich, but to get wealthy, a difference principally between earning a high income and creating dynastic wealth through long-term business dealings with elites.

Santos explained it like this: by virtue of being from Colombia, he was in a position to accumulate ties to Latin American oil supply companies, and he had recently got to know the heads of Gulf States, who were regular fixtures in the French Riviera. He intended to someday introduce these suppliers and buyers, and collect commissions off of the ensuing exchanges. His plan went like this:

> I don't want a million or two million, I want a billion. I put people in touch but I haven't asked for a fee even though people do business together because of me. But in five, ten years, when I know them a long time, I'll say listen, "I'll put you in touch with petroleum but let's make a contract." Even if I take one percent or half a percent on each barrel of oil from Venezuela to the Middle East, that's a billion dollars in a year.

"But I have to wait," he reasoned, because he couldn't just ask for this kind of business relationship right now. Right now, he was building up ties, and putting people in touch with each other, and letting them do business because of him, not with him. He first needed to prove himself a worthy business collaborator. While the scenario Santos imagined was likely exaggerated, he claimed to have come close to brokering business deals between his clients in the past, and he genuinely believed he could leverage his ties to become wealthy.

But while promoters certainly put businessmen in touch with each other, it was actually pretty rare that they were ever able to extract a broker's commission or fee from making those connections. Explained the forty-year-old promoter Michel:

> Like, billions and billions of dollars have been negotiated or initiated in clubs. Billions-of-dollar deals. Like, we used to put people together, and next thing you know, they are doing freaking development. They're building hotels, and this and that. . . . That's also one of the things that made us who we were, that made people come to us.

But when it came to taking a cut, Michel conceded that they were unable to monetize their ties: "We actually never did. We should have. We realized very late that we should have. But who cares? The past is past."

When pressed to describe just how their social connections might enable them to broker business deals among elites, promoters were vague. For one thing, promoters were not experienced or trained in financial dealmaking. Trevor, for example, sent Malcolm a text message one afternoon that read, "hey I got a deal for a building you know anybody with 200–300 mil, know anyone that wants to buy it?"

Malcolm laughed as he described his response: "I was like 'Yo, you need profit margins, more details, a full prospectus. It's a lot of work to piece these deals together.'"

Malcolm himself wasn't cut out for brokering complex deals either, though he aspired to. "Even the other day," he told me, "a friend of mine, he's in banking, venture capitalism. He's like, 'Yo, if you have anybody who has great ideas, let me know. I got people who put up money to sponsor good ideas . . . And if it works, we'll go ahead and cash out, sell out. Because that's what's going on now. Technology is really where everything's going.' And that's something I like, and I'll keep in mind. I know a lot of bright people who may not necessarily have the funding, I can get into that, and next thing I know, I'm—I'll be a part-owner who can facilitate." This vague plan did not come to fruition in the three years that I knew him.

Perhaps the biggest dreamer of them all was Dre. Every night it seemed he spun a different tale about his music career just about to blow up, his hip-hop album about to drop, his car company, or his import company. One evening at the Downtown restaurant, he noticed a pair of famous and wealthy businessmen sitting across the room. He nodded to them and winked, and the wealthy partners waved back to Dre, who said:

I knew that those guys were rich, but I didn't know just how much. When I see them out, we talk. They like me and I say, let me get you a table, let me help you. When you come out, you ask for me. Now I have a business proposal for them, who do you think they are going to listen to? Dre, who they know and they like. Not Enrico. Not Santos. . . . Those other promoters out at night, running after models and acting stupid and drinking? Not me. I'm sober. I know exactly who is that person over there, who's in the room. I introduce myself to them, become friends with them, and make it happen.

"It seems kind of like a fantasy," I interjected. "Does it really happen?"

"Ash, yes. *Yes*, Ash, it can happen. All the people that make money in this world, it's a question of relationships. It doesn't happen any other way. No other way. You introduce them and you take your cut." Typical of the way promoters narrated their careers, Dre disregarded his past failures and emphasized his tremendous potential for future deals.

The most promising deal he described was the one involving a Serbian telecommunications company, the owner of which was looking to expand his coverage across European markets. The businessman had come to New York for meetings with potential partners arranged by one of Dre's collaborators, and Dre organized their business dinners accompanied by six beautiful girls, whom the men apparently liked. Dre's partner was supposedly negotiating in Europe to sign a contract to secure their broker's fee, and, rather ambiguously, Dre spoke of his impending "30 percent for the next ten fifteen twenty years. I just got the text message." He quickly added, "This is one of twenty deals." Ostensibly, as Dre told it, because he brought the girls to help make the business dinner a success, he was to be paid a cut from the deal.

Over the next few days, Dre kept me abreast of the unfolding deal by text messages:

I feel like all my life I worked so hard now it's happening
Signing contract today.

When asked about how the telecommunications coverage would expand from the Balkans and to which parts of Europe, Dre did not know the details; he'd have to check with his partners. The deal never materialized.

Promoters entered their jobs through their ease with and passion for partying, but being around rich businessmen could reorient their aspirations to become millionaires—billionaires, even—on par with their clients. Their success in the VIP circuit was also a source of frustration, for it escalated their aspirations to unattainable heights. Service relationships do not generally enable the accumulation of ties that yield social mobility. Yet promoters believe otherwise—that they could convert their connections into profit—in part because they saw their job not as conducting a service relationship, but as leisure time spent with friends.

My Best Friends

When I asked promoters for introductions to their clients for interviews, some of them bristled. "Don't use that word to them," Santos told me, because they think of themselves as just friends, not clients, given their shared partying experiences around the world and the frequency and duration of their fun outings. Talk of friendship with clients was ubiquitous among promoters; Santos even described some of them as his "best friends" and "really good friends."

Promoters and clients came from different social worlds. Most promoters weren't nearly as educated or rich as their clients, resulting in an obvious social distance, one to be expected in any patronage relation.[8] Promoters tried to close that social distance by building up the strength and intimacy of their relationships, and imbuing what was fundamentally a service-based transaction with meaning, just as they did in their interactions with girls.

This began from the moment promoters met clients, often through introductions from mutual acquaintances or by strategically being in upscale spaces. To meet potential clients, promoters relied on word of mouth from, for example, hotel concierges (to whom they gift drinks and event tickets), and personal introductions. They made sure to insert themselves in the right kinds of places, like fashion label events and luxury hotels. One promoter deliberately worked out in one of Manhattan's most expensive gyms, where he met a lot of his bottle clients. Dre met a lot of rich men at clubs, and when he heard their names, he made sure to google them later, and then, he said: "Oh wow, look who he is, and the next day I follow up, send an email: 'It was very good to meet you. I'm going out, I organized a dinner with three models, one celebrity, whatever it is, let me know if you'd like to come.'" At this meal, Dre would choose a restaurant that would comp the bill, allowing him to treat his guests while paying only the tip.

For those few promoters who came from wealthy backgrounds, meeting prospective clients was comparatively easy. Enrico, the thirty-year-old promoter from a wealthy Spanish family, tapped into his family connections to find clients. He even dressed like his wealthy European friends, in tailored slacks and suspenders over dress shirts embroidered with his initials. Enrico regularly showed me pictures on his phone of his "good friends" and "best friends," such as famous European soccer players, and business tycoons and their college-aged sons and daughters.

Promoters who lacked preexisting connections instead had to form friendships with rich men over the course of many shared experiences. Bobby, a white American promoter for eight years from Long Island, said about his clients: "You get them via relationships, from your contacts. And when they come, you make sure your guys take care of him so he comes back," meaning that the club's doormen, service personnel, and his team's subs offer great service. "Over time," he said, "real friendships develop."

The nature of that friendship is ambiguous, for it is based on an economic transaction. Promoters stood to profit from clients' bottle expenditures, as we have seen, receiving a cut from the club owners of up to 20 percent of what their clients spend. This can add up to thousands of dollars. Plus there are the perks of invitations to private parties and, eventually, getting hired to organize such private parties. However, promoters did not want their friendships with clients to be perceived as too economically motivated. They downplayed their financial motivations by investing their time in infusing friendships with meaning, not dissimilarly from how they strategically built intimacy with girls. Dre noted that the very big spenders in the world are usually "younger guys," under age forty, who like to party. To develop ties with them, Dre explained, he had to hang out with them: "A guy might spend a lot of money in the club, but it's a lot of work. A lot of work to get him in there. It takes your whole day," including brunch, lunch, going to the movies, and sometimes securing him drugs or arranging dates with models.

Once inside the club, the promoter also serves the role of easing interactions between girls and clients, making introductions around the table and leading small talk at dinners. A promoter usually sits near the client at dinner and at the club, to ensure his enjoyment. Thibault and Felipe cleverly made sure to have at least one outgoing Russian girl in their company when one of their biggest bottle clients, a Russian businessman, attended.

Enrico was so uncomfortable with the thought of making money on his friends that he often turned down commissions from their bottle sales. He explained: "It's not right [that] I make my friends buy bottles and I make money from them, is it?" he asked. "I go out with people I like. I don't want to tarnish my soul by making money off them, like, 'Come out, Marcos, buy two bottles and I take commission from you?' They know I don't work like that, and if I did they would know I'm getting paid off my friends."

In fact, Enrico did profit handsomely from his friends, but indirectly. They frequently recommended him to friends visiting New York as their go-to person for reservations at top restaurants and clubs in the city. For booking their reservations, Enrico typically received a commission, around 10 percent of the bill. Still, by creating distance *between friendship and money*, promoters could redefine their dealings with clients as meaningful ties to *friends with money*, essentially reframing their economic incentives into "hanging out" among equals.

In interviews, clients sometimes also described their relationships with promoters as friendships, though they were less emphatic than the promoters were. All clients know promoters' friendliness can be motivated by money. But this did not rule out the possibility of friendship. One client, a forty-year-old in finance whom I met at Thibault's table, put it this way, "Most friendships you have are supposed to be kind of mutually beneficial, right? So it doesn't have to be, like, explicitly transactional, but I think it usually has to make some sense for both sides. . . . If it's kind of always a transaction, then you should probably question the relationship." This client said he used promoters for dinner and club reservations when he needed to go out to entertain financial investors, and he added, a night out with promoters' girls is always more enjoyable than a night out with other businessmen. However, he would be careful not to ask such favors too often of promoters if they weren't getting paid for it. "If there's too much abuse in one direction, then it gets bad. Because if you overuse that person, you break that bond, and that guy goes away," he said.

For other clients, promoters made them feel comfortable and welcome in the club scene, as Sanford, a sixty-year-old white celebrity lawyer from New York exclaimed: "I have a friendship with the guys who own the club, the guys who promote the club, and I feel comfortable there. That's the primary reason that I would go. But the fact that there are beautiful models floating around is certainly not a deterrent."

Despite their efforts to close social distance, promoters and clients still faced a gulf typical of that between service employee and their customers. And while promoters were skilled in charming girls, this ease did not necessarily translate to their interactions with clients. I frequently observed clients ignoring or dismissing the very promoters who claimed to be their dear friends.

This happened to Santos, back at the port in Cannes lined with yachts. Santos had bragged that he was taking the girls to an afterparty aboard the yacht of his "really good friends," a family of wealthy South American financiers we happened to see at a nearby table in the club earlier that night. Once on board the yacht, it became clear that Santos was at best loosely acquainted with one son of the family, twenty-three-year-old Ricardo, whose uncle at one point asked me in confusion if Santos was a pimp and if the girls now aboard his ship were possible victims of sex trafficking.

When I later interviewed Ricardo, he said that he had indeed met Santos just once, more than a year earlier. In his view, some promoters can become true friends, so long as they don't obviously try to get him to order more bottles to increase their commission; or, as he put it: "If they don't bust my balls." Santos was a good guy, he reasoned, because he never tried to upsell him champagne.

However much Santos and other promoters inflated the depth of their ties to elite men, their friendships with clients seemed largely a discursive framing strategy and part of a practice of hiding economic exchanges, including the rather unsavory trade of girls for profit. Sharing moments of leisure and the illusion of friendly relations with clients—thereby denying the economic importance of those friendships—put the promoter in a difficult position. It set up asymmetrical expectations between the two parties: clients expected fun and short-term contact, while promoters expected long-term ties with economic-mobility opportunities.

The Double Edge of Color Capital

Race was another marker of promoters' outsider status. During my fieldwork at night, most of the men of color I came across were promoters or other club personnel like bouncers. Perhaps there would be up to ten black people in a club like the Downtown out of a hundred people on any given night, and several of them would be promoters. Doormen were careful not to let too many brown and black people inside.

Promoters are ethnically and racially diverse—during my fieldwork, about one-third of the promoters I came across in New York identified as black and/or Latino, and often they were immigrant men. Of the forty-four promoters I interviewed, nineteen identified as black, twenty as white, five as Asian, and five as ethnically Latino (three black and two white). Twenty-five of them were immigrants working in America, and just eight of them were white Americans.[9]

As anomalies in the VIP circuit's mostly white spaces, black promoters were aware of their marginality and how they were viewed through the lens of racial stereotypes. It was common for girls to sexualize black and brown promoters, and for clients to assume that black promoters were engaged in pimping or drug dealing. However, in some instances, promoters could exploit what sociologists have called "color capital," by tapping into stereotypes about black bodies, exoticism, and carnality. Color capital refers to the objectification of people of color in, for instance, stereotypical associations of blackness with "soul" and exoticism, which white people can appropriate to increase their own status. Whites can use black color capital by claiming ties to black people to portray themselves as capable of being sensual or connected to African culture. Because color capital is defined by whites, black promoters can use it only when they embody stereotyped notions of blackness and only in certain spaces. Yet, surprisingly, I found that some black promoters used dominant racial stereotypes to their advantage in their work, carving out a narrow space of agency from of the larger structure of racial capitalism.[10] These men described blackness as an advantage in the VIP scene, exploitable for personal gain, in three ways.

First, some black promoters embraced a prevailing notion in the club world that black men can hustle, a positive stereotype that they could use, for instance, in haggling with the club management to get their paychecks. Like Mustafa, a black man from Senegal, who said that black men work harder, because they are not entitled to anything, so "they push and they seize, and that's what you have to do as a promoter." Black immigrant men, in particular, were seen as the hardest working because of their double disadvantage. Explained Wayne, an African American man from Brooklyn: "A lot of the black ones are from Africa, French African, and they know the value of the dollar. . . . They don't have anything else. Like, this is their life. So they're very, very driven. Unlike a lot of the ones that aren't, which are from America, or they went to college already."

Second, these promoters felt that their blackness helped them stand out. While tokenism can certainly have drawbacks in professional settings, in VIP clubs, most of the black men described benefitting from their heightened visibility as the token black people in the room.[11] Michel, forty, got his start in nightlife like most promoters:

by hanging out and being well-liked. As a teenager, he and his cousin Loïc, both black men from the Caribbean, were regulars at a biker bar in Miami, where they became familiar faces:

> People loved us. We were the only two black guys in there. And the owner of the place asked to meet with us, and he offered us to become promoters. Like, he told us, like, "I've never seen anything like this. People just love you guys. You guys are so fun. . . . Have you guys ever thought of being promoters?" And we didn't even know what that was. I was nineteen years old. I was not even legally supposed to be in the place! And actually, when he asked to meet with us, I thought he was gonna tell us we can't come there anymore, because he found out my age.

Michel quit his job as a busboy in a Miami tourist café, but, still in disbelief, he asked the owner, "Hold on. You mean that I can get paid for doing what I'm already doing for free?" Recognizing value in their color capital, clubs provided unusual opportunities for black men to crack into elite circles. Or as Michel explained, "Look, I'm a black kid from Jamaica and I can call up for lunch tomorrow a CEO of a finance firm if I want to."

Third and most pronounced, pervasive stereotypes of black masculinity and hypersexuality were described as assets when it came to attracting girls. "I love American black guys" was something that Malcolm, the twenty-nine-year-old from Brooklyn, frequently heard from European women, to whom he responded:

> I'm your man! Like, you know, I'm a guy. I've hooked up with girls based on the fact that I was probably the only, or one of the few, attractive black men in the building. You hear what I'm saying? All the guys are short white boys in suits, or whatever. And it's just, like, I capitalized on it. I'm not gonna lie to you. If it's not me, it was gonna be somebody else anyway.

Black masculinity has long been a source of fascination and fear for white society. Old colonial tropes of black men as hypersexual threats and exotic entertainers are still prevalent.[12] Despite the violence inherent in these tropes, black promoters found that, in the space of VIP clubs, their racialized identity made them seem exotic and desirable to white girls. As Dre explained, since a large part of promoters' work was to meet women and hold their interest, they could use racial stereotypes to their advantage:

> Women love us. The girls love us. These young girls, they come from small towns or from Eastern Europe and their parents tell them to stay away from black men—they are dangerous, they are trouble—and when they get to New York, young girls always rebel against their parents. They see us, they think, wow, he's cool, he smells good, he can dance. They think we are sexy, we are fun. We have an edge the white guys don't have . . . We have cool style; they think we are fun and they think we have drugs.

Dre knew this was a stereotype, but he did not mind playing it up: "There are black men I know that are terrible in bed, and white guys that are great, but that's the stereotype . . . they see us and they see the fun, they see a good fuck, a guy that can dance." In fact, Dre had to explain over and over to girls that he was not a drug dealer and that he was unwilling to procure them drugs. On the other hand, he wholeheartedly embraced the sexual stereotype that black men are good in bed.

Black promoters' success with white girls could even override the racism black men like Malcolm expected to face in a mostly white elite environment of the VIP scene. Lately Malcolm had been hosting tables at an upscale club in London with Santos. He was residing in a London townhouse that cost 3,800 pounds a week to rent, shared with Santos and some girls. Malcolm dressed his large frame in hip-hop-inspired outfits. He liked his pants to sag enough to show a couple of inches of his boxer shorts, and he always wore sleek rare-edition sneakers and a baseball cap turned backward. When he first turned up at the VIP clubs in London, he was stopped by the doormen, who told him, "No trainers, no hats." This is a familiar code of racial exclusion, an implicit method to exclude blacks on the basis of stylistic choices, for wearing the "wrong" shoes or clothes, those usually associated with poor, black, and marginal populations—the very people credited with creating the hip-hop music that is now celebrated by white clubbers.[13]

Malcolm began laughing as he told me this story. He replied to the doorman, "'You see these ten, twelve models? They not coming in if I don't come in!' Now I walk in with my pants bagging down to here"—he pointed below his butt—"and they be like, 'What up, Malcolm? Come in, come in!'"

But black men's color capital was double-edged, posing risks as well as creating opportunities. While they described race as an asset to help them stand out and attract girls, promoters also acknowledged the drawbacks of being coded as nonwhite, both in and out of the VIP arena. Dre explained:

> In elite societies, the higher you go the fewer of us there are. The truth is, and I know it, at Downtown, do you think that they would let me in without the girls, without the connections? They wouldn't let me in. They'd treat me like a monkey, or treat me badly.

Promoters also knew that negative, damaging stereotypes of blackness were always nearby, threatening both their image and their security. Dre was wary of girls who did drugs or were underage, because he thought the police were eager to arrest black men who associated with white women. Malcolm shared similar fears when, once, a white girl went missing. Police questioned him because he was in her phone contacts. It turned out that she had run off to Atlantic City without telling anybody, which relieved Malcolm: "Thank God she turned up! You know I'm a black man, and this is a white girl gone missing. I be like, I'm screwed!"

Finally, beyond the VIP space, black male promoters were liable to encounter acts of bigotry and racism every day. "As a black man, you have to be the best, best dressed, best behaved, always," Dre explained at an art show opening one night. "So many times I go to dinners and events like these," he continued, "and some smart guy is there trying to push my buttons, telling racist jokes. I smile, say, 'Ha, ha, ha.' I don't get upset."

Indeed, Dre kept his cool in the face of egregious bigotry one sunny afternoon in downtown New York, as we strolled through the streets shopping for a birthday present for a modeling agent. Before we set off, he announced, "Okay, now let me look like someone," and he put on his vintage Ray-Ban sunglasses and pulled down his black beanie low over his brow. With that, he linked arms with me and walked with a swagger in his low-slung distressed designer blue jeans.

People sometimes think he's a celebrity when he walks like this, and frequently he gets stopped on the street by passerby wanting to know who he is and where he is from. People look up from sidewalk cafés and street corners to follow him with their eyes.

But Dre's stylized black masculinity did not impress everyone, and on this afternoon walking with him, someone began to follow us. An older white man trailed us for a few blocks, and when he caught up to us at the next street light, he aggressively scolded Dre for wearing his pants too baggy—a popular look among hip-hop artists and well accepted as stylish in the VIP club.

"In *this* society, this *white* society, we wear our pants over our asses," the man shouted to him on the sidewalk. Dre was cordial and calm during the incident, brushing it off, but he didn't soon forget it. Weeks later he remarked to me, "'This is a white society.' That's offensive, no?"

Like the inflated value of the champagne bottle, the value of blackness drops precipitously when one steps beyond the velvet rope. The worth of color capital, like all forms of capital, is field-specific; beyond the VIP club walls, blackness could quickly become a liability to promoters. This is the double edge of blackness in the VIP circuit: cool but dangerous, exotic but polluting, desirable only in small quantities, and rarely fitting in fully with the elite.

The Limits of Social Capital

Promoters could mobilize their sex appeal to build ties with girls, which were then convertible into social capital among elite networks. But even with a formidable amount of ties to elites, few promoters were able to leverage the value of their networks in the ways they could see happening for the elite men around them.

In addition to being constrained by the social distance that divided them from their clients, promoters had to reckon with the fact that the kinds of ties they had to rich men were shallow: acquaintance-ships based on leisure, frequently centered on drunken interactions in loud nightclubs.

Partying with elites gave the promoter access to valuable social capital, but it also limited how he could "spend" that capital. How one acquires social capital has an effect on the perceived legitimacy of its holder.[14] Despite promoters' efforts to redefine transactional clients into genuine "friends," physical proximity couldn't compensate for the social distance between promoters and their clients, a predica-ment shared among flight attendants, chauffeurs, and other personal service workers who cater to elites.[15] And while race could lend an aura of exoticism to black promoters in mostly white spaces, black-ness also threatened to define them as low status.

This was the overwhelming sentiment among the twenty clients that I spoke with. If a promoter managed to start his own club or bar, clients said they might invest in it, thereby ensuring their unlimited access to a new club. However, no client would seriously do busi-ness with a promoter or rely on a promoter to make business deals happen. One club owner looked at promoters and their big dreams with some pity:

> They think they're gonna make it. They *think*. There's a big dif-ference between that and actually making it. And they do have the connections. They do know the families. But—here, I was talking with Donni [a promoter] and he says, "I've got an idea. I've got a project I'm working on and I talked to this person or that guy about it and I'm just waiting for them to confirm they're investing . . ." I said, "Donni, look, they're not gonna call you back. They like you only for the party. They don't like you for a business partner."

Realizing this, some promoters took pains to minimize their identi-fication with nightclubs. They avoided calling themselves promoters, knowing its associations with frivolity. When Trevor, for example, meets a new businessman, he tells them he's an event consultant: "I avoid the P-word," he said. Even Dre, a master of cultivating ties as a promoter, was uncomfortable with the label. When I first proposed to study his world, back in 2011, he immediately cut me off to say that he did not want to be seen as a promoter because he wanted to be known for his music career.[16]

There was a sense among promoters that they shouldn't do the job for too long, that it was unseemly to be an "old man" working off of young girls at night. Said twenty-five-year-old Travis:

> I don't want to be stuck in the industry. I'm twenty-five, and get-ting older. I don't want to be confined to getting married and having a kid, and I'm working in a nightclub, you know? That's very embarrassing.

By the age of forty, a man still in the job of promoter was likely to be seen as a loser and a failure, stuck in the role of "party boy," or worse, of a "creepy old man" chasing after girls in the streets. Men like Thibault were described by other promoters and girls as a warning of what could befall a young man if he didn't make smart decisions to transition out of nightclubs and into a more respectable career. Like the young models for whom time was a threat to their value, older promoters felt the precariousness of a position that depended heavily on looks and sex appeal.

Yet it was easy to coast on the job once a promoter had his net-work of girls and clients; in fact, it was hard for many of them to walk away from such lucrative work. Enrico, for instance, turned thirty-four around the time of our final interview. He felt ready to move into his ideal future business venture—an upscale European-style coffee shop like the ones he frequented in Soho so often—but at the moment, he didn't have any plan solid enough to give up the flow of easy cash and fun nights. Though the job became unseemly at a certain age, it paid very well—or so it seemed if one didn't think too much about the hidden expenses. "I make a lot of money," as Travis put it. "I make more money than families."

By 2018, six years after they first told me of their dreams, Dre, Santos, Enrico, and Malcolm were still promoting at other people's clubs. By the time Dre was nearing forty, his friends with day jobs were getting married, having children, and advancing in their careers. Dre wanted those things too; he talked often of wanting to have a family with the right woman, and he searched for her among the many girls he met at night. But he believed that first he needed to establish his business ventures, and for that, he was still waiting.

Likewise, Santos continued to wait for his business brokerage career to take off, when he could say he finally made it. It's hard to say Santos hadn't "made it" already, in the sense that nightlife had propelled him to heights far greater than could be predicted for an uneducated mixed-race immigrant from a poor family in Central America. In fact, a year after we met, he told me with pride that he had bought a home for his mother in Colombia. She came to Cannes for a short visit while I was there, to help with the housekeeping in his villa and also to see his brother, himself a promoter in nearby Milan. Their mother beamed with pride for her sons, who were working with VIPs in some of the wealthiest enclaves in the world. But in Santos's world, there was a lot farther to climb before closing the gap between him and his rich "friends."

"For how much more I'm gonna do this job?" he asked rhetorically as he drove me to the Cannes train station. He smirked and shook his head. "I can go forever. Thibault is forty-six, did you know that? He's doing the same shit as me, taking girls around the world. Chasing girls in the street. You know why I wanna do this job? I'm twenty-seven and working for the king of [a Gulf State]. When I'm fifty I'm gonna be ruling everything. You gonna see."

At the station Santos and I parted ways with a hug and I boarded a train bound for Saint-Tropez. That was the summer of 2013, and the last time I saw him.

On the train, I looked out the window as the luxury hotels of Cannes slipped away, giving way to green fields and modest homes. After a few minutes, the gentleman sitting next to me tapped my arm. He introduced himself as a local businessman living in Cannes, and in fact he was a regular at Club Holla, where Santos promoted. The gentleman had seen me hugging Santos goodbye on the platform, and he immediately asked me something he had long wanted to know about that distinctive black man with long dreadlocks always surrounded by beautiful white girls in the club: "Is he a pimp, you know, trafficking women?"

7

Closure

This book has analyzed the VIP party circuit as a transnational stage for the display of luxury consumption in which status, connections, and economic value accrue to the new global elite. To understand status dynamics among the upper echelons of an unequal class structure, we must come to grips with the social significance of their consumption. Hardly a fringe phenomenon, the VIP circuit demonstrates a historically significant moment, a form of status acquisition made possible by the conditions of twenty-first-century capitalism.

It is perhaps counterintuitive to think of consumption as a means of producing value. Consumption has historically been defined as a loss of value, even as waste. Early uses of the word *consumption* in seventeenth-century Europe were pejorative, signaling an impulse "to devour" or "to use up."[1] Pulmonary tuberculosis, a disease in which the body wasted away, was commonly called "consumption" until the early twentieth century.

As the science of economics emerged during the Industrial Revolution, experts considered production to be the central means of creating value. Production and value creation were what men did; early economists looked to the male wage as the indicator of the health of capitalism.[2] Consumption was women's frivolous business, even declared an "act of madness" by the church prior to industrialization.

Especially in Protestant Europe, which spearheaded the capitalist transformation and its personal imperatives to accumulate rather than spend, the consumption of luxury was considered highly pathological and extravagant, the folly of lustful women and effeminate men.[3]

Luxury consumption was also considered dangerous because of its potential to destabilize social hierarchies. For centuries in Europe, the highest social status belonged to titled families with inherited wealth. True gentility took generations of affluence, and the real mark of high status was the possession of fine old objects, those with the patina of respectable age, passed down through the family lineage.[4] The circulation of new luxuries like household wares and dress in early modernity posed a political and social crisis of sorts: now the nouveau riche mercantile classes could potentially look like their higher-ups, confusing distinctions among social groups.

That one could acquire status simply by buying luxury things was a radical idea.[5] Aristocrats responded to the threat with legal restrictions on what lower classes could wear or consume. Under sumptuary laws in the seventeenth and eighteenth centuries, an aristocrat could own crystal, but a merchant could not, or if the latter did, he had to pay an extra tax. Sumptuary laws especially targeted women's dress and presentation. The heel of a woman's shoe, her necklace, and the lace on her sleeves each marked her social position and the position of the men in her family. Wives and daughters of knights were allowed long trains of precious gold and silk on their dresses; wives of merchants were subject to fines if they dared such display.[6]

Today, three centuries into the spread of consumer capitalism, trying to legally enforce class distinctions seems silly. Anyone with enough money can try to enter the upper echelons of high society. Thorstein Veblen was struck by such efforts to consume for status among the nouveau riche in the late nineteenth century, considering it a distinctly modern and American phenomenon. As booming industries overfilled the pockets of self-made men, their rush to display new riches exemplified the promise of a capitalist democracy: that anyone, regardless of rank or heritage, could make a bid to join the upper class—race and gender, of course, still posed acceptable ceilings. Over the course of the twentieth century, with legal statutes striking down gender and racial exclusions, America could increasingly really appear to be the land of golden opportunity, where any person from humble beginnings could imagine themselves climbing their way into the 1 percent.

To be rich has never been a guarantee of being elite. Everyone knows that money does not guarantee status. The challenge of trying to translate money into elite status is illustrated by plenty of famous cases, like that of billionaire turned president Donald Trump, whose gold-plated penthouse elicits sneers from New York's high society.[7] Money is only a means to status. It can buy prestige through philanthropy.[8] It can buy high-status objects like artworks and fine wines to impress visitors. Money can buy your residence in an affluent neighborhood and your children's place in the right school. The sum total of all of these efforts creates valuable "cultural capital," what French social theorist Pierre Bourdieu identified as the mastery of upper-class cultural codes. The mannerisms and habits of the elite may appear "natural," but, to Bourdieu, they are the product of a long process of socialization into the tacit rules of upper-class taste and distinction. Only through experience, Bourdieu argued, could a person master the right skills and knowledge to claim belonging within elite society.

Academics avidly took up Bourdieu's concept of cultural capital, fine-tuning analyses of professionals, parents, teachers, students, and everyday consumers who convert familiarity with upper-class culture into relative social advantage. How, they wanted to know, did upper-class parents, schools, and workplaces transmit to their children, students, and employees the culturally appropriate ways of being upper-class? Varieties of the cultural capital concept flourished in sociology, alongside a proliferation of nuanced analyses of the symbolic economy of legitimate claims to status.[9]

In all of the attention to cultural capital, however, academics lost sight of the importance of displays of economic power, or, in Veblen's terms, "pecuniary might." Cultural capital is just one strategy for acquiring status. Some elites have *only* economic capital with which to seek status. In fact, Bourdieu himself noted that, for the highest strata of the wealthy classes—the "most dominant fraction of the dominant classes"—economic domination can be a strategy to compete for recognition.[10] For some, sheer economic might powers the quest for status without concern for highbrow sophistication.

Veblen saw blunt financial competition at the heart of American capitalism. But, today, our focus on the cultural aspects of distinction blinds us to escalating displays of pecuniary might all around us: in the growing size and popularity of megayachts, record prices for artwork, and extravagant birthday parties—including the notorious multimillion-dollar thirty-first birthday celebration in 2012 for Jho Low, hosted by Strategic Group's Noah Tepperberg and Jason Strauss at LAVO in Las Vegas. The party featured celebrity guests like Leonardo DiCaprio, Kanye West, and Britney Spears, who was reportedly paid six figures to burst out of his birthday cake and sing.[11]

Economists have called the rise of luxury consumption "luxury fever," a ratcheting upward of price-driven distinction resulting in an arms race for positional, or status-affirming goods.[12] These dynamics drive new markets for high-status objects like artworks and fine wines, which French theorists Luc Boltanski and Arnaud Esquerre call "exceptional objects," things that are sold by the rich to the rich and are valued mostly for the fact of their expensiveness.[13]

Luxury objects like art and wine appreciate in value the longer they are preserved; more recently, a related market in luxury experiences has emerged, predicated on the opposite process: waste. The VIP club is part of the "experience economy," in which the experience of consuming goods is more important than their possession. Since the 1990s, businesses have increasingly been advised to adopt themes and to sell not just goods and services but memorable moments to their customers; the experience itself, as well as its memory, is the product.[14]

The growing market for luxury experiences is necessary context for understanding the emergence of the VIP club, which facilitates a carefully choreographed display of waste. It is perhaps the ultimate expression of economic domination. From Saint-Tropez and St. Barts to downtown New York, big clients burn through large pools of cash in ritualized squandering: the bottle girls, the models, the "bottle trains," the shaking and spraying of champagne bottles as if they were water guns. The opposite of accruing value through the collection of things like artworks, the VIP party offers the experience and the memory of wasting money. Like casinos and luxury music festivals, the VIP party offers a stage for customers to experience ostentation. Potlatches such as these celebrate money in its pure, unconverted form: that is, money as economic domination.

You will likely not see all of the organized work it takes to mobilize rich men into ostentation, behaviors that even big spenders themselves describe as "ridiculous," even "disgusting." Depending on the context, conspicuous consumption generates not status but disdain; one need only consider journalistic critiques of elite lifestyles, as well as the way clients themselves talked with disdain about their own expenditures. VIP clubs have to enable the potlatch to unfold in a way that suspends the deliberateness of status-seeking, primarily by making it seem spontaneous and playful. It takes an enormous amount of labor to pull off a successful potlatch performance. Like any organized social form, the potlatch is a collective ritual that unfolds in carefully scripted situations; it is constituted by a shared culture of excess and the collective valorization of waste.

Rather than being frivolous and inconsequential behavior, consumption and even waste are in fact organizing principles of the global economy, argued the mid-twentieth-century philosopher Georges Bataille.[15] Every society, in one way or another, designs ways to destroy excess in a ritualized way, Bataille argued. How a society offloads its excess, or its "unproductive expenditure," shapes and reveals social relations. Spraying a bottle of champagne into the air at a VIP table is not an anomaly, but a ritual expression of our manifestly unequal society in twenty-first-century capitalism. Rituals of sacrifice, war, gladiator games, monuments, and, today, luxury retail, casinos, and nightclubs are shows of waste that are constitutive of social life; they shape our dreams and desires, and they merit careful attention.

The champagne potlatch reveals volumes about the new global leisure class and its gender and racial hierarchies. The "ownership of women," noted Veblen over a century ago, is one of the most prominent means for men to conspicuously display their status, a gendered relation of power that continues to govern the VIP scene and beyond.[16] The exclusion and devaluation of persons of color, meanwhile, characterizes VIP spaces and reveals assumptions that the elite spaces are largely white. The performance of economic domination hinges on masculine domination and white supremacy.

The champagne potlatch gestures, too, toward transformations in the lifeworld of the globally mobile elite. The VIP club has emerged in a time of both the democratization and globalization of extreme wealth. Previous generations of wealthy people were rooted in local communities where they knew each other and shared social space and social rules—think of the Brahmins of Boston and the elites in the social register of Chicago.[17] Then there was the European aristocracy and its boarding school descendants—all of those independent islands of wealth were governed by internal codes of behavior and restraint, reproduced through elaborate sets of arranged marriages. In contrast, the new elite includes Internet entrepreneurs and Russian oligarchs who are globally connected and hypermobile. They share social space and compete for social importance with Saudi princes and hedge fund titans. Within this flattened global field of wealth, elites are no longer anchored to the normative holds of local communities. They are also more anonymous. Anyone with an Amex Black Card can access the VIP party, and here, out of sight of family, neighbors, and local customs, one can act as wild as one pleases. With claims to distinction much more up for grabs, potlatching has become one of many sensible strategies for status marking in a way that would make little sense in the structured local orders prevalent only a few generations ago.

To satisfy these uniquely mobile newly rich, whole towns, islands, and local economies have transformed into centers for wasteful consumption. At VIP parties from Las Vegas to Dubai, from Miami to Cannes, you will see the rich wasting money without restraint and showcasing their economic power on a carefully curated and free-floating global stage.

In a time when elites control more and more of the world's resources, cities like New York have transformed to cater to the transient superrich, for whom the city has become a desirable destination within global circuits of business and leisure. As a result, New

Yorkers, like residents of other global cities, are living through a crisis of affluence.[18] Luxurious amenities, like upscale restaurants and entertainment, have flourished while public goods and public spaces have languished. Home prices throughout the city have soared as wealthy buyers invest in real estate only to leave prime units empty. The *New Yorker* noted in 2016 that in large parts of midtown Manhattan, almost one apartment in three sits empty for at least ten months a year, promoting some to call New York a "rich ghost town."[19] Meanwhile, middle-class families have been pushed out of a housing market where the average condo sale price in Manhattan is about two million dollars. The rate of homelessness is approaching record levels; in 2016 roughly one in five New Yorkers was living below the official poverty rate.

But the party goes on in the glamorous city and its glittering enclaves. The VIP scene reveals dynamics of value creation in the modern experience economy, in which an extremely wealthy minority benefit from, and take pleasure in, the emotional and aesthetic labor of women and marginalized men. It is "ridiculous," promoters and their rich clients agreed, that thousands of dollars of champagne are shaken and sprayed into the air, and yet, to the very important people in that carefully orchestrated moment, it feels perfectly right.

Exiting the VIP

Shortly before midnight, on a summer Tuesday evening in 2013, Dre was at his table at Club X, mingling among the models, bankers, realtors, and celebrities. It was a typical evening, full of air kisses, fist bumps, and endless glasses of champagne from comped bottles.

I had been following him for a year and a half at this point, and not much had changed in Dre's life, notwithstanding his constant talk of pending business deals. He was still using girls to cultivate connections to more powerful men.

The girls, however, changed. Many of them grew up into women with professional careers or families, or they simply got too weary of the scene, or too old to be invited out anymore. This did not pose much of a problem for Dre, since he could always replenish his supply with newcomers eager to experience his glamorous world for free. If she were pretty, thin, and tall, any girl could be his friend. Girls cycle in and out in a never-ending circuit of beauty and status that drives the luxury economy.

One can conceive of the VIP party scene as a series of complex exchanges between promoters, clients, and beautiful women. Through the scene, girls can access fabulous destinations and spend time with wealthy and famous people. Irrespective of their own socioeconomic or educational backgrounds, they are invited to mingle with some of the world's richest and most accomplished men, in exclusive settings like Saint-Tropez and the Hamptons. In exchange, girls help promoters and clients project masculine prowess. Like a kind of currency, *girl capital* can be converted by men into status, social connections, and lucrative business deals. Clients can also use girls to climb elite hierarchies by building social ties to other very important people. The economic value of girls is enormous if one considers their centrality to a network of industries spanning finance, fashion, entertainment, and urban development. Measured by the volumes of capital they generate for men, girls are priceless. But they are seen as worthless as long-term relationship partners and are largely unpaid for their work

Still, girls are compensated, and even highly so, just not in the financially lucrative ways that men in the VIP scene aimed to be. We can break down girls' motivations to participate in these arrangements into three central overlapping types: the practical, the relational, and the sensual. Concerning practical incentives, girls have basic needs such as meals, housing, and arguably entertainment, which are all rather expensive things in a city like New York, a conundrum generalizable to other young and precariously employed people living in affluent cities. VIP nightlife satisfies those needs in a "win-win" arrangement in which girls get to consume luxury amenities they otherwise couldn't afford in exchange for participation in the gendered theatrics of the VIP club. While their participation usually occurs under fairly favorable conditions, those conditions are dictated by men. Second, girls have relational motivations, such as forging friendships with promoters to facilitate meeting new friends or professional contacts in an unfamiliar city. When girls entered into such arrangements, they could experience a scale of attachment from, at the least, an obligation to repay promoters' treats, to, at the most, falling in love with them. There is a third compelling consideration that motivates girls to go out night after night under exploitative conditions of which they are often remarkably self-aware. This is the sensual motivation, through which girls seek the pleasures of "the vibe" and the ego stroke of being pretty enough to be included in it. A promoter seeks girls for whom all three motivations align: if she needs subsidized meals, if she is loyal to his friendship, and if she genuinely enjoys whatever fun can be shared in during the night, she will likely become a regular presence at his table. Lacking all three of these motivations, she is unlikely to come out at all.

For sites designed for the display and squander of money, VIP clubs undertake elaborate efforts to conceal economic exchanges. Money is front and center in the champagne potlatch, yet it is also carefully hidden in the relations between clients, clubs, promoters, and girls. Direct monetary exchanges between these groups is taboo. For clients, clubs afford them the chance to act out domination over each other and over girls' bodies, without the taboo that comes with hiring women directly, a relation that teeters dangerously close to the brink of sex work. In paying for wildly inflated prices on alcohol, clients buy the invisibility of the labor it took to bring girls to them; they pay to not have to bring girls themselves, or to pay a broker outright to procure girls. They are buying, in part, the illusion of spontaneity.

For promoters, relational strategies help to frame their ties to clients as more than economic, even as they strive to accumulate valuable social ties to businessmen in hopes of joining their business ventures. Relational work plays out night and day in the promoter's hustle to maintain a flow of gifts, sex, and friendship in order to obfuscate girls' economic value and assert themselves as something other than pimps. Promoters make visible the typically invisible privileges that disproportionately flow to beautiful women, and they reveal the benefits that men can access through their company.[20]

Looking around the room of Club X, it's easy to miss all of the labor that brings together such high volumes of beauty and money each night. As Dre worked the room, I told him I was writing a section about him in my book, and he nodded in approval.

"Because of all the people, I tell you the truth. I tell you how it is," he said, perched on the upper back of the sofa, surveying his table and the beautiful girls drinking from his bottle of champagne. He nodded at passing guests: "He's a multimillionaire. He's a *multi*millionaire. Those guys"—he pointed out three sharply dressed men in the corner—"own all the water in Serbia, or so they say; if so, that's a billion dollars. And then there's me, right in the middle of them, trying to make it."

Dre was right in one sense. Promoters indeed bridge two related economies, global finance and beauty, both at the center of New York City's booming nightlife. Mostly uneducated men, many of them non-white immigrants, promoters were keenly aware of their unlikely presence in this rich world, and they were eager to capitalize on the access to the elite that girls open up for them. But Dre was wrong in his assumption that his social capital and ties to elite businessmen would catapult him into their financial orbit. Like girls, promoters are instrumental to making the party, but full membership in the elite is closed off to them. Social closure happens when groups hoard opportunities among themselves and keep outsiders from joining.[21] Rich clients and club owners extract the benefits of girl capital while dangling dreams of joining their ranks to men like Dre. The VIP party looks like an arena in which outsiders can join elite networks, but sexist tropes and social distance mark girls and promoters as unfit for long-term relationships. Dre's rise into elite circles showed both the limits of social capital, and the frustrations of extreme wealth inequality. In this dreamworld of billionaires, his own success would always look small-time.

A few moments later, I tucked my Chanel bag under my arm and kissed Dre on each cheek, bidding him goodnight. That was my last night at Club X, which closed not long afterward.

RESEARCH APPENDIX

I began this project in 2011, by reconnecting with promoters I had met during my previous fieldwork in the fashion modeling industry. I met Dre, Thibault, and Felipe in 2004–2005, when I was a graduate student at New York University, and I saved their contact information. They texted me party and dinner invitations over the years, and I replied to thank them and to say hello periodically even after I had moved to Boston to begin my job as a sociology professor. In the summer of 2010, I began to rekindle relationships to promoters by replying to their text messages and even meeting Dre out at Club X to say hello after all those years. In 2011, I approached Dre with a request to research his world of VIP clubs, and he invited me to accompany him out to observe him at night on the condition that I did not use his real name in any publications. After a few long talks and several nights out with Dre at the Downtown and Club X in 2011, I was fascinated.

With permission from the Boston University Institutional Review Board for research with human subjects, I began to observe and interview promoters systematically in 2012 and 2013. In the winter and spring of 2012, with fellowship support from the BU Center for the Humanities, I moved back to New York and immersed myself in the scene. I got in touch again with Thibault and Felipe, who invited me to follow them, as did numerous other promoters I quickly met at clubs and through these initial contacts. I returned to Boston to resume teaching in the fall of 2012 but returned to New York regularly to see promoters on weekends, maintaining a partial foot in the field. I again moved back to New York to resume fieldwork and interviews the following summer, of 2013. I returned less frequently in 2014, and checked in on Dre and other promoters mostly by text and Facebook messages.

Over the course of roughly eighteen months between 2011 and 2013, I went out with promoters on over a hundred different nights in seventeen different clubs in New York. I frequented the Downtown on over fifteen different Sunday nights, usually with Dre but sometimes with other promoters.

I focused my initial recruitment of research subjects on promoters, because they act as brokers in the global field of clubs, women, and clients. Dre and Thibault were so well connected from years in the scene that it was easy to meet other promoters through them. In fact, I met promoters almost every night those first weeks going out and, usually, we exchanged numbers and the next day I sent them a Facebook or text message asking for an interview. Facebook and Instagram were useful tools to identify "girls" and promoters. I also got on WhatsApp to keep in touch with promoters working and living abroad, such as Santos.

I accepted invitations to VIP destinations on four occasions: five nights in Miami, with Santos (March 2012), two separate weekends in the Hamptons (June 2012, with Malcolm and Sampson; June 2013, with clients I met via Jonas), and one week in Cannes and Saint-Tropez, with Santos (July 2013). Accommodations were arranged and paid for by promoters, clubs, and clients, which is a typical arrangement for women attending VIP parties. However, unlike most other "girls," I paid for my own airfare to these destinations, to maintain greater autonomy over my flight times.

Ethnography is well suited to the observation of practices behind coordinated action like a potlatch; here, supplementary interviews were necessary to understand the surprisingly conflicted meanings participants constructed about ostentation and its underlying social relations.[1] Methodologically, I followed Margarethe Kusenbach's "go-along" method, a hybrid of interviewing and participant observation where researchers follow participants on their daily (and nightly) rounds, recording their interactions through space and their interpretations of events as they unfold in situ, as a way to study the social architecture around physical places.[2] With their permission, I recorded promoters' responses either by audio or by typed notes on my phone. I accompanied most of the forty-four promoters whom

I interviewed to their parties at least once and as frequently as ten times, sometimes visiting three or four clubs over the course of one night, which generally began at 10 p.m. with dinner free of charge and ended between 3 and 4 a.m., with occasional after-parties stretching past 8 a.m. Promoters generally welcomed my presence, since their job is chiefly to get women to hang out. In exchange for letting me shadow and interview them during the day, I dressed like a "girl" and went out with them at night, thus using my bodily capital to maneuver the access problem known in ethnography as "studying up."[3]

Copious amounts of alcohol and drugs are supplied to women free of charge in these settings. I usually held a drink during the parties, taking occasional sips to fit in, but rarely consuming enough to cloud my senses. Taking notes was easy, as everyone is constantly tapping on their phones inside clubs.

Of the forty-four promoters I interviewed, most of whom I met at clubs or through other promoters in New York, seven are transitioning or have already become owners/operators of clubs or restaurants. I also interviewed three club owners, each of whom began their careers as promoters. Interviews were sometimes conducted over the course of several days, and promoters got used to seeing me typing notes on my phone as they offered insights on our outings together. Sometimes I ducked into the bathrooms of restaurants and clubs to write down the details of conversations and observations. I invited forty-seven promoters to participate; three declined out of privacy concerns.

Reflecting the demographics of promoters, my sample is mostly men (n=39), and five women. Over half of the forty-four promoters interviewed are immigrants (n=25). They are ethnically and racially diverse; more than a third of the promoters are black, and just eight of them are white Americans. Most speak multiple languages and can converse with international clients and models. They ranged in age from twenty to forty-five years old, with an average age of thirty. Most of the promoters I interviewed, twenty-eight out of forty-four, had not attended college or did so without completing a degree. Nineteen of them described their backgrounds as poor or lower-middle-class, and only eight of them identified as from upper-middle-class or wealthy families (see table 2).

TABLE 2. Descriptives of Promoter Sample

Promoters	
Total	44
Men	39
Race and Ethnicity	
White	20
Black	19
Latino	5
Asian	5
Education	
High School Only	16
Some College	12
College	16
Class Background	
Poor	6
Lower-middle	13
Middle	17
Upper	3
Wealthy	5
Future Goals	
Owner in FNB*	19
Creative Field	9
B2B**	6
PR/Marketing	5
Real Estate	5

* Food and Beverage Industry
** Business-to-Business Dealmaking

I interviewed twenty women, whom I recruited primarily from the tables. Interviews with women focused on their relationships with promoters and clients and their careers in the scene. Among the twenty women in this sample, the average age was twenty-three. As a thirty-one- to thirty-two-year-old myself during this period, I was regularly the oldest woman at promoters' tables, but I blended in because I looked younger than my age.

I also interviewed a sample of twenty bottle clients, all in New York. Clients were the most difficult to access, even if I saw them repeatedly at parties. I might be one of two dozen women in their presence, and few opportunities arose inside clubs in which I might speak with them about my research, given the loud music. On quieter nights or if clients attended pre-party dinners, I was able to explain my research and invite them to participate in my project. I mostly recruited clients by relying on introductions from promoters and from other clients. Dre and Enrico usefully introduced me to clients as a writer, working on a book about nightlife. I focused discussions with clients on their party careers, motivations, and relationships forged in nightclubs. Among the clients in this study, the average age was forty years old; half of them worked in finance, two were cosmetic dentists, one an insurance salesman, and the rest identified as entrepreneurs. Just over half of them (eleven) were from the United States; the rest either were visiting or living permanently in New York, having arrived from various locations in South America, Asia, and Western and Eastern Europe.

I coded interview transcripts and field notes in several waves using the software Nvivo to organize the themes of these chapters, which emerged inductively over multiple rounds of reading, rereading, and listening to my recordings. As a condition of access, I have replaced all names of persons and places with pseudonyms, except when requested otherwise, and I have removed potentially identifying information.

Chapter 1. We Are the Cool People

1. Niemietz 1999.

2. See, for example, *Primetime Nightline*, "A Model Life," aired September 14, 2011, on ABC.

3. This varies according to context. For instance, in Copenhagen, a company called Cult hires young women ("Cult girls") to attend clubs to make them look good (Johnsen and Baharlooie 2013). In the States, women are hired as promoters, or "models," for alcohol and cigarette companies in clubs and bars. In Serbia, such women are called *promoterke*, literally "promoter girls." An important difference in VIP clubs is that women attend clubs without pay, though promoters they accompany are paid.

4. While some scholars (e.g., Khan 2012) conceptualize elites as those who have influence, others (e.g., Savage 2015) consider elites those who have great financial resources, i.e., "economic elites" or "wealth elites." Because "VIP" is a purchasable status, I use Savage's conceptualization of wealth elites, to indicate persons with large stores of economic capital, which typically though not necessarily come with greater social and political influence. My conceptualization of class position foregrounds the power of economic resources, as opposed to Weberian notions of status (see Savage 2015).

5. Jacobs 1999.

6. Halle and Tiso 2014.

7. On rising commercial retail rents, see Siwolop 2001.

8. As Thomas Piketty (2014) shows in *Capital in the Twenty-First Century*, the greatest wealth gap in recent decades has been not that between the 1 percenters and everyone else, but that between the 1 percenters and the 0.1 percenters. Mike Savage (2015) has made similar observations about economic inequalities among the top 1 percent of households in the UK. For an overview on difference and divergence among the elite, see Cousin, Khan, and Mears 2018. See also Freeland 2012.

9. On Studio 54, see Blum 1978. On wealth inequality trends, see Saez and Zucman 2016. See also Saez 2009.

10. According to a 2017 report by Credit Suisse; see Neate 2017.

11. Saez and Zucman 2016. On wealth disparities, see Inequality.org, n.d.

12. The rich also find increasingly inventive ways to preserve and hide their fortunes from taxation; see Harrington 2016. Most scholars working with quantitative and historical data peg the growth of inequality to a surge in very high incomes, the financialization of assets, and a relaxation in government efforts to redistribute wealth. See Lin and Tomaskovic-Devey 2013.

13. Godechot 2016; Piketty and Saez 2003. On growth of incomes, see Saez 2009.

14. Story 2008.

15. Office of the New York State Comptroller 2018.

16. Story 2008.

17. Currid 2007, p. 3.

18. On the upscaling of the Meatpacking District, see Halle and Tiso 2014, p. 11.

19. Elberse 2013.

20. Ritual champagne waste arguably originated in hip-hop club culture. The club Tunnel, home to the famous Sunday night hip-hop party "Mecca" in the early 1990s, before hip-hop music went mainstream, was among the pioneer places for customers to display champagne purchases. Famous rappers like Puff Daddy and Jermaine Dupri and other rich men would order bottles at the bar, sometimes forgoing glasses, and even gift whole bottles to strangers in the crowd. Though Tunnel didn't have tables, customers found ways to display even their empty bottles. Owner Peter Gatien recounts, "There were nights where you would have competing groups trying to see who could have more Cristal sitting on the bar." See Scarano 2012.

21. Jeffrey Jah and Mark Baker began an inexpensive form of bottle service in the club Tunnel's VIP section, charging $90 per bottle. Originally, bottle service at Tunnel was actually cost-effective for customers otherwise paying $6 a drink. Jah and Baker claim to have first seen the practice of bottle service at a club called Les Bains Douches, in Paris, during the late 1980s. See Niemietz 2006; Urken 2011. Pink Elephant owner David Sarner noted that a bottle of Grey Goose that he bought for $29 was sold for $350—a markup of more than 1,100 percent in 2006. See Milzoff 2006.

22. Wallace 2013.

23. Willett 2013.

24. Eells 2013; see also Elberse 2013.

25. Goffman 1967. Goffman defined *action* as "activities that are consequential, problematic, and undertaken for what is felt to be their own sake" (p. 185), as supplied by institutions such as casinos and other arenas for thrills. In his observations of "action," Goffman wrote that in the city's commercialized spaces of action, such as casinos, bowling alleys, amusement parks, and the taxi dance hall, the opportunity for ephemeral ennoblement abounds (Goffman 1967, p. 199), an astute description of contemporary nightclubs.

26. Cressey 1952, p. 11.

27. Veblen 1899.

28. This "leisure inequality"—unequal time for enjoyment—is evidenced by the changing ratio of work versus leisure hours. Low-educated men saw their leisure hours grow to 39.1 hours a week in 2003 from 36.6 hours in 1985. Highly educated

men saw their leisure hours shrink to 33.2 hours from 34.4 hours in that time period. However, highly educated, high-income professionals also have more control over their hours and more fulfilling work than the working poor (Attanasio, Hurst, and Pistaferri 2015).

29. As Veblen noted, conspicuous consumption is only possible in an open society that allows for social mobility. However, this societal condition also allows for the possibility that people can "fake" their status by consuming things they cannot actually afford, such as on credit. In the VIP club, clients may make extravagant purchases only to refuse payment at the end of the night, for instance by paying with a bad credit card or disputing the purchase after the fact. Payment disputes occasionally go to court in high-profile lawsuits. For instance, one Brazilian financial executive ordered $340,000 worth of champagne and liquor over two nights at the Meatpacking District club Provocateur in 2016 only to have the charges rejected by his credit card company; the dispute was resolved privately six months later after the club initiated litigation (Bekiempis 2017).

30. For a comparative analysis of urban youth culture and the embrace of hip-hop, see Warikoo 2011. On black masculinity and the embrace of especially African American hip-hop in Côte d'Ivoire, see Matlon 2016, p. 1029.

31. According to the US Federal Reserve, the 2008 economic crash destroyed 38.8 percent of the wealth held by the median American family, for whom the recovery has been slow. The wealthiest Americans, in contrast, lost far less and experienced a quick recovery and growth of their fortunes. See Harrington 2016, p. 213.

32. Roose 2014.

33. Studying the door screening process at one high-end club, Lauren Rivera observed how nightclub personnel preferred to admit more women than men as a way to manage risk and reduce potential conflicts among patrons. Rivera 2010.

34. The term "girl" came into popular usage in England in the 1880s to describe working-class and middle-class unmarried women who occupied a social space between childhood and adulthood. Imagery of the girl spread globally between the 1920s and 1930s, such as with the American flapper "It Girl," was and continues to be associated with the "frivolous" pursuits of consumption, romance, fashion (Weinbaum et al. 2008).

35. Webster and Driskell 1983.

36. Bourdieu 1986, p. 27, n. 3.

37. This is the logic of hiring attractive women in a range of settings, from Hooters and hotels to airlines. Goffman (1967, p. 198) observed that consumer spaces ranging from casinos to commercial airlines were "laid on with ambience through the display of women," including "scantily clad waitresses."

38. Wacquant 2004; Mears 2014.

39. *BlackBook* 2010. On face control in Moscow, see Yaffa 2009. In her study of doormen screening practices in a Northeastern city, Lauren Rivera (2010) described significant efforts to identify security threats, such that doormen code race and class into symbolic hierarchies corresponding to potential threats. They discriminate between dangerous and safe black men, and Latinos from South America versus Europe. Rivera found that girls are always welcome, for they pose few security

threats. At the more exclusive VIP clubs in New York, security is a major concern, but doorman are also keenly attuned to women's status signifiers, namely their bodies, clothes, and beauty. This suggests that at the upper echelons of businesses serving a primarily male clientele, women's beauty is distinctly important, consistent with historical accounts of elite leisure (e.g., Veblen 1899) and contemporary analyses of "beauty economies" (Osburg 2013).

40. May 2018. Federal lawsuits occasionally claim race discrimination against patrons in bars and restaurants; see, for instance, Balsamini 2016.

41. By bounding my analysis to the production of status in this particular global circuit, I necessarily miss others, such as in Asia and the Gulf States, where large pools of capital are increasingly concentrated and racial exclusion dynamics likely differ. On racial bias against white foreigners in Asia, see Farrer and Field 2015 on Shanghai nightlife; see Hoang 2015 on Ho Chi Minh City nightlife. There are also many distinct and overlapping party circuits in New York that cater to specific scenes of primarily black, Asian, or young "hipster" customers, each with their own local hierarchies and capitals. For example, see Thornton 1995 on club dynamics in the youth underground club scene in London.

42. Wright and Hope 2018

43. Wright and Hope 2018, pp. 253, 267.

44. PageSix.com Staff 2009.

45. Battan 2016.

46. On the variable meanings of zero-priced goods, see McClain and Mears 2012.

47. Cultural capital refers to embodied dispositions, correlated to class, that emit lifestyle markers, such as clothing, posture, body type, and mannerisms; see Bourdieu 1986.

48. Goffman 1959, pp. 151–53.

49. Giuffre and Williams 1994; Spradley and Mann 1974.

50. Marquee club owner Jason Strauss noted, "We make an effort to develop our own promoters, but as they get more successful, it ends up costing the club more money . . . We create monsters." Elberse 2013, p. 258.

51. Elberse 2013, p. 255: "Revenues for Marquee NYC even trended upward in its first years, from just under $10 million in 2004 to more than $15 million, and a net of around $2.5 million, three years later." See also S. Evans 2010; McIntyre 2015; and Nightclub & Bar Staff, n.d.

52. Elberse, Barlow, and Wong 2009.

53. Tao Group, n.d. See also Elberse, Barlow, and Wong 2009.

54. Elberse 2013.

55. Additionally, the rise of EDM clubs in Vegas has brought hoteliers greater profits than their casinos, transforming Vegas entertainment and profitability (Eells 2013). On the rise of Vegas as a luxury entertainment destination, see Al 2017.

56. Nightclub & Bar Staff, n.d. 2015; McIntyre 2015.

57. Eells 2013.

58. Sky 2014.

59. Harrington 2016, pp. 114–17.

60. For ethnographic accounts of the Hamptons, see Dolgon 2005; on Aspen, see Park and Pellow 2011; Elias 2008.

61. Cousin and Chauvin 2013.

62. For example, one of the most popular private plane routes is between Moscow and the Cote d'Azur, in the south of France (Fox 2015). On elite mobilities through and in "fast" spaces, see Beaverstock, Hubbard, and Short 2004, pp. 402–6. In a parallel case, the art world and its wealthy patrons materialize in a global circuit of events from Art Basel in Miami to the Venice Biennial. Such "scenes" are physical manifestations of subculture rooted in locally based social interaction (Silver and Clark 2016).

63. With globalization and the decoupling of state and citizenship, the wealthy have become globally dispersed and hypermobile and segregated (Hay and Muller 2012). For more on elite mobilities, see Birtchnell and Caletrío 2013.

64. Elliott 2017.

65. Wallace 2013.

66. The globally mobile party scene is part of what Mimi Sheller and John Urry (2006, p. 200) have described as touristic mobility characteristic of late capitalism, evident in the movement of people to places like "good beaches, clubs, views, walks, mountains, unique history, surf, music scene, historic remains, sources of good jobs, food, landmark buildings, gay scene, party atmosphere, universities and so on."

This is not to assume that the VIP party scene I studied is representative of all global clubbing experiences. I do not aim to generalize to nightlife scenes globally. Though this case spans disparate locations in an international party circuit, its participants disproportionately live and work in New York, and my findings are US- and Western-centric. US sociologists have long written unreflexively about the American context as though their country were not parochial or particular. The fact that whiteness was so highly valued in the spaces I studied—and that blackness was so problematic—suggests one important and potentially unique feature of American cultural logics in operation here that may operate differently in other contexts. For instance, James Farrer and Andrew Field's (2015) research on clubbing in Shanghai points to the rapid decline in the value of whiteness exactly during the time in which the VIP clubbing model arose in that city to cater to mostly Asian elites. On changing hierarchies of racialized masculinities in Vietnam, see Hoang 2015.

Even with these limitations, the international VIP party circuit is a valuable case not so much as a study of global nightlife, but as a case to empirically examine dynamics of waste and wealth, following Thorstein Veblen's (1899) classic analysis. Other in-depth qualitative studies of clubbing and leisure in non-US and non-Western settings echo my findings especially on the staged nature of conspicuous consumption, the uses of women's bodies to signal men's status, and men's struggles to position themselves vis-à-vis each other. See, e.g., Osburg 2013.

67. Urry 2010, p. 2016; see also Davis and Monk 2007 for a discussion of neoliberal dreamworlds around the world.

68. For a discussion of how to incorporate race and gender analyses in studies of elites, see Cousin, Khan, and Mears 2018.

69. Hay and Miller 2012, pp. 77–78. For an in-depth study of upper-class retreats and how they foster social cohesiveness among the American business elite, see Domhoff 1975.

70. For exceptions, see Bruno and Salle 2018 on Saint-Tropez; Cousin and Chauvin 2013 on St. Barts; Domhoff 1975 on the private club camping grounds Bohemian Grove in Northern California; Elias 2008 on Aspen.

71. Social closure, according to Max Weber ([1922] 1978, pp. 43–46, 339–48, 926–55), occurs wherever the competition for a livelihood creates groups interested in reducing that competition. These exclusions may be based on any convenient or visible characteristic, including race, social background, language, religion, and gender (p. 342), although with the passage of formal legal protections over the twentieth century, exclusion based on ascribed criteria has been replaced by exclusion based on "individualistic" criteria such as educational credentials, knowledge, or property ownership (Collins 1979).

Chapter 2. Daytime

1. Jacobs (1961) 1992, p. 68. Jacobs further suggested that the social structure of sidewalk life depended in part on the engagement of self-appointed public characters.

2. The five women promoters I interviewed were regulars going out in the scene or had ready access to pretty girls. See Chapter 5.

3. See chap. 1, n. 21.

4. In the words of labor scholars, promoters are performing aesthetic and affective labor all the time; they are "always on," even when not working in the clubs, ostensibly during their time off (Entwistle and Wissinger 2006).

5. Being at ease among elites is a hallmark of privilege, argued Shamus Khan (2011). Promoters like Enrico would thus have an advantage in integrating with upper-class clients with whom he shares cultural similarities, compared to promoters like Sampson. However, because both he and Sampson are working with newly rich and mostly young clientele, such advantages seemed not to translate into big differences in their opportunities in the clubs.

Chapter 3. The Potlatch

1. See Bourdieu (1998) 2001.

2. Boaz 1921. See also Graeber 2001, pp. 203–4.

3. Mauss (1954) 1990, p. 74; see also Graeber 2001, p. 260.

4. Boas's (1921) original interpretation was that potlatch generated status to advance a noble's rank; see also Graeber 2001, pp. 188–210. Within anthropology, there are several competing explanations for why potlatch existed, but perhaps the strongest challenge to Boas's original, status-focused interpretation has come from ecological anthropologists who proposed that potlatching was primarily redistributive: the gifting ritual provided a form of social insurance against local hardship, such as the occasional failed salmon run (Suttles 1960). However, the

results of empirical tests of the ecological thesis have been inconsistent (Wolf 1999, pp. 117–18). There seems to be consensus that potlatch was mostly, if not entirely, a status-generating ritual. On slave sacrifice as potlatch, see Bataille (1949) 1988, pp. 45–61. On big-men, see Sahlins 1963.

5. Mauss (1954) 1990. In fact, Mauss interpreted Boas's observations as evidence for his theory of general exchange, but anthropologists have since critiqued this as an overgeneralization, since the potlatch was a highly variable practice with internal logic specific to local context (see Wolf 1999).

6. Sahlins 1963, pp. 289–91.

7. Graeber 2001, p. 203.

8. The Canadian government disagreed, outlawing potlatches from the late nineteenth century until 1951, in an attempt to curb what they saw as natives' economically irrational behavior.

9. Quinones 2015; see also Rossman 2017.

10. Quinones 2015, p. 261.

11. See, e.g., Hoang 2015.

12. Osburg 2013.

13. *Rich Kids of Instagram*, or *RKOI*, was a Tumblr blog of curated public images of wealthy people's consumption habits, largely selfies of young people from around the world. See therkoi.com.

14. On Dutch wealth, see Schama (1987) 1997; on Silicon Valley, see Sengupta 2012; on rich New Yorkers, see Sherman 2017.

15. Like any metaphor, the potlatch has limitations, and there are of course substantial differences between the champagne potlatch and the Pacific Northwest tribal one. The nineteenth-century potlatches that Boas observed were mostly somber affairs characterized by restraint in food and drink consumption. Another difference for VIP partygoers is that they face almost no political consequences for social hierarchy in the long term, even as their performances reach amplified audiences via social media. Despite these differences, in considering the VIP wasting ritual as potlatch-like, we gain important insights into the dramaturgy of waste and the interaction rituals through which waste produces status. For an overview of interaction rituals, see R. Collins 2004.

16. For example, renovating Marquee New York City cost nearly $3.5 million (Elberse 2013, p. 254). Provocateur, in downtown New York, was a $5 million investment, designed to be the "most luxurious" of VIP clubs in the city (Gray 2010).

17. According to Anita Elberse (2013, p. 257), top spinners like Avicii could command as much as $10 million for a high-profile Las Vegas nightclub residency. See also LeDonne 2014.

18. Elevated seating is a frequent marker of status. In an eclectic example, Wesley Shrum and John Kilburn (1996) analyzed the spatial arrangements of New Orleans' Mardi Gras parties, and found that masked float-riders only throw gifts of beads downward to persons below, an arrangement they call the "command paradigm," a physical emblem of hierarchical class relations.

19. Restaurant & Bar Design Staff 2015.

20. Guy 2003, pp. 10–18.

21. On champagne, wine experts agree that bubbles bring joy and are "magical" (Bell 2015).

22. Cousin and Chauvin 2013, p. 198, n. 8.

23. Goffman (1967, p. 207) notes, quoting Hemmingway, that "Bullfighting is worthless without rivalry."

24. The role of rivalry and one-upmanship has many anthropological antecedents, most prominently the cock fight in Balinese culture documented by Clifford Geertz (1973, chap. 15).

25. On potlatch destruction by fire, see Mauss (1954) 1990, p. 114.

26. Vankin and Donnelly 2011.

27. Hip-hop music plays an important role in these venues, even as the popularity of electronic music and superstar DJs has driven the expansion of nightclubbing. Girls, promoters, and clients are likely familiar with the genre and its prevalent discourses of striving to succeed, escaping poverty, and "bling," or consumption fantasies (see Watson 2016, p. 190).

28. See Buckley 2012.

29. Jho Low, with his brother, in fact spent about 2 million euros, or $2.6 million, at the club Les Caves in Saint-Tropez in July 2010, winning a bottle war against Winston Fischer, a member of a prominent New York family in the real estate industry. Low's total bill was announced by the DJ at the end of the competition (PageSix.com Staff 2010).

30. Stuyvesant 2009.

31. MDMA, or "Molly," is a form of the synthetic psychoactive drug ecstasy, which has properties of both a stimulant and a hallucinogen. Typically ingested as a pill, or by mixing the powder in a drink, MDMA produces feelings of high energy and euphoria.

32. The pleasures of being at a club with promoters can yield intense highs, as described in studies of cultural consumption (Benzecry and Collins 2014).

33. Tutenges 2013.

34. Durkheim (1912) 2001, pp. 283–5.

35. Tutenges 2013.

36. In his ethnography of opera consumption, Claudio Benzecry (2011, pp. 39–62) likewise finds that the opera fan describes his sensation of emotional uplift to the music as though he's falling in love, or losing himself to the crowd of his fellow opera devotees.

37. Tutenges 2013.

38. Shrum and Kilburn 1996. This is another organizational challenge to the club, to facilitate certain kinds of transgressions—wild dancing, shouting, wasting huge sums of money—while keeping others in check, like vandalism and fighting. Physically imposing security personnel survey the room to clamp down on dangerous emotional energies, while the club provides some symbols to channel other, more positive, crowd energies.

39. Mauss (1954) 1990.

40. Murray 1984.

41. Max Weber (1930) famously linked the Protestant virtues of restraint, reinvestment, and worldly asceticism to the development of modern capitalism. On the belief in equality and social discomfort with hierarchy, see Khan 2011; Sherman 2017. Researching an elite boarding school, Shamus Khan (2011) found that students from privileged backgrounds truly believed that they deserved their place among the elite because of the sheer force of their individual efforts. On the discomfort with entitlement and economic inequality among the upper-class homeowners in New York, see Sherman 2017.

42. Rossman 2014, p. 53.

43. Sherman 2017, pp. 92–122.

44. On the social meanings of money see Zelizer 1994; on the meanings of money derived from work, see Delaney 2012. On social characterizations of prices and the people who pay high and low prices, see Wherry 2008.

45. James Farrer and Andrew Field (2015, pp. 76–83), for instance, describe the transformation of nightclubbing in Shanghai from a scene that valued white customers for their perceived economic superiority, in the 1990s, to one that catered mostly to rich Asians. While white women may have a novelty value in some clubs in Asia still, they do not represent a hegemonic form of sexual currency such as that described in this ethnography. Likewise, Hoang 2015 (pp. 131–38), documents how white Western women's bodies are explicitly devalued in high-end clubs in Ho Chi Minh City.

46. Sociologists have identified nightlife as a resource for lower-income participants, a chance to make social connections and gain access to job leads and even childcare contacts in the "nightly round" at clubs (Hunter 2010). My fieldwork revealed the importance of nightlife for building ties to and among economic elites, as well, though less so for girls in the scene.

47. *The Star* 2010.

48. Status is a function of a person's positioning vis-à-vis other actors, including in terms of the number and prestige of those around him. See Podolny 2005.

49. I heard this often as a graduate student when I researched the fashion modeling industry and its curious practice of paying male models lower rates than women for the same jobs. Agency owners and designers reasoned that women are paid more because, quite simply, "sex sells." See Mears 2011, p. 226.

50. The historian Abigail Solomon-Godeau (1986) has argued, following French feminist theorist Luce Irigaray ([1977] 1985), that femininity and commodities merged together as desirable objects over the course of the nineteenth century in Europe with the rise of visual culture. The first pictures to be widely circulated were engraved lithographs, a fair share of them erotically charged images of women in public view, like coquettes on Paris streets; then came pinups, nudes, demimondaines, fashion plates, and underground illegal pornography. As erotic images of femininity bloomed, they pushed out the male body as a visual object that had been the dominant ideal for centuries. Male bodies in painting and on ballet stages drew less and less attention, pushed to the background as secondary props to the female form.

Meanwhile, European and American cities flush with new industrial money developed arcades, promenades, and eventually department stores featuring the open display of goods. These new public spaces of leisure and consumption flourished especially as the nascent advertising industry stoked desire for new products. All of these historic developments reinforced a visual culture premised on appearance, display, exposure, and spectacle. The simultaneous emergence of the public display of women and the display of goods solidified and structured attention into one and the same thing: commodity fetishism. Irigaray ([1977] 1985) has argued that femininity is both emblem and lure of the commodity, such that the feminine image operates as a conduit and mirror of desire. This close historic relation between feminine eros and commodities helps to explain why women's bodies are so centrally displayed to compel the consumption of things, literally anything, from cigarettes to cheeseburgers. Arguably, femininity does even further work in nightclubs, to sublimate homosexual desire and confirm the assumption that heterosexual men desire femininity.

51. Mulvey 1989.

52. Lise Sanders (2006) notes that the shopgirl emerged as an important cultural figure in the nineteenth century, just as labor forms were shifting from the sweaty manual laborer to a genteel employee in retail, who was supposed to be above working-class labor. With her softness of both body and manners, the shopgirl was integral to the display culture of the department store, a new consumer space that opened up both the public desirability of commodities and the public availability of women's bodies for men's spectatorship. However, working conditions in the department stores were physically and emotionally grueling, as documented by Annie Marion MacLean, who published an early ethnographic account of working as a shopgirl in a store's toy department, published in 1899 in the *American Journal of Sociology*. "It was an openly acknowledged fact among the girls," wrote MacLean (1899, p. 736), "that the paths of dishonor were traversed to supplement their small incomes . . . Lecherous men were always around ready to offer aid. They came, professedly, to buy, but it was not the wares of the store they wanted. The young and pretty girls yielded most easily. They would weep, sometimes, and say: 'Good people look down on us. But they don't know—they don't know. We have to earn our living.'"

53. Bailey 1998, p. 151.

54. See chap. 1, n. 37. In what it is now called *aesthetic labor* by sociologists, companies in the service industries hire workers that have the right personalities and the right appearances to sell their brand. Aesthetic labor is gendered and sexualized, because businesses use women's bodies specifically to sell their services, most obviously to attract male consumers to places like Hooters, a restaurant renowned for scantily clad waitresses serving chicken wings. In addition to uniforms, companies commodify sexualized female bodies by positioning women to attract a male gaze in offices (Gottfried 2003), or by encouraging women to give off the impression of being heterosexually available, for instance in the tourism sector (Adkins 1995). Indeed, for women, there is a blurry distinction between aesthetic and sexualized labor (Warhurst and Nickson 2009). Employers seek out particular

types of women's bodies because they signify distinction; for instance, tall and svelte women add value, or "feminine capital," in luxury hotels (Otis 2011).

55. Salmon 2015.

56. Similarly, Erving Goffman (1969) described various urban nightspots as offering vicarious teases that reinvigorate fantasy, such as a women's skimpy dress, which lays the basis for action that is very likely not going to lead to sexual action occurring. The club too affords a "vicarious tease" (p. 269) of a sizable magnitude.

57. I learned later that Santos was stressed by potential economic losses. When he failed to show up at a clients' after-party as promised, he was told he wouldn't be paid about $2,000. "I said I'd have ten girls, now I have five, and my girls go and hang at the table with another promoter, so I lost the client. I'm not gonna get paid. All the tickets and investments, it cost me $4,000 to organize . . . It's harmful, too, for me, later on, because of this."

Over the next couple of days in Miami, Santos's financial situation grew more dire. He had a habit of giving any surplus money in his bank account to his family back home in Colombia. ("What am I gonna do with $3,000?" he rhetorically asked; for instance, when his mom is calling him for money, or when he knows his grandmother needs medication. "I'm not gonna keep $3,000 in my account for my ego.") By the middle of his stay in Miami, he was out of cash, still awaiting his payment from the clubs, and since he didn't own a credit card, Tanya began paying for our lunch and even a last-minute stay at a hotel, when he had to vacate the Star Island villa with no place to go.

Chapter 4. Trafficking at Model Camp

1. Dolgon 2005, p. 1–13.

2. While the Hamptons are regularly associated with economic elites, this collection of hamlets and villages is in fact a mix of working-class residents and immigrant laborers, and historically the land has been mired in class and ethnic struggle between Native Indians and white newcomers. However, the class, immigrant, and ethnic diversity described by sociologist Corey Dolgon (2005) goes relatively unseen by the upper-class tourists and part-time residents.

3. Men's dominance seeped into every aspect of VIP club culture, including the ways men talked about women as prey to be conquered, or as objects to be collected, akin to infamous pick-up artists. In fact, two clients recommended I read Neil Strauss's *The Game: Penetrating the Secret Society of Pickup Artists*, a 2005 book that explains how to pick up women, widely criticized for its predatorial and dehumanizing approach to women. One client described his style of talking to women as using "Jedi mind tricks." Another praised the lessons he learned from reading *Some Girls: My Life in a Harem*, Jillian Lauren's 2010 memoir about living in the harem of the prince of Brunei and his psychological games of attention and rejection. Then there was Dre, who claimed to ignore specific girls in order to "break" their confidence so they would give in to sex with him more easily. Much of this talk was just that, ritualized talk, much like "girl watching," that collective male ritual of appraising women for their looks (Quinn 2002), and "girl hunting" (Grazian 2007a),

the collective male sport of pursuing women for hookups. However, in Dre's case, I observed in practice at the Downtown how he in fact ignored particular women in order to spur their interest.

But talk and ritual can have profound significance for the social order. David Grazian, a sociologist who examined his undergraduate students' experiences in nightlife in Philadelphia, observed that the "girl hunt" looks like men's efforts to get sex, whereas it is in fact a homosocial ritual college men play with each other to heighten their own performance of masculinity (2007a, p. 224). Similarly, sociologist Beth Quinn (2002) argues that girl watching functions as a form of gendered play among men. This play is productive of masculine identities and premised on a studied lack of empathy with the feminine other.

In the VIP world, girls bolstered men's claims to hegemonic masculinity; that is, to be a powerful, heterosexually successful, and dominant man (see also Spradley and Mann 1974, for a classic study of cocktail waitressing). Masculinity is never a static identity, but rather must be constantly reclaimed (Connell 1995). Girls provide the stage for men to display their heterosexuality and assert their dominance and masculinity. Even if the men don't have sex with girls, even if they don't talk with the girls, men get to perform their dominance over women. A man's male peers are the intended audience for competitive games of sexual reputation and peer status and public displays of situational dominance, as well as a means by which a certain type of masculinity is produced and heterosexual desire displayed (Bird 1996).

4. Goffman 1967, 149–280. Nightclubs and bars are so heavily sexualized that sociologists call them "sexual marketplaces" (e.g., Grazian 2007b, p. 142; Laumann et al. 2004).

5. In Asian markets, sex work is deeply intertwined with deal-making. Hostess and karaoke clubs help men to forge connections, symbolic debts and credits, and reputation and, ultimately, to seal business deals (Osburg 2013). In Ho Chi Minh City, sociologist Kimberly Hoang (2015) found, the beauty of sex workers in hostess clubs was central to Vietnamese men's pitches to investors. In Japan in the 1980s, anthropologist Anne Allison has shown, hostess clubs were vital to boosting masculine identity and morale among corporate salarymen, and upholding a system of male-controlled capitalism (1994). On the role of gentlemen's clubs in forging business deals, see Llewellyn Smith 2006; for an academic treatment, see Mobley and Humphreys 2006.

6. The American journalist and magazine editor H. L. Mencken (1919, p. 72), writing on Thorstein Veblen's *The Theory of the Leisure Class*, asked: "Do I prefer kissing a pretty girl to kissing a charwoman because even a janitor may kiss a charwoman—or because the pretty girl looks better, smells better and kisses better?" But Mencken's critique points to the challenge of untangling motivations and meanings from behaviors: we often have multiple and poorly understood reasons for liking the things that we like.

7. In her study of wealth managers, Brooke Harrington (2016, pp. 92–105) found a similar concern to project a sense of belonging among elite social worlds.

8. Bogardus 1933.

9. Elberse 2014.

10. Weinbaum et al. 2008, p. 9.

11. Gebhart 1929.

12. While a dressmaker named Gagelin is credited as the first to have employed a house mannequin to walk around the premises of his salon modeling shawls, Charles Frederic Worth increased the number of house mannequins available to try on dresses for clients (C. Evans 2001).

13. Latham 2000; Sanders 2006.

14. When John Robert Powers opened the first modeling agency in New York, in 1923, he steered this ambivalence with clever marketing. His models were called "Powers Girls" and they had to keep to strict professional standards, like no drinking in public, and they carried makeup and accessories in uniform hat boxes, a mark of feminine refinery (De Marly 1980; Entwistle and Wissinger 2012, p. 140).

15. Similarly, on college campus, women draw symbolic boundaries between "good girls" and "sluts," a distinction that supposedly signifies sexual behavior but is, in fact, largely determined by women's class positions and correlated status groups. In a five-year study of college women at a Midwestern public university, sociologists found that working-class and poor college women were deemed "slutty" because they lacked upper-class markers of femininity, e.g., they lacked the right clothes and makeup, even though upper-class women had more sexual partners (Armstrong et al. 2014).

16. Among the twenty girls I interviewed, twelve of them were in professional jobs or studying in college, and the remaining eight were models or part-time retail workers looking for modeling agencies.

17. Contrary to the popular belief that women with beauty can "marry up," upper-class men tend to marry similarly privileged women. Since the 1980s, the earnings of husbands and wives have converged, with high-earning men increasingly coupled with similarly high-earning women (Graf and Schwartz 2010; Schwartz 2010). For demography work on homogamy in assortative mating, see Mare 2016.

18. All but four of the twenty clients I interviewed said that they did not expect to form a long-term relationship with girls they met in the VIP scene, though half of them had in fact dated girls they met in clubs.

19. Horowitz 2016. When Paolo Zampolli, now a United Nations ambassador of Dominica (by appointment), held his high-profile birthday party at the exclusive club Provocateur in 2011, in attendance were celebrities, moguls, and Arab royalty. Zampolli 2011.

20. Quoted in Lee 2015.

21. Regardless of her actual class positon, a woman's performance of class position was central to these assessments of her virtue and potential. That is, the perception of women's class, marked in her manners and cultural capital, guided men in determining whether she had superior morality, manners, and resources. On the close coupling of class and women's perceived virtue, see Bettie 2003.

22. Bruno and Salle 2018. On the transformation of Saint-Tropez into a seasonal playground for the global elite, see Bruno and Salle 2018.

23. The ordeal of Rachel Uchitel, a club hostess who became well known for servicing Tiger Woods in New York, popularized the sexualized demands on women who work in high-end nightclubs. See Taddeo 2010.

24. On the sexualization of cocktail waitresses, see Spradley and Mann 1974. Additionally, there are symbolic links among nonwhite bodies, voluptuous bodies, and perceived sexual availability, for instance in the ways that nonwhite women have been represented as more sexually exotic (Mears 2010).

25. Conti 2014.

26. For most of the history of the world, men and women married *solely* for economic reasons, and mostly a union came down to a man's explicit ability to provide for his wife. Sometimes this contractual obligation was explicit, as when a man secured his wife by paying a dowry to her patriarchal family. Marriage was always an economic arrangement. While it may have led to love later on, love was hardly its precondition (Coontz 2005, pp. 15–23). The idea of a woman marrying primarily for economic reasons turned unsavory against the emerging ideal of the "pure" relationship, unspoiled by economic interests (Illouz 2007). Over the course of the twentieth century, idealized intimate relationships were those rooted in equality, open communication, and sexual pleasure, while instrumental matches would come to be maligned as inauthentic, the purview of gold diggers and trophy wives.

27. As the practice of "treating" women emerged in American cities, in the early twentieth century, and before it transformed into what we know as modern dating culture, journalists, crusaders, and police all grappled to differentiate between "working girls" on the streets (that is, prostitutes) and charity girls—young women who accepted men's treats in exchange for intimacies. Charity girls were morally distinct from prostitutes because they didn't take money, but subject to critiques of sexual immorality because they capitalized on intimacy or the potential for it. Records from the New York City vice squad in 1913 recount an investigation of a popular working-class nightclub frequented by women identified as "near whores" or "whores in the making" and "professional prostitutes," all types of women who were compensated for their intimacy in various ways (Clemens 2006, p. 1).

Scholars now describe "treating" and "sugar" relationships as "compensated dating," a practice of exchanging intimacy for some material compensation (Swader et al. 2013). There are multiple ways to make sense of transactional sex, which vary depending on local cultural contexts and women's structural constraints. Transactional sex is a routine part of both courtship and women's economic survival in many societies; for instance, gifts for sex are widespread in present-day Malawi (Poulin 2007).

28. Parreñas 2011.

29. Such labeling of women as "good girls" or "party girls" reflects a system of social status ranking. As Elizabeth Armstrong and Laura Hamilton (2015) argue in their study of college women, men play a critical role in establishing women's rankings by rewarding particular femininities. Women, they show, also sexually evaluate

and rank each other. Thus, femininities are never wholly derivative of masculinities, and women do not passively accept criteria established by men. See also Waller 1937 for a foundational statement.

30. Hakim 2010.

31. Bourdieu 1984, p. 193. While such marriages imply exchange, classically the trade of men's money for women's beauty, they may in fact be based on other logics of matching; the importance of men's looks and women's success, for instance, has been overlooked in past research (McClintock 2014). Prior to the mid-twentieth century, the norm was that people married horizontally, within their ascribed class—the one they were born into—and from their same geographic location, while prioritizing economic, not romantic, sensibilities (Coontz 2005, pp. 15–23).

32. Mare 2016; Schwartz 2010.

33. Paula England and Elizabeth McClintock (2009, p. 814) found that the older men are when they marry, the more years senior to their brides they are, whether it is a first or any other marriage. The authors argue that because the prevailing standards of beauty favor young women, the older men are when they marry, the less they find women their own age attractive relative to younger women. Starting at thirty-five years of age, and increasing with each year, a woman's probability of being single is significantly greater than a man's (p. 807).

34. Sontag 1972.

35. This suggests that nightclubs, while a source of opportunities for men such as promoters and clients, do not offer a pathway to crack into business networks. This is on top of the well-documented exclusions of women (and persons of color) from powerful financial business circles (see, e.g., Ho 2009; Roth 2006). Hedge funds, in particular, emphasize socializing and loyalty via patrimonial networks that exclude women and nonwhites (Tobias 2018).

36. While it can very fun to participate as a girl in the VIP scene, those thrills are cheap in relation to the vast and fungible sums generated by corporate nightclub companies like Strategic Group.

37. In Pierre Bourdieu's (1984, p. 328) terms, nightlife offered a "heretical mode of acquisition" of cultural-capital acquisition; that is, it exposed people from lower-class backgrounds to some aspects of upper-class lifestyles, but, as "non-certified cultural capital" gained from experience in elite leisure space rather than true upbringing via elite institutions, this could lead to the acquisition of disjointed or unpredictable tastes that could potentially always be recognized by true elites as illegitimate. On non-certified cultural capital, see Lise Bernard's (2012) study of real estate brokers, who also come from diverse social backgrounds but gain more reliable familiarity with upper-class buyers and their tastes.

38. Since Pierre Bourdieu (1986) expanded the concept of capital beyond human capital to account for the cultural foundations of class inequality, new concepts of cultural capital have proliferated. Some are in response to changes in the world, like changing class structure and, hence, are emergent forms of cultural capital (Prieur and Savage 2013), while others are efforts to understand specific fields, like sexual capital (Martin and George 2006), or the role of the body in carrying forms of

capital, from aesthetic (Anderson et al. 2010), bodily (Wacquant 1995), and physical capital (Shilling 2012). Marx's concern with capital accumulation centered on owners and the unequal extraction of value, yet in sociology's accumulation of forms of capital (Neveu 2013), there is a relative absence of attention to appropriation and ownership. The case of the VIP scene illustrates the importance of attending to appropriation in the study of capital: here, men and women unequally profit from women's embodied symbolic capital, or *girl capital*, for short. Men use girl capital to generate status and social connections in an exclusive world of businessmen, but girls have difficulty leveraging their own bodily capital to the same extent.

39. Using sex appeal and "erotic capital" may in fact exacerbate women's exclusion from masculine realms, which tend to be more authoritative, higher status, and better paid. For example, Heidi Gottfried, in her study of temp work firms, found the primacy of women's bodies made them suitable as frontline workers, but this association with embodiment hindered their chances in managerial positions (2013). My findings here suggest that perceptions of sexual virtue are another way that opportunities become closed to women with "erotic capital."

Furthermore, approaching beauty as a form of capital, as Catherine Hakim (2011) does, exemplifies a neoliberal philosophy of the personal imperative for self-investment but disregards systemic power relations that unequally distribute bodily capital across populations (for a critique of Hakim's work, see Green 2013). By keeping the focus on capital as a personal asset with individual outcomes, this perspective embraces the imperative for self-investment that is assumed to lead to better "marriage market" outcomes, paradigmatic of neoclassical economists' human capital theory. Such arguments, however, rely on the assumption that the primary value of someone's embodied capital resides with the capital holder herself. In the VIP club, women's beauty is worth more in men's hands than in women's own, given the cultural penalties on strategic women. By considering appropriation and ownership, sociologists can move away from analyses of capital as personal advantage, to consider how systems of power relations enable value accumulation from bodily resources that are not one's own (See Mears 2015b).

40. That women perform unpaid domestic work is, argue Marxist feminists, an exploitative arrangement necessary for the reproduction of workers in a capitalist system (Federici [1975] 2012).

41. For an overview of display work and its proliferation across the labor market, especially for women workers, see Mears and Connell 2016.

42. In sociological terms, we could call this a "gender strategy" that girls enact, consenting to the appropriation of their feminine bodily capital in order to access worlds that men control, because, like Katia, they believe in the value and pleasures of being a part of those worlds. For parallels in Greek life and college women's consent to being used by fraternity men, see Hamilton 2007.

43. Rubin (1975) 1997.

44. Here, Rubin ([1975] 1997), pp. 34–39) draws from the anthropology of Lévi-Strauss (1969).

45. On US financial industries and the role of strip clubs, see Mobley and Humphreys 2006. On dealmaking in Asian markets, see Allison 1994; Hoang 2015; Osburg 2013.

46. Blair 2010.

47. Hanser 2008, p. 106; see also Otis 2011; Warhurst and Nickson 2001, 2009.

48. As "sign-bearing" capital, Beverley Skeggs (2004, p. 22) argues, women are a gender and class resource that men appropriate. Because men are the majority shareholders and owners of companies in the service and sex industries, profits accumulate disproportionately to men (see also Mears and Connell 2016). For an empirical example of the structural inequalities in the stripping industry, see Sanders and Hardy 2012.

49. On "little sisters," see Martin and Hummer 1989, pp. 466–69. This system of trafficking women through fraternity houses is not without risks to the women. In a five-year longitudinal study of college women at a "party school," the sociologists Elizabeth A. Armstrong and Laura T. Hamilton observed that on Friday nights, fraternity men sent large SUVs to women's dorms to offer one-way rides to their parties (Hamilton 2007, p. 153). Hamilton and Armstrong (2015) found that working-class women who joined the frat scene faced greater risks of sexual disrespect and academic derailment. The more popular they were at frat parties, the worse their financial and educational futures looked.

50. Rubin 1975 (1997).

51. Choosing to be an object necessitates subjecthood and the enactment of agency. Post-structuralist feminist theory reconsidered sites that had been previously conceptualized in terms of their oppressive conditions for women, for instance sex work, as spaces of negotiation and potential female empowerment. For an analysis of women in sex work as shrewd agents, see Hoang 2015.

52. Odell 2013.

53. Here I draw from Eva Illouz's (2017) analysis of the heterosexual bargain in popular culture narratives.

54. Sociologist Susan Ostrander (1984) described a similar kind of patriarchal bargain in her interview study with upper-class women. These women had married wealthy men and put their own careers on hold to tend to their families and support their husbands' careers. They accepted their subordinate gender positions to access class privilege relative to other women and men.

Chapter 5. Who Runs the Girls?

1. Barrionuevo 2010.

2. Sociologist Viviana Zelizer (2012) has outlined "relational work" as the efforts people expend to match interpersonal relations with economic transactions.

3. On sex work, see Bernstein 2007 on the girlfriend experience and Hoang 2011 on varieties of relationships among different types of sex work in the class hierarchy, from high-end hostess workers to street-level prostitutes.

4. For a theoretical treatment of strategic intimacies, see Mears 2015b. Beyond sex work and romantic intimacies, strategic intimacies can apply to realms where people try to capitalize on their intimate exchange partners, most obviously in cases like "sugar dating" or "compensated dating" (Swader et al. 2013), but such dynamics appear also in the electronics industry, where seller firms give gifts to construct obligations among potential buyer firms (see Darr 2003).

5. Ellis and Hicken 2016a.

6. Ellis and Hicken 2016b.

7. Mears 2011, pp. 64–69.

8. Ziff 2014.

9. Barrionuevo 2010.

10. Darr and Mears 2017, pp. 4–5.

11. Mauss (1954) 1990. On potlatch, the anthropologist Georges Bataille ([1949] 1988, pp. 70–71) argues that giving a gift looks like a loss, but that outdoing another bestows the giver with a power over the recipient: "He is now rich for having ostentatiously consumed what is wealth only if it is consumed." In other words, gifting confers rank upon the one who has the last word. Squandering gives prestige.

12. Mauss (1954) 1990.

13. As Michel Callon (1998, pp. 13–15) notes, whether or not an item given is understood as a quid pro quo or as a gift depends on how the exchange is framed and, crucially, when the transaction occurs. If enough time passes after the gifting, the obligation to reciprocate, while still very real, goes unnoticed and "amnesia" prevails in framing the exchange as disinterested non-calculatedness. The accumulation of social capital, noted Pierre Bourdieu (1984, p. 253), presupposes a specific labor, often the apparently gratuitous expenditure of time, attention, and care, which allows the economic nature of an exchange to be understood and felt as a meaningful relationship.

14. McGoey 2016, p. 19.

15. Clemens 2006.

16. In her book *Women and the Everyday City*, historian Jessica Sewell (2010, pp. 3–6) documents a historic shift in San Francisco, from when women in public invited a dangerous male gaze that was typically aimed at prostitutes, not "polite" middle-class women, to the newly consumerist city with its mixed-gendered spaces and greater movement of women into public space, by the turn of the twentieth century (see also Bernstein 2007, p. 24). Newly emboldened as workers going out in public in the daytime, girls began going out in mixed-sex groups at night. Kathy Peiss (2004) further shows how "charity girls" upended Victorian strictures of sexual respectability.

17. Clemens 2006, p. 1.

18. Clemens 2006, p. 70.

19. Similar strategies of differentiation are clear in the practice of sugar dating (Rowe 2018).

20. Olga disagreed that there was a meaningful difference between a comped promoter dinner and a dinner in which the promoter pays the full bill out of pocket.

From her viewpoint as Enrico's girlfriend, both were work. She complained that in seven months together they had dinner alone together just ten times. "We are always with somebody, always it's a promoter dinner with the girls, always he is texting and working. I can't take it." They broke up soon after this exchange.

21. Dre was an exception in that he let me pay for our lunches a few times, when I wanted to ask him follow-up interview questions.

22. However, two girls I met disputed Felipe's account. One model told me about the time Thibault and Felipe accidentally left her behind in the bathroom of a restaurant in the Hamptons, not checking on her until half an hour later (she secured a ride with a different promoter, who happened to be going to the same club). "They don't care about the girls," she told me. Another model underwent an ordeal after being left without secure accommodations in Miami when she came for the March parties with Nicolas and Thibault.

23. Mikelberg 2016.

24. On the transformative power of money to redefine social relations, see Zelizer 1994.

25. Hardly a New York phenomenon, sexy women are bundled with other commodity purchases in lots of other contexts around the world. For instance, in Iceland in 2010, the government outlawed strip clubs on the grounds that they objectify and dehumanize women, a legal move widely celebrated as a feminist victory and emblematic of the progressive Icelandic state. But some men in Iceland still want to see strippers, so a workaround was created. They now go to a "champagne club," where, for the right price, a bottle of champagne comes to the customer with a scantily clothed dancing woman. The champagne sale is an exchange form known as "bundling" (Rossman 2014, pp. 47–49), which enables champagne clubs to operate within the law while strip clubs remain illegal (*Iceland Review* 2015). Bundling is a common way of obfuscating a disreputable exchange, to transform a suspicious trade into a legitimate one. For a famous case of bundling performed by the bottle hostess Rachel Uchitel, see Taddeo 2010.

26. Gabriel Rossman (2014, p. 47–49) analyzed exchanges in the bottle service club, arguing that clients understand payments to a broker as involving the purchase of drinks, a case of bundling or, in the terms of Viviana Zelizer (2005, p. 35), differentiated ties, which enable actors to reframe disreputable trades as relatively unobjectionable. This allows their spending on price-inflated bottles of champagne to remain an exchange separate from the hiring of a broker to procure girls.

27. Pimps must keep the sexual interest of their prostitutes to maintain a legitimate claim on ownership of them (Bernstein 2007, pp. 53–57). For example, in Holland the term "lover boy" refers to a nonwhite adult man who recruits young and socially vulnerable women, mostly white women, into prostitution, by developing relationships cemented with gifts and favors to entice them into transactional sex with other men, to the lover boy's profit (Al Jazeera 2012).

28. Considering a broad definition of sex work as "any commercial sexual service, performance, or products given in exchange for material compensation," girls' circulation in the VIP scene shares similarities with sex work, and most certainly promoters' strategic efforts to target models for sex (Weitzer 2000, p. 3).

The promoter performs a version of sex work by flirting and sleeping with girls for economic gain. He trades his sexuality for money, in the form of wages from the club and commission on bottle sales. Plenty of work resembles transactional sex, as feminist scholars have argued. If you stretch your imagination far enough, breadwinner marriage resembles prostitution, since it involves the exchange of men's economic support for women's domestic work and sexual access. What keeps these realms separate—marriage and prostitution—are the meanings and interpretations of different relationships. Viviana Zelizer (2006, p. 308) offers a typology of relationships in which commerce and intimacy comingle, and she notes that relationships vary by their depth and duration. A shallow and brief social connection, like sex work, is the opposite of a deep and enduring one such as breadwinner marriage. Promoters and their girls would seem to have shallow and brief, quid pro quo relations, but promoters described their ties as having greater depth than those of girls and clients, both of whom described relationships with promoters as relatively shallow. This discursive divide exists in part due to the promoter's position; as a broker, he depends on social capital and has incentives to inflate the value of it. In practice, the fact of shallow ties between promoters, girls, and clients mattered little. It was enough that ties between participants be recurring to enable a shared sense of belonging in the VIP scene.

29. This emotional labor is similar to that of higher-end sex workers who must perform intimate connections in the "girlfriend experience" (Bernstein 2007, p. 126).

30. Sex with girls is both the promoter's resource and his weakness. The possibility of sex stoked competitive rivalries between girls that could be useful, but risky. Promoters faced emotional and practical challenges involved in managing multiple sex partners, particularly if they were all at the same party and expecting his full attention. Even one sex partner at the table alters the group dynamic from friends to jealous competitors if he talks too much to the other girls. Promoters can exploit this weakness by telling a rival's girlfriend that her man is cheating. When Thibault found out that Dre was sleeping with three models without their knowing about the others, he told them, precipitating a dramatic fight at a club and hindering Dre's connections to several models. "That's against the code," Dre said. They no longer talk. By far the most extreme example of a promoter using sex to undercut his competition was Duke, the promoter whose heyday was in the late 1990s. He explained that the way to be the best promoter in town is to sleep with other promoters' girlfriends.

31. On the spread of the "hookup culture" ethos among young people, see England, Shafer, and Fogarty 2012.

32. Still, this promoter declined an interview for this book about promoters because he didn't want to further the industry's bad image. On promoters' response rate and collecting the interview sample, see the research appendix.

33. When upselling is directly organized by clubs and bars, it is known as illegal extortion, as exemplified by the case of criminal rings of women in Miami who drug unsuspecting men and take them to bars to pay inflated prices on bottles. The women receive a 20 percent commission (Conti 2014).

34. One promoter, Celia, told me that she has to pay extra tip at the restaurant to accommodate civilian women: "Because the club, they'll charge me more at the dinner to have her. The tip was $200; it will go up $500 to have her there."

"Just from one girl?" I asked.

"It's not one girl," she explained. "It's the whole principle. It's an image table, and they want a certain image, you see?"

35. Warhurst and Nickson 2001; Williams and Connell 2010.

36. Thibault never raised an issue about me hanging out with other promoters, except to caution me not to share his roster of model apartment numbers with anyone.

37. While the amount of commentary on women's bodies seemed high in the nightlife to me, it is also commonplace for men to publicly comment on women's looks in other contexts, from consumer spaces to professional workplaces (Quinn 2002).

38. For a brief discussion of the negative outcomes of relation work, see Bandelj 2012, p. 189.

39. In his essay "Rival Views of Market Society," the economist Albert O. Hirschman (1986) calls this the "destructive" view of market society, in which intimate life comes under the logic of cold rational calculation, and inalienable properties like love and sex and friendship are traded like any other good.

40. On direct-selling organizations, see Biggart 1990. Additionally, in the electronics sector, firms exchange gifts and favors to maintain ties as they trade electronics components (Darr 2003). And in the upper ends of the sex work industry, women are paid not only for sex, but also for the feeling of authentic connection that is safely bounded by the terms of economic exchange (Bernstein 2007).

41. In the factory that Michael Burawoy (1979, pp. 77–95) studied, he observed that workers played a game of "making out" on the shop floor, in which they tried to match or outdo one another's output and managers' expectations, and which allowed them to make choices about when and how much effort to exert. The game produced a sense of social and psychological achievement, and because it dominated shop floor culture, it led workers to consent to their own exploitation, even enthusiastically so. Thus the labor process in capitalist production simultaneously obscures and secures surplus labor, legitimizing exploitation through consent. Burawoy's intervention was an important break with both industrial sociologists and Marxist sociology, because it shifted the analysis to the labor process at the point of production—the moments of transformation of raw materials into surplus value—thereby explaining the organization of consent through work activities independent of outside orientations like school, family, and the state. This move, from structure to symbolic interactions, and from ideology to situations, could now explain how workers' motivations emerged from the work process itself.

42. For an expansion of this argument, see Mears 2015a.

43. Indeed, we can say that relational work is an important tool to maintain labor exploitation. The trade in organs (Healy 2006), reproductive materials (Almeling 2007), and cadavers (Anteby 2010) are illustrative cases. Operators in these industries use relational work to sell "priceless" human goods. Company owners

gain vast profits while drawing on cultural discourses of altruism and pricelessness to secure gifts from unpaid donors. Similarly, relational practices in markets for intimate human services facilitate labor exploitation, as when care workers are underpaid on the grounds that their work is altruistic and beyond the market (Folbre and Nelson 2000, pp. 129–133). In these cases, relational work redefines labor processes by constructing symbolic boundaries around work activities as gifts, donations, and intimacy.

44. Strategic intimacy is not necessarily a bad thing, so long as the parties involved share equivalent understandings of the degree of economic utility. When two exchange partners have different understandings of their relationship—as, say, true love on the one hand and paid sexual services on the other—emotional and legal problems ensue. Viviana Zelizer (2005) documents many such misunderstandings that end up in court.

Chapter 6. Started from the Bottom

1. See the research appendix for a full description of the promoters I interviewed.

2. Chetty et al. 2014; Jäntti et al. 2006.

3. For a programmatic statement on the value of social capital, see Burt 1992.

4. Bourdieu 1986, p. 257.

5. On the rapid turnover of clubs and their short shelf lives, estimated between eighteen and twenty-four months, see Elberse, Barlow, and Wong 2009.

6. Sociologist Taylor Laemmli develops the concept of the "lifestyle wage" to account for upscale service workers, who, like promoters, work in the unusual gap between class and status, two social categories that overlap for most people. Such jobs involve "class laundering," a process by which people get to consume a higher-class lifestyle than they can afford given their formal material capabilities. See Laemmli 2019.

7. In network science, "brokers" connect exchange partners to profit for symbolic or material rewards (Burt 1992).

8. Interactive services are typically characterized by clear asymmetries between workers and customers, and luxury services in particular have been described as performances of subordination, requiring workers to display deference, professionalism, and courtesy as a way to produce a sense of superiority in their customers (see, e.g., Sherman 2007, pp. 44–48). But the promoter, in an effort to craft an "authentic" consumption experience, cultivates and performs a relationship of equality with clients. His work is better described as "proximal service," as sociologist Eli Wilson (2016) has termed the provision of service among equals increasingly characteristic of high-end commercial settings. In proximal service, workers attempt to construct relationships of closeness and equality, rather than distance and deference, for instance by using fewer markers of formality and more personalized exchanges between servers and customers. Such efforts attempt to narrow social distance, which is considerable for promoters who aren't nearly as educated and rich as their clients. For an outline of social distance, see Bogardus 1933.

9. See the research appendix for a full description.

10. The "capital" in "color capital" refers here to value or worth. The concept is not derived from a Bourdieusian framework, nor does it imply that people of color can mitigate the effects of institutional racisms via their symbolic capital. See Hughey 2012. "Racial capitalism" refers to economic systems that generate profit from the racial identity of others.

11. In her theory of the negative effects of tokenism in the workplace, Rosabeth Moss Kanter (1977) argued that any numerical minority, whether women or racial minorities, will suffer disadvantage in the workplace under heightened scrutiny and the emotional pressures of performing not as an individual but as a representative of a group. Subsequent research has shown that the context and type of work matter very much for how tokens experience their work. For instance, in nursing, marked as a woman's job, white men can benefit and be tracked upward into supervisory positions (Williams 1995), while black men are less likely to benefit from their masculinity in the same context (Wingfield 2009).

12. See Patricia Hill Collins (2004, pp. 151–164) on race and representations, particularly on the historically entrenched associations between black sexuality, exoticism, and, for black men, colonial legacies of danger.

13. May and Chaplin 2008, pp. 60–68.

14. Cousin and Chauvin 2012.

15. See Mears, 2019.

16. Three promoters I reached out to for interviews declined to participate in this book (see the research appendix for more on interview recruitment). Two of them explained that they did not want to be associated with promoters nor with any book about promoters, because of the connotations of reckless behavior and a lifestyle that is incompatible with their larger goals of business entrepreneurship. One promoter declined to even take my business card, telling me that that he has nothing in common with "those people"—meaning other promoters—and that he planned to put his own background in finance to use, unlike other promoters who "think small" and don't know how to use their ties in nightlife.

Chapter 7. Closure

1. de Grazia 1996, pp. 12–13.

2. de Grazia 1996, pp. 12–13. Likewise, historians have generally emphasized the significance of the industrial revolution to the exclusion of the "consumer revolution," which in eighteenth-century Europe was equally transformative and necessary to spur changes in industrial development (McCracken 1988, pp. 3–4). See also Sombart (1913) 1967.

3. For a review of historical variations over expressions of distinction via consumption, from Greek and Roman societies to sumptuary laws, see Daloz 2009.

4. McCracken 1988, pp. 31–43.

5. The economist Werner Sombart ([1913] 1967), in *Luxury and Capitalism*, identified luxury goods as one of the earliest means to acquire social distinction, and desire for luxury unleashed an important force spurring capitalism.

6. Muzzarelli 2009 Before codified in laws, religious norms regulated status positioning via dress.

7. In *Politico*, for instance, Michael Kruse (2017) writes, "The city, for the admittedly shallow, ever-transactional Trump, was a place not to be experienced so much as exploited. The interest was not mutual: To most of New York's elite, whose acceptance he sought, Trump was far too brash and gauche. He was an outer-borough outsider, bankrolled by his politically connected father. He wanted to be taken seriously, but seldom was."

8. On status-seeking through philanthropy among the wealthy, see Ostrower (1997, pp. 36–47). Writing about the new vastly rich classes of Russia, Elisabeth Schimpfossl (2014, pp. 38–64) documents how oligarchs have moved from ostentation to bourgeoisie legitimacy by participating in the arts and donating to cultural development projects.

9. While an abundance of literature around cultural capital in the upper-middle and middle classes attends to the convertibility of varieties of cultural and symbolic capital (e.g., Khan 2011; Lareau 2003; Rivera 2010), the dynamics of status around displays of money are not very well understood (but see Schulz 2006 for an empirical case). Given the focus on distinction, scholars have rarely accounted for ostentation. Perhaps this is because academics themselves found legitimation in the concept of cultural capital, a game at which academics could win if played, in contrast to the game of economic domination, at which they would almost assuredly lose.

10. However, Bourdieu (1984, p. 31) described efforts to compete for status through wealth display as "the naïve exhibitionism of 'conspicuous consumption,' which seeks distinction in the crude display of ill-mastered luxury." He added that such strategies for economic domination are "nothing compared to the unique capacity of the pure gaze" (p. 31), that is, the aesthetic disposition of the bourgeoisie whose superior taste appears embodied and effortless, and which he studied in detail.

11. For colorful details on Jho Low's birthday party and other extravagances, see Wright and Hope 2018. Even with his spectacular and ill-gotten wealth, Low is hardly an outlier in terms of lavish birthday celebrations. When Blackstone Group founder Stephen Schwarzman turned sixty, in 2007, he celebrated with a $5 million party hosting dozens of friends and finance industrialists; reports estimate that his seventieth birthday party cost double (Holson 2017).

12. Frank 1999. Luxury fever spurs what Veblen termed pecuniary emulation— that is, willful attempts to compete, outdo, and intimidate upper-class peers (Veblen 1899, chap. 2). Pecuniary denomination, the show of raw economic power, is, and always has been, a powerful tool for the nouveau riche to gain status. Ostentation, argues sociologist Jean-Pascal Daloz (2009, pp. 61–80), is an overlooked but powerful form of distinction around the world. Based on comparative and historical case studies, Daloz claims that, in addition to the forms of distinction identified by Bourdieu, elites have often marked their superiority with outright ostentatious display.

13. Boltanski and Esquerre 2017. In the enrichment economy, a few goods are sold at very high prices to the very rich, unlike in mass consumerism, where the goal is to sell a lot of stuff at low profit margins to a lot of people who were not very rich. This represents the exploitation of the rich by the rich, and the generation of riches almost autonomous from the rest of society. In this economy, goods can be endowed with value by strategically tying them to narratives of heritage and tradition, resulting in spectacularly expensive objects that may have been comparatively worthless without the narrative framing of their heritage.

14. Pine and Gilmore 1999.

15. Bataille (1949) 1988.

16. Veblen 1899, chap. 4.

17. See, for example, Zorbaugh 1929 on Chicago elites and their social rules.

18. Baker 2018.

19. Keefe 2016; see Thompson 2018 on New York as a "ghost town."

20. Economists have identified numerous social advantages to being perceived as good-looking, including wage premiums in the labor market, higher-earning spouses, and greater likelihoods of promotion to leadership positions (Hamermesh 2011).

21. Weber (1922) 1978, pp. 43–46.

Research Appendix

1. Rachel Sherman (2017), too, uses interviews to document conflicted consumption among New York's upper classes and wealthy homeowners, who try very hard to minimize their privilege, especially when forced to justify their consumption in an interview with a sociologist.

2. Kusenbach 2003.

3. Nader (1969) 1974.

REFERENCES

Al, Stefan. 2017. *The Strip*. Cambridge, MA: MIT Press.

Adkins, Lisa. 1995. *Gendered Work: Sexuality, Family and the Labour Market*. Buckingham: Open University Press.

Al Jazeera. 2012. "Lover Boys." *Witness*, May 15. http://www.aljazeera.com/programmes/witness/2012/05/20125115345899123.html.

Allison, Anne. 1994. *Nightwork: Sexuality, Pleasure, and Corporate Masculinity in a Tokyo Hostess Club*. Chicago: University of Chicago Press.

Almeling, Rene. 2007. "Selling Genes, Selling Gender: Egg Agencies, Sperm Banks, and the Medical Market in Genetic Material." *American Sociological Review* 72 (3): 319–40.

Anderson, Tammy L., Catherine Grunert, Arielle Katz, and Samantha Lovascio. 2010. "Aesthetic Capital: A Research Review on Beauty Perks and Penalties." *Sociology Compass* 4 (8): 564–75.

Anteby, Michel. 2010. "Markets, Morals, and Practices of Trade: Jurisdictional Disputes in the U.S. Commerce in Cadavers." *Administrative Science Quarterly* 55 (4): 606–38.

Armstrong, Elizabeth A., and Laura T. Hamilton. 2015. *Paying for the Party: How College Maintains Inequality*. Cambridge, MA: Harvard University Press.

Armstrong, Elizabeth A., Laura T. Hamilton, Elizabeth M. Armstrong, and J. Lotus Sweeney. 2014. "'Good Girls:' Gender, Social Class, and Slut Discourse on Campus." *Social Psychology Quarterly* 77 (2): 100–122.

Attanasio, Orazio, Erik Hurst, and Luigi Pistaferri. 2015. "The Evolution of Income, Consumption, and Leisure Inequality in the United States, 1980–2010." In *Improving the Measurement of Consumer Expenditures*, edited by Christopher D. Carroll, Thomas F. Crossley, and and John Sabelhaus, 100–140. Chicago: University of Chicago Press.

Bailey, Peter. 1998. "Parasexuality and Glamour: The Victorian Barmaid as Cultural Prototype." In *Popular Culture and Performance in the Victorian City*, 151–74. Cambridge: Cambridge University Press.

Baker, Kevin. 2018. "The Death of a Once Great City: The Fall of New York and the Urban Crisis of Affluence." *Harper's*, July. https://harpers.org/archive/2018/07/the-death-of-new-york-city-gentrification/?src=longreads.

Balsamini, Dean. 2016. "'We Don't Want Them Here': Suit Claims Eatery Used Race to Seat Patrons." *New York Post*, December 25. https://nypost.com/2016/12/25/we-dont-want-them-here-suit-claims-eatery-used-race-to-seat-patrons/.

Bandelj, Nina. 2012. "Relational Work and Economic Sociology." *Politics & Society* 40 (2): 175–201.

Barrionuevo, Alexei. 2010. "Off Runway, Brazilian Beauty Goes beyond Blonde." *New York Times*, June 8. https://www.nytimes.com/2010/06/08/world/americas/08models.html.

Bataille, Georges. (1949). 1988. *The Accursed Share*. Vol. 1. Translated by Robert Hurley. New York: Zone Books.

Battan, Carrie. 2016. "Money for Nothing: The Lucrative World of Club Appearances." *GQ*, April 4. https://www.gq.com/story/how-celebs-get-paid-for-club-appearances.

Beaverstock, Jonathon, Philip Hubbard, and John Rennie Short. 2004. "Getting Away with It? Exposing the Geographies of the Super-rich." *Geoforum* 35 (4): 401–7.

Bekiempis, Victoria. 2017. "Brazilian Banker Finally Settles Suit over Unpaid $340G Bar Tab at Club Provocateur." *New York Daily News*, February 2. https://www.nydailynews.com/new-york/brazilian-banker-finally-settles-suit-unpaid-340g-bar-tab-article-1.2962814.

Bell, Emily. 2015. "The Total and Profound Illogic of Relegating Champagne to 'Occasions.'" *Vine Pair*, October 5. https://vinepair.com/wine-blog/the-total-and-profound-illogic-of-relegating-champagne-to-occasions/.

Benzecry, Claudio. 2011. *The Opera Fanatic: Ethnography of an Obsession*. Chicago: University of Chicago Press.

Benzecry, Claudio, and Randall Collins. 2014. "The High of Cultural Experience: Toward a Microsociology of Cultural Consumption." *Sociological Theory* 32 (4): 307–26.

Bernard, Lise. 2012. "Le capital culturel non certifié comme mode d'accès aux classes moyennes: L'entregent des agents immobiliers." *Actes de la recherche en sciences sociales*, no. 191–92, 68–85.

Bernstein, Elizabeth. 2007. *Temporarily Yours: Intimacy, Authenticity, and the Commerce of Sex*. Chicago: University of Chicago Press.

Bettie, Julie. 2003. *Women without Class: Girls, Race, and Identity*. Berkeley: University of California Press.

Biggart, Nicole Woolsey. 1990. *Charismatic Capitalism: Direct Selling Organizations in America*. Chicago: University of Chicago Press.

Bird, Sharon R. 1996. "Welcome to the Men's Club: Homosociality and the Maintenance of Hegemonic Masculinity." *Gender & Society* 10 (2): 120–32.

Birtchnell, Thomas, and Javier Caletrío, eds. 2013. *Elite Mobilities*. London: Routledge.

BlackBook. 2010. "Industry Insiders: Michael Satsky, Agent Provocateur." January 7. https://bbook.com/nightlife/industry-insiders-michael-satsky-agent-provocateur/.

Blair, Elizabeth. 2010. "Strip Clubs: Launch Pad for Hits in Atlanta." NPR, December 23. https://www.npr.org/sections/therecord/2010/12/23/132287578/strip-clubs-launch-pads-for-hits-in-atlanta.

Blum, David. 1978. "Drawing the Line at Studio 54." *New York Times*, June 14.

Boas, Franz. 1921. "Ethnology of the Kwakiutl, Based on Data Collected by George Hunt." *Thirty-Fifth Annual Report of the Bureau of American Ethnology*. 2 parts. Washington, DC: Government Publishing Office.

Bogardus, Emory S. 1933. "A Social Distance Scale." *Sociology & Social Research* 17: 265–71.

Boltanski, Luc, and Arnaud Esquerre. 2017. *Enrichissement: Une critique de la marchandise*. Paris: Gallimard.

Borris, Eileen, and Rhacel Salazar Parreñas. 2010. *Intimate Labors: Cultures, Technologies, and the Politics of Care*. Stanford, CA: Stanford University Press.

Bourdieu, Pierre. 1984. *Distinction: A Social Critique in the Judgement of Taste*. Translated by Richard Nice. London: Routledge.

———. 1986. "The Forms of Capital." In *Handbook of Theory and Research for the Sociology of Education*, edited by John G. Richardson, 241–58. New York: Greenwood Press.

———. (1998) 2001. *Masculine Domination*. Translated by Richard Nice. Cambridge: Polity.

Bruno, Isabelle, and Grégory Salle. 2018. "'Before Long There Will Be Nothing but Billionaires!' The Power of Elites over Space on the Saint-Tropez Peninsula." *Socio-Economic Review* 16 (2): 435–58.

Buckley, Cara. 2012. "In Celebrity Brawl at Club, a Scene of Flying Bottles and Ice Cubes." *New York Times*, June 16. https://www.nytimes.com/2012/06/16/nyregion/in-brawl-involving-drake-and-chris-brown-flying-bottles-and-ice.html.

Burawoy, Michael. 1979. *Manufacturing Consent: Changes in the Labor Process under Monopoly Capitalism*. Chicago: University of Chicago Press.

Burt, Ronald S. 1992. *Structural Holes: The Social Structure of Competition*. Cambridge, MA: Harvard University Press.

Callon, Michel. 1998. "Introduction: The Embeddedness of Economic Markets in Economics." In *The Laws of the Markets*, edited by Michel Callon, 1–56. Oxford: Blackwell.

Chetty, Raj, Nathaniel Hendren, Patrick Kline, and Emmanuel Saez. 2014. "Where Is the Land of Opportunity? The Geography of Intergenerational Mobility in the United States." *Quarterly Journal of Economics* 129 (4): 1553–1623.

Clemens, Elizabeth Alice. 2006. *Love for Sale: Courting, Treating, and Prostitution in New York City, 1900–1945*. Chapel Hill: University of North Carolina Press.

Collins, Patricia Hill. 2004. *Black Sexual Politics: African Americans, Gender, and the New Racism*. New York: Routledge.

Collins, Randall. 1979. *The Credential Society: A Historical Sociology of Education and Stratification*. Cambridge, MA: Academic Press.

———. 2004. *Interaction Ritual Chains*. Princeton, NJ: Princeton University Press.

Connell, R. W. 1995. *Masculinities: Knowledge, Power and Social Change*. Berkeley: University of California Press.

Conti, Alie. 2014. "Prostitutes Steal Millions and Walk Free." *Miami New Times*, January 23. https://www.miaminewtimes.com/news/prostitutes-steal-millions-and-walk-free-6394610.

Coontz, Stephanie. 2005. *Marriage, a History: From Obedience to Intimacy, or How Love Conquered Marriage*. New York: Viking.

Cousin, Bruno, and Sébastien Chauvin. 2012. "The Symbolic Economy of Social Capital." *Actes de la recherche en sciences sociales* 193: 96–103.

———. 2013. "Islanders, Immigrants and Millionaires: The Dynamics of Upper-Class Segregation in St Barts, French West Indies." In *Geographies of the Super-Rich*, edited by Iain Hay, 186–200. Cheltenham: Edward Elgar.

———. 2014. "Globalizing Forms of Elite Sociability: Varieties of Cosmopolitanism in Paris Social Clubs." *Ethnic and Racial Studies* 37 (12): 2209–25.

Cousin, Bruno, Shamus Khan, and Ashley Mears. 2018. "Theoretical and Methodological Pathways for Research on Elites." *Socio-Economic Review* 16 (2): 225–49.

Cressey, Paul Goalby. 1952. *The Taxi-Dance Hall: A Sociological Study in Commercialized Recreation and City Life*. Chicago: University of Chicago Press.

Currid, Elizabeth. 2007. *The Warhol Economy*. Princeton, NJ: Princeton University Press.

Daloz, Jean-Pascal. 2009. *The Sociology of Elite Distinction: From Theoretical to Comparative Perspectives*. Basingstoke: Palgrave Macmillan.

Darr, Asaf. 2003. "Gifting Practices and Interorganizational Relations: Constructing Obligation Networks in the Electronics Sector." *Sociological Forum* 18 (1): 31–51.

Darr, Asaf, and Ashley Mears. 2017. "Local Knowledge, Global Networks: Scouting for Fashion Models and Football Players." *Poetics* 62: 1–14.

Davis, Mike, and Daniel Monk, eds. 2008. *Evil Paradises: Dreamworlds of Neoliberalism*. New York: New Press.

Davis, Natalie Zemon. 2006. "Women on Top." In *Early Modern Europe: Issues and Interpretations*, edited by James B. Collins and Karen L. Taylor, 398–411. Oxford: Blackwell.

Delaney, Kevin. 2012. *Money at Work: On the Job with Priests, Poker Players, and Hedge Fund Traders*. New York: NYU Press.

de Grazia, Victoria, 1996. Introduction to part 1, "Changing Consumption Regimes." In *The Sex of Things: Gender and Consumption in Historical Perspective*, edited by Victoria de Grazia, with Ellen Furlough, 11–24. Berkeley: University of California Press

De Marly, Diana. 1980. *The History of Haute Couture, 1850–1950*. Ann Arbor: University of Michigan Press.

Dolgon, Corey. 2005. *The End of the Hamptons: Scenes from the Class Struggle in America's Paradise*. New York: NYU Press.

Domhoff, G. William. 1975. *Bohemian Grove and Other Retreats: A Study in Ruling-Class Cohesiveness*. New York: Harper and Row.

Durkheim, Émile. (1912) 2001. *The Elementary Forms of Religious Life*. Translated by Karen E. Fields. Oxford: Oxford University Press.

Eells, Josh. 2013. "Night Club Royale." *New Yorker*, September 30. https://www.newyorker.com/magazine/2013/09/30/night-club-royale.

Elberse, Anita. 2013. *Blockbusters: Hit-making, Risk-taking, and the Big Business of Entertainment*. New York: Henry Holt.

———. 2014. "Marquee: Reinventing the Business of Nightlife." Harvard Business School Multimedia/Video Case 515-702, September 2014.

Elberse, Anita, Ryan Barlow, and Sheldon Wong. 2009. "Marquee: The Business of Night Life." Harvard Business School Case 509-019, February.

Elias, Sean. 2008. "Investigating the Aspen Elite." *Contexts* 7 (4): 62–64.

Ellis, Blake, and Melanie Hicken. 2016a. "The 'Model Apartment' Trap." CNN Money, May 12. https://money.cnn.com/2016/05/11/news/runway-injustice-model-apartments/index.html.

———. 2016b. "The Outrageous Cost of Being a Model." CNN Money, May 12. https://money.cnn.com/2016/05/09/news/runway-injustice-model-expenses/index.html.

Elliott, Hannah. 2017. "How One Nightclub Defied the Odds to Last a Decade—and Make $250 Million." Bloomberg.com, February 21. https://www.bloomberg.com/news/articles/2017-02-21/secrets-of-success-from-1oak-the-250-million-nightclub.

England, Paula, and Nancy Folbre. 1999. "The Cost of Caring." *ANNALS of the American Academy of Political and Social Science* 561 (1): 39–51.

England, Paula, and Elizabeth Aura McClintock. 2009. "The Gendered Double Standard of Aging in US Marriage Markets." *Population and Development Review* 35 (4): 797–816.

England, Paula, Emily Fitzgibbons Shafer, and Alison C. K. Fogarty. 2012. "Hooking Up and Forming Romantic Relationships on Today's College Campuses." In *The Gendered Society Reader*, 5th ed., edited by Michael Kimmel and Amy Aronson, 559–72. New York: Oxford University Press.

Entwistle, Joanne, and Elizabeth Wissinger. 2006. "Keeping up Appearances: Aesthetic Labour in the Fashion Modelling Industries of London and New York." *Sociological Review* 54 (4): 774–94.

———. 2012. *Fashioning Models: Image, Text and Industry*. London: Berg.

Evans, Caroline. 2001. "The Enchanted Spectacle." *Fashion Theory* 5 (3): 271–310.

Evans, Sean. 2010. "Marquee NYC: Still Hip After Seven Years." *Nightclub & Bar*, September 2. https://www.nightclub.com/operations/marquee-nyc-still-hip-after-seven-years.

Farrer, James, and Andrew David Field. 2015. *Shanghai Nightscapes: A Nocturnal Biography of a Global City*. Chicago: University of Chicago Press.

Federici, Silvia. (1975) 2012. "Wages Against Housework." In *Revolution at Point Zero: Housework, Reproduction, and Feminist Struggle*, 15–22. Oakland: PM Press.

Folbre, Nancy, and Julie A. Nelson. 2000. "For Love or Money—Or Both?" *Journal of Economic Perspectives* 14 (4): 123–40.

Fox, Emily Jane. 2015. "Here's Where People Are Flying Private Jets." CNN Business, March 5, 2015. http://money.cnn.com/2015/03/04/luxury/top-ten-private-jet-routes/index.html.

Frank, Robert H. 1999. *Luxury Fever: Why Money Fails to Satisfy in an Era of Excess*. New York: Free Press.

Freeland, Chrystia. 2012. *Plutocrats: The Rise of the New Global Super-Rich and the Fall of Everyone Else*. New York: Penguin Press.

Gebhart, Harriet. 1929. "Woodside Girl Scores High as Kicker in Galaxy of Ziegfeld Beauties." *Daily Star Queens Borough*, January 3.

Geertz, Clifford. 1973. *The Interpretation of Cultures*. New York: Basic Books.

Godechot, Olivier. 2016. *Wages, Bonuses and Appropriation of Profit in the Financial Industry: The Working Rich*. London: Routledge.

Goffman, Erving. 1959. *The Presentation of Self in Everyday Life*. New York: Doubleday.

———. 1967. *Interaction Ritual: Essays in Face to Face Behavior*. New York: Pantheon.

Gottfried, Heidi. 2003. "Temp(t)ing Bodies: Shaping Gender at Work in Japan." *Sociology* 37 (2): 257–76.

Graeber, David. 2001. *Toward an Anthropological Theory of Value*. New York: Palgrave Macmillan.

Graf, Nikki L., and Christine R. Schwartz. 2010. "The Uneven Pace of Change in Heterosexual Romantic Relationships." *Gender & Society* 25 (1): 101–7.

Gray, Billy. 2010. "Provocateur Is So Crowded That Nobody Goes There Anymore." *Guest of a Guest*, May 10. http://guestofaguest.com/nightlife/provocateur-is-so-crowded-that-nobody-goes-there-anymore.

Grazian, David. 2007a. "The Girl Hunt: Urban Nightlife and the Performance of Masculinity." *Symbolic Interaction* 30 (2): 221–43.

———. 2007b. *On the Make: The Hustle of Urban Nightlife*. Chicago: University of Chicago Press.

Green, Adam Isaiah. 2013. "'Erotic Capital' and the Power of Desirability: Why 'Honey Money' Is a Bad Collective Strategy for Remedying Gender Inequality." *Sexualities* 16 (1–2):137–58.

Gusterson, Hugh. 1997. "Studying Up Revisited." *Political and Legal Anthropology Review* 20 (1): 114–19.

Guy, Kolleen M. 2003. *When Champagne Became French: Wine and the Making of a National Identity*. Baltimore: Johns Hopkins University Press.

Hakim, Catherine. 2010. "Erotic Capital." *European Sociological Review* 26 (5): 499–518.

Halle, David, and Elizabeth Tiso. 2014. *New York's New Edge: Contemporary Art, the High Line, and Urban Megaprojects on the Far West Side*. Chicago: University of Chicago Press.

Halttunen, Karen. 1982. *Confidence Men and Painted Women: A Study of Middle-Class Culture in America, 1830–1870*. New Haven, CT: Yale University Press.

Hamermesh, Daniel S. 2011. *Beauty Pays: Why Attractive People Are More Successful*. Princeton, NJ: Princeton University Press.

Hamilton, Laura. 2007. "Trading on Heterosexuality: College Women's Gender Strategies and Homophobia." *Gender & Society* 21 (2): 145–72.

Hanser, Amy. 2008. *Service Encounters: Class, Gender, and the Market for Social Distinction in Urban China.* Stanford, CA: Stanford University Press.

Harrington, Brooke. 2016. *Capital without Borders: Wealth Managers and the One Percent.* Cambridge, MA: Harvard University Press.

Hay, Iain, and Samantha Muller. 2012. "'That Tiny, Stratospheric Apex That Owns Most of the World': Exploring Geographies of the Super-Rich." *Geographical Research* 50 (1): 75–88.

Healy, Kieran. 2006. *Last Best Gifts: Altruism and the Market for Human Blood and Organs.* Chicago: University of Chicago Press.

Hirschman, Albert. O. 1986. *Rival Views of Market Society and Other Recent Essays.* Cambridge, MA: Harvard University Press.

Ho, Karen. 2009. *Liquidated: An Ethnography of Wall Street.* Durham, NC: Duke University Press.

Hoang, Kimberly Kay. 2011. "'She's Not a Low-Class Dirty Girl!': Sex Work in Ho Chi Minh City, Vietnam." *Journal of Contemporary Ethnography* 40 (4): 367–96.

———. 2015. *Dealing in Desire: Asian Ascendancy, Western Decline, and the Hidden Currencies of Global Sex Work.* Oakland, CA: University of California Press.

Holson, Laura. M. 2017. "Camels, Acrobats and Team Trump at a Billionaire's Gala." *New York Times,* February 14. https://www.nytimes.com/2017/02/14/fashion/stephen-schwarzman-billionaires-birthday-draws-team-trump.html.

Horowitz, Jason. 2016. "When Donald Met Melania, Paolo Was There." *New York Times,* September 1. https://www.nytimes.com/2016/09/01/fashion/donald-trump-melania-modeling-agent-paolo-zampolli-daily-mail.html.

Hunter, Marcus Anthony. 2010. "The Nightly Round: Space, Social Capital, and Urban Black Nightlife." *City & Community* 9 (2): 165–86.

Hughey, Matthew W. 2012. "Color Capital, White Debt, and the Paradox of Strong White Racial Identities." *Du Bois Review: Social Science Research on Race* 9 (1): 169–200.

Illouz, Eva. 2007. *Cold Intimacies: The Making of Emotional Capitalism.* London: Polity.

———. 2017. "From Donald Trump to Christian Grey: Are Women Secretly Drawn to Beasts?" *Haaretz,* March 2.

Inequality.org. n.d. "Wealth Inequality in the United States." Accessed October 24, 2019. https://inequality.org/facts/wealth-inequality/.

Irigaray, Luce. (1977) 1985. *This Sex Which Is Not One.* Ithaca, NY: Cornell University Press.

Jacobs, Andrew, 1999. "Dance Clubs Heeding Call to Tame Wild Life." *New York Times,* August 31. http://www.nytimes.com/1999/08/31/nyregion/dance-clubs-heeding-call-to-tame-wild-life.html.

Jacobs, Jane. (1961) 1992. *The Death and Life of Great American Cities.* New York: Vintage.

Jäntti, Markus, Bernt Bratsberg, Knut Røed, Oddbjørn Raaum, Robin Naylor, Eva Österbacka, Anders Björklund, and Tor Eriksson. 2006. "American

Exceptionalism in a New Light: A Comparison of Intergenerational Earnings Mobility in the Nordic Countries, the United Kingdom and the United States." IZA Discussion Paper no. 1938 (January).

Johnsen, Rasmus, and Navid Baharlooie. 2013. "Cult Girl: Responsible Management and Self-management of Subjectivity at Work." Case 713-070-1. Case Centre, Copenhagen Business School.

Kanter, Rosabeth Moss. 1977. *Men and Women of the Corporation*. New York: Basic Books.

Keefe, Patrick Radden. 2016. "The Kleptocrat in Apartment B." *New Yorker*, January 21. https://www.newyorker.com/news/daily-comment/the-kleptocrat-in-apartment-b.

Khan, Shamus Rahman. 2011. *Privilege: The Making of an Adolescent Elite at St. Paul's School*. Princeton, NJ: Princeton University Press.

Kruse, Michael. 2017. "How Gotham Gave Us Trump." *Politico*, July/August. https://www.politico.com/magazine/story/2017/06/30/donald-trump-new-york-city-crime-1970s-1980s-215316.

Kusenbach, Margarethe. 2003. "Street Phenomenology: The Go-Along Method." *Ethnography* 4 (3): 455–85.

Laemmli, Taylor. 2019. "Class Laundering: Perks and the Lifestyle Wage." Presentation at the annual meeting of SASE (Society for the Advancement of Socio-Economics), New York, NY, June.

Lareau, Annette. 2003. *Unequal Childhoods: Class, Race, and Family Life*. Berkeley: University of California Press.

Latham, Angela J. 2000. *Posing a Threat: Flappers, Chorus Girls, and Other Brazen Performers of the American 1920s*. Hanover, NH: University Press of New England.

Laumann, Edward O., Stephen Ellingson, Jenna Mahay, Anthony Paik, and Yoosik Youm. 2004. *The Sexual Organization of the City*. Chicago: University of Chicago Press.

Lauren, Jillian. 2010. *Some Girls: My Life in a Harem*. New York: Plume.

Lee, Adrian. 2015. "Could the THIRD Mrs. Trump move into the White House?" *Express*, September 8. http://www.express.co.uk/life-style/life/603772/Third-Mrs-Trump-Melania-Donald-Trump-president-White-House.

LeDonne, Rob. 2014. "Opening a Dance Club in the Era of the $100,000-a-Night DJ." *Observer*, November 10. https://observer.com/2014/11/opening-a-dance-club-in-the-era-of-the-100000-a-night-dj/.

Lévi-Strauss, Claude. 1969. *The Elementary Structures of Kinship*. Translated by James Harle Bell, John Richard von Sturmer, and Rodney Needham. Boston: Beacon Press.

Lin, Ken-Hou, and Donald Tomaskovic-Devey. 2013. "Financialization and US Income Inequality, 1970–2008." *American Journal of Sociology* 118 (5): 1284–1329.

Llewellyn Smith, Julia. 2006. "No More Sex and the City." *Telegraph*, January 15. https://www.telegraph.co.uk/news/uknews/1507860/No-more-sex-and-the-City.html.

MacLean Annie Marion. 1988. "Two Weeks in Department Stores." *American Journal of Sociology* 4 (6): 721–41.

Mare, Rob. 2016. "Educational Homogamy in Two Gilded Ages: Evidence from Inter-generational Social Mobility Data." *Annals of the American Academy of Political and Social Science* 663 (1): 117–39.

Martin, John Levi, and Matt George. 2006. "Theories of Sexual Stratification: Toward an Analytics of the Sexual Field and a Theory of Sexual Capital." *Sociological Theory* 24 (2): 107–32.

Martin, Patricia Yancey, and Robert A. Hummer. 1989. "Fraternities and Rape on College Campuses." *Gender & Society* 3 (4): 457–73.

Matlon, Jordanna. 2016. "Racial Capitalism and the Crisis of Black Masculinity." *American Sociological Review* 81 (5): 1014–38.

Mauss, Marcel. (1954) 1990. *The Gift: Forms and Functions of Exchange in Archaic Societies*. Translated by W. D. Halls. New York: Norton.

May, Reuben A. Buford. 2018. "Velvet Rope Racism, Racial Paranoia, and Cultural Scripts: Alleged Dress Code Discrimination in Urban Nightlife, 2000–2014." *City and Community* 17 (1): 44–64.

May, Reuben A. Buford, and Kenneth Sean Chaplin. 2008. "Cracking the Code: Race, Class, and Access to Nightclubs in Urban America." *Qualitative Sociology* 31 (1): 57–72.

McClain, Noah, and Ashley Mears. 2012. "Free to Those Who Can Afford It: The Everyday Affordance of Privilege." *Poetics* 40 (2): 133–149.

McClintock, Elizabeth Aura. 2014. "Beauty and Status: The Illusion of Exchange in Partner Selection?" *American Sociological Review* 79 (4): 575–604.

McCracken, Grant. 1988. *Culture and Consumption: New Approaches to the Symbolic Character of Consumer Goods and Activities*. Bloomington: Indiana University Press.

McGoey, Linsey. 2016. *No Such Thing as a Free Gift: The Gates Foundation and the Price of Philanthropy*. New York: Verso.

McIntyre, Hugh. 2015. "American's 10 Biggest Nightclubs Earned over $550 Million in Revenue Last Year." *Forbes*, May 26. https://www.forbes.com/sites/hughmcintyre/2015/05/26/americas-10-biggest-nightclubs-earned-over-550-million-in-revenue-last-year/#ba2418a4514e.

McKendrick, Neil, John Brewer, and J. H. Plumb. 1982. *The Birth of a Consumer Society: The Commercialization of Eighteenth-Century England*. New York: HarperCollins.

Mears, Ashley. 2010. "Size Zero High-End Ethnic: Cultural Production and the Reproduction of Culture in Fashion Modeling." *Poetics* 38 (1): 21–46.

———. 2011. *Pricing Beauty: The Making of a Fashion Model*. Berkeley: University of California Press.

———. 2014. "Aesthetic Labor for the Sociologies of Work, Gender, and Beauty." *Sociology Compass* 8 (12): 1330–43.

———. 2015a. "Working for Free in the VIP: Relational Work and the Production of Consent." *American Sociological Review* 80 (6): 1099–122.

———. 2015b. "Girls as Elite Distinction: The Appropriation of Bodily Capital." *Poetics* 53: 22–37.

———. 2019. "Des Fêtes très Exclusives. Les Organisateurs de Soirées VIP, des Intermédiaires à la Mobilité Contrariée." *Actes de la recherche en sciences sociales* 230 (December).

Mears, Ashley, and Catherine Connell. 2016. "The Paradoxical Value of Deviant Cases: Toward a Gendered Theory of Display Work." *Signs* 41 (2): 333–59.

Mencken, H. L. 1919. "Professor Veblen." In *Prejudices: First Series*, 59–82. New York: Knopf.

Mikelberg, Amanda. 2016. "NYC's Nightclubs Filled with Imported Models Who Live for Free, Insiders Reveal." *Metro*, October 13. https://www.metro.us /new-york/nyc-s-nightclubs-filled-with-imported-models-who-live-for-free -insiders-reveal/zsJpjl---r8xia58wgFOHM.

Milzoff, Rebecca. 2006. "Taking the Fifth: Can Clubland Survive without Bottle Service?" *New York Magazine*, October 13. http://nymag.com/news/intelligencer /22834/.

Mobley, Mary Edie, and John Humphreys. 2006. "How Low Will You Go?" *Harvard Business Review* (April). https://hbr.org/2006/04/how-low-will-you-go.

Mulvey, Laura. 1989. "Visual Pleasure and Narrative Cinema." In *Visual and Other Pleasures*, 14–26. London: Macmillan.

Murray, Charles A. 1984. *Losing Ground: American Social Policy, 1950–1980*. New York: Basic Books.

Muzzarelli, Maria Giuseppina. 2009. "Reconciling the Privilege of a Few with the Common Good: Sumptuary Laws in Medieval and Early Modern Europe." *Journal of Medieval and Early Modern Studies* 39 (3): 597–617.

Nader, Laura (1969) 1974. "Up the Anthropologist: Perspectives Gained from Studying Up." In *Reinventing Anthropology*, edited by Dell H. Hymes, 284–311. New York: Random House.

Neate, Rupert. 2017. "Richest 1% Own Half the World's Wealth, Study Finds." *Guardian*, November 17. https://www.theguardian.com/inequality/2017/nov/14 /worlds-richest-wealth-credit-suisse.

Neveu, Érik. 2013. "Les sciences sociales doivent-elles accumuler les capitaux?" *Revue française de science politique* 63 (2): 337–58.

Niemietz, Brian. 1999. "Model Mayhem." *New York Post*, November 30. https:// nypost.com/1999/11/30/model-mayhem/.

———. 2006. "Bottle Service: A Brief History." *New York Magazine*, June 15. http:// nymag.com/nightlife/features/17308/.

Nightclub & Bar Staff. n.d. "2015 Top 100 List." *Nightclub & Bar*. Accessed October 24, 2019. https://www.nightclub.com/industry-news/2015-top-100-list.

Odell, Amy. 2013. "10 Ways to Get Into New York's 'Hottest' Nightclub." *Buzzfeed*, March 21. https://www.buzzfeed.com/amyodell/10-ways-to-get-into-new-yorks -hottest-nightclub?utm_term=.lrQ3MmP66A#.kdQZnDadd9.

Office of the New York State Comptroller. 2018. "New York City Securities Industry Bonus Pool." March 26. https://www.osc.state.ny.us/press/releases/mar18/wall -st-bonuses-2018-sec-industry-bonus-pool.pdf.

Osburg, John. 2013. *Anxious Wealth: Money and Morality among China's New Rich*. Stanford, CA: Stanford University Press.

Ostrander, Susan A. 1984. *Women of the Upper Class*. Philadelphia: Temple University Press.

Ostrower, Francie. 1997. *Why the Wealthy Give: The Culture of Elite Philanthropy*. Princeton, NJ: Princeton University Press.

Otis, Eileen. 2011. *Markets and Bodies: Women, Service Work, and the Making of Inequality in China*. Stanford, CA: Stanford University Press.

PageSix.com Staff. 2009. "Clubs Court Low-Key Mr. Low." *Page Six*, November 10. https://pagesix.com/2009/11/10/clubs-court-low-key-mr-low/.

PageSix.com Staff. 2010. "Billionaires Vie to See Who Can Order More Champagne in Saint Tropez." *New York Post*, July 24. https://pagesix.com/2010/07/24/billionaires-vie-to-see-who-can-order-more-champagne-in-saint-tropez/.

Park, Lisa Sun-Hee, and David N. Pellow. 2011. *The Slums of Aspen: Immigrants vs. the Environment in America's Eden*. New York: NYU Press.

Parreñas, Rhacel Salazar. 2011. *Illicit Flirtations: Labor, Migration, and Sex Trafficking in Tokyo*. Stanford, CA: Stanford University Press.

Peiss, Kathy. 2004. "Charity Girls and City Pleasures." *Magazine of History* 18 (4): 14–16.

Piketty, Thomas. 2014. *Capital in the Twenty-First Century*. Translated by Arthur Goldhammer. Cambridge, MA: Belknap Press of Harvard University Press.

Piketty, Thomas, and Emmanuel Saez. 2003. "Income Inequality in the United States: 1913–1998." *Quarterly Journal of Economics* 118 (1): 1–39.

Pine, B. Joseph II, and James H. Gilmore. 1999. *The Experience Economy: Work Is Theatre and Every Business a Stage*. Boston: Harvard Business School Press.

Podolny, Joel. 2005. *Status Signals: A Sociological Study of Market Competition*. Princeton, NJ: Princeton University Press.

Poulin, Michelle J. 2007. "Sex, Money, and Premarital Relationships in Southern Malawi." *Social Science Medicine* 65 (11): 2382–93.

Prieur, Annick, and Mike Savage. 2013. "Emerging Forms of Cultural Capital." *European Societies* 15 (2): 246–67.

Quinn, Beth A. 2002. "Sexual Harassment and Masculinity: The Power and Meaning of 'Girl Watching.'" *Gender & Society* 16 (3): 386–402.

Quinones, Sam. 2015. *Dreamland: The True Tale of America's Opioid Epidemic*. London: Bloomberg.

Restaurant & Bar Design Staff. 2015. "Restaurant & Bar Design Award Shortlist 2015: Nightclub." *Restaurant & Bar Design*, July 29. https://restaurantandbardesign.com/2015/07/29/restaurant-bar-design-awards-shortlist-2015-nightclub/.

Rivera, Lauren. 2010. "Status Distinctions in Interaction: Social Selection and Exclusion at an Elite Nightclub." *Qualitative Sociology* 33 (3): 229–55.

Roose, Kevin. 2012. "A Raucous Hazing at a Wall St. Fraternity." *New York Times*, January 20. https://dealbook.nytimes.com/2012/01/20/raucous-hazing-at-a-wall-st-fraternity/.

Rossman, Gabriel. 2014. "Obfuscatory Relational Work and Disreputable Exchange." *Sociological Theory* 32 (1): 43–63.

———. 2017. "They Meant Us No Harm, But Only Gave Us the Lotus." *Code and Culture*, January 27. https://codeandculture.wordpress.com/2017/01/27/they-meant-us-no-harm-but-only-gave-us-the-lotus/.

Roth, Louise Marie. 2006. *Selling Women Short: Gender and Money on Wall Street*. Princeton, NJ: Princeton University Press.

Rowe, Carmen. 2018. "Girls Just Wanna Have Funds." Paper presented at the Annual American Sociological Association Conference, Philadelphia, August.

Rubin, Gayle. (1975) 1997. "The Traffic in Women: Notes on the 'Political Economy' of Sex." In *The Second Wave: A Reader in Feminist Theory*, edited by Linda Nicholson, 27–62. New York: Routledge.

Saez, Emmanuel. 2009. "Striking it Richer: The Evolution of Top Incomes in the United States (Update with 2007 Estimates)." August 5, update of "Striking it Richer: The Evolution of Top Incomes in the United States." *Pathways Magazine* (Winter 2008): 6–7. https://eml.berkeley.edu/~saez/saez-UStopincomes-2007.pdf.

Saez, Emmanuel, and Gabriel Zucman. 2016. "Wealth Inequality in the United States since 1913: Evidence from Capitalized Income Tax Data." *Quarterly Journal of Economics* 131 (2): 519–78.

Sahlins, Marshall D. 1963. "Poor Man, Rich Man, Big-Man, Chief: Political Types in Melanesia and Polynesia." *Comparative Studies in Society and History* 5 (3): 285–303.

Salmon, Felix. 2015. "Plutocrats Gone Wild." *New York Times*, May 17. https://www.nytimes.com/2015/05/17/t-magazine/plutocrats-gone-wild.html.

Sanders, Lise Shapiro. 2006. *Consuming Fantasies: Labor, Leisure, and the London Shopgirl, 1880–1920*. Columbus: Ohio State University Press.

Sanders, Teela, and Kate Hardy. 2012. "Devalued, Deskilled and Diversified: Explaining the Proliferation of the Strip Industry in the UK." *British Journal of Sociology* 63 (3): 513–32.

Savage, Mike. 2015. "Introduction to Elites: From the 'Problematic of the Proletariat' to a Class Analysis of 'Wealth Elites.'" *Sociological Review* 63 (2): 223–39.

Scarano, Ross. 2012. "The Oral History of the Tunnel." *Complex*, August 21. https://www.complex.com/pop-culture/2012/08/the-oral-history-of-the-tunnel.

Schama, Simon. (1987) 1997. *The Embarrassment of Riches: An Interpretation of Dutch Culture in the Golden Age*. New York: Vintage.

Schimpfossl, Elisabeth. 2014. "Russia's Social Upper Class: From Ostentation to Culturedness." *British Journal of Sociology* 65 (1): 63–81.

Schulz, Jeremy. 2006. "Vehicle of the Self: The Social and Cultural Work of the H2 Hummer SUV." *Journal of Consumer Culture* 6 (1): 57–86.

Schwartz, Christine R. 2010. "Earnings Inequality and the Changing Association between Spouses' Earnings." *American Journal of Sociology* 115 (5): 1524–57.

Sengupta, Somini. 2012. "Preferred Style: Don't Flaunt It in Silicon Valley." *New York Times*, May 18.

Sewell, Jessica. 2010. *Women and the Everyday City: Public Space in San Francisco, 1890–1915*. Minneapolis: University of Minnesota Press.

Sheller, Mimi, and John Urry. 2006. "The New Mobilities Paradigm." *Environment and Planning A: Economy and Space* 38 (2): 207–26.

Sherman, Rachel. 2007. *Class Acts: Service and Inequality in Luxury Hotels.* Berkeley: University of California Press.

———. 2017. *Uneasy Street: The Anxieties of Affluence.* Princeton, NJ: Princeton University Press.

Shilling, Chris. 2012. "The Body and Physical Capital." In *The Body and Social Theory*, 3rd ed., 135–60. London: SAGE.

Shrum, Wesley, and John Kilburn. 1996. "Ritual Disrobement at Mardi Gras: Ceremonial Exchange and Moral Order." *Social Forces* 75 (2): 423–58.

Silver, Daniel, and Terry Clark. 2016. *Scenescapes: How Qualities of Place Shape Social Life.* Chicago: University of Chicago Press.

Siwolop, Sana. 2001. "A Warehouse Turns into Retail Space." *New York Times*, August 15. https://www.nytimes.com/2001/08/15/nyregion/commercial-real -estate-a-warehouse-turns-into-retail-space.html.

Skeggs, Beverley. 2004. "Context and Background: Pierre Bourdieu's Analysis of Class, Gender and Sexuality." In *Feminism after Bourdieu: International Perspectives*, edited by Lisa Adkins and Beverley Skeggs, 19–33. Oxford: Blackwell.

Sky, Jennifer. 2014. "Young Models Are Easy Pickings for the City's Club Promoters." *Observer*, September 22. https://observer.com/2014/09/young-models -are-easy-pickings-for-the-citys-club-promoters/.

Solomon-Godeau, Abigail. 1986. "The Legs of the Countess." *October* 39 (Winter): 65–108.

Sombart, Werner. (1913). 1967. *Luxury and Capitalism.* Translated by W. R. Dittmar. Ann Arbor: University of Michigan Press.

Sontag, Susan. 1972. "The Double Standard of Aging." *Saturday Review*, September 23.

Spradley, James P., and Brenda E. Mann. 1974. *The Cocktail Waitress: Woman's Work in a Man's World.* New York: Wiley.

Story, Louise. 2008. "On Wall Street, Bonuses, Not Profits, Were Real." *New York Times*, December 17. https://www.nytimes.com/2008/12/18/business/18pay .html.

Strauss, Neil. 2005. *The Game: Penetrating the Secret Society of Pickup Artists.* Los Angeles: ReganBooks.

Stuyvesant, Stanley. 2009. "Group behind Bagatelle to Take Over the Merkato 55 Space." *Guest of a Guest*, September 29. http://guestofaguest.com/new-york /restaurants/breaking-group-behind-bagatelle-to-take-over-the-merkato-55 -space.

Suttles, Wayne. 1960. "Affinal Ties, Subsistence, and Prestige among the Coast Salish." *American Anthropologist* 62 (2): 296–305.

Swader, Chris S., et al. 2013. "Love as a Fictitious Commodity: Gift-for-Sex Barters as Contractual Carriers of Intimacy." *Sexuality and Culture* 17 (4): 598–616.

Tao Group. n.d. "About." Accessed October 29, 2018. https://taogroup.com/about/.

Taddeo, Lisa. 2010. "Rachel Uchitel Is Not a Madam." *New York Magazine*, April 2. http://nymag.com/news/features/65238/.

The Star. 2010. "Right Place, Right Time, Right People." July 29. https://www.thestar.com.my/news/nation/2010/07/29/right-place-right-time-right-people/.

Thompson, Derek. 2018. "How Manhattan Became a Rich Ghost Town." *CityLab*, October 15. https://www.citylab.com/life/2018/10/how-manhattan-became-rich-ghost-town/573025/.

Thornton, Sarah. 1995. *Club Cultures: Music, Media and Subcultural Capital*. London: Polity.

Tobias, Megan Neely. 2018. "Fit to Be King: How Patrimonialism on Wall Street Leads to Inequality." *Socio-Economic Review* 16 (2): 365–85.

Tutenges, Sébastien. 2013. "The Road of Excess: Young Partyers Are Searching for Communion, Intensity, and Freedom." *Harvard Divinity School Bulletin*. Accessed October 29, 2018. https://bulletin.hds.harvard.edu/book/export/html/264281.

Urken, Ross Kenneth. 2011. "The Origin of Bottle Service: The Scintillating Backstory to Club Flashiness." *Guest of a Guest*, March 1, 2011. https://guestofaguest.com/new-york/nightlife/the-origin-of-bottle-service-the-scintillating-backstory-to-club-flashiness.

Urry, John. 2010. "Consuming the Planet to Excess." *Theory, Culture & Society* 27 (2–3): 191–212.

Vankin, Deborah, and Matt Donnelly. 2011. "Nightclubs Having a Whale of a Time." *Los Angeles Times*, October 15. http://articles.latimes.com/2011/oct/15/entertainment/la-et-bottle-service-20111015.

Veblen, Thorstein. 1899. *The Theory of the Leisure Class: An Economic Study of Institutions*. New York: Macmillan.

Wacquant, Loïc J. D. 1995. "Pugs at Work: Bodily Capital and Bodily Labour among Professional Boxers." *Body & Society* 1 (1): 65–93.

———. 2004. "Following Pierre Bourdieu into the Field." *Ethnography* 5 (4): 387–414.

Wallace, Benjamin. 2013. "A Very Exclusive Brawl." *Vanity Fair*, April 2. https://www.vanityfair.com/style/scandal/2013/05/model-mogul-nightclub-brawl-double-seven.

Waller, Wallard. 1937. "The Rating and Dating Complex." *American Sociological Review* 2: 727–34.

Warhurst, Chris, and Dennis P. Nickson. 2001. "Looking Good and Sounding Right: Style Counselling and the Aesthetics of the New Economy." *Industrial Society* 33 (1): 51–64.

———. 2009. "'Who's Got the Look?' Emotional, Aesthetic and Sexualized Labour in Interactive Services." *Gender, Work and Organization* 16 (3): 385–404.

Warikoo, Natasha. 2011. *Balancing Acts: Youth Culture in the Global City*. Berkeley: University of California Press.

Watson, Allan. 2016. "'One Time I'ma Show You How to Get Rich!' Rap Music, Wealth, and the Rise of the Hip-hop Mogul." In *Handbook on Wealth and the*

Super-Rich, edited by Iain Hay and Jonathon V. Beaverstock, 178–98. Northampton, MA: Edward Elgar.

Weber, Max. (1922) 1978. *Economy and Society: An Outline of Interpretive Sociology*. Translated by Guenther Roth. Berkeley: University of California Press.

———. 1930. *The Protestant Ethic and the Spirit of Capitalism*. Translated by Talcott Parsons. New York: Charles Scribner's Sons.

Webster, Murray, Jr., and James E. Driskell Jr. 1983. "Beauty as Status." *American Journal of Sociology* 89 (1): 140–65.

Weinbaum, Alys Eve, Lynn M. Thomas, Priti Ramamurthy, Uta G. Poiger, Madeline Y. Dong, and Tani E. Barlow. 2008. "The Modern Girl as a Heuristic Device: Collaboration, Connective Comparison, Multidirectional Citation." In *The Modern Girl around the World: Consumption, Modernity, and Globalization*, edited by Alys Eve Weinbaum, Lynn M. Thomas, Priti Ramamurthy, Uta G. Poiger, Madeline Y. Dong, and Tani E. Barlow. Durham, NC: Duke University Press.

Weitzer, Ronald. 2000. *Sex for Sale: Prostitution, Pornography, and the Sex Industry*. New York: Routledge.

Wherry, Frederick F. 2008. "The Social Characterizations of Price: The Fool, the Faithful, the Frivolous, and the Frugal." *Sociological Theory* 26 (4): 363–79.

Willett, Megan. 2013. "The Days of VIP Bottle Service at New York City's Nightclubs Are So Over." *Business Insider*, March 8. https://www.businessinsider.com /bottle-service-is-over-at-nyc-clubs-2013-3.

Williams, Christine L. 1995. *Still a Man's World: Men Who Do Women's Work*. Berkeley: University of California Press.

Williams, Christine L., and Catherine Connell. 2010. "'Looking Good and Sounding Right': Aesthetic Labor and Social Inequality in the Retail Industry." *Work and Occupations* 37 (3): 349–77.

Wilson, Eli. 2016. "Matching Up: Producing Proximal Service in a Los Angeles Restaurant." *Research in the Sociology of Work* 29: 99–124.

Wingfield, Adia Harvey. 2009. "Racializing the Glass Escalator: Reconsidering Men's Experiences with Women's Work." *Gender & Society* 23 (1): 5–26.

Wolf, Eric R. 1999. *Envisioning Power: Ideologies of Dominance and Crisis*. Berkeley: University of California Press.

Wright, Tom, and Bradley Hope. 2018. *Billion Dollar Whale: The Man Who Fooled Wall Street, Hollywood, and the World*. New York: Hachette.

Yaffa, Joshua. 2009. "Barbarians at the Gate." *New York Times*, September 27. https:// www.nytimes.com/2009/09/27/style/tmagazine/27moscoww.html.

Zampolli, Paolo. 2011. "Zampolli's World: Paolo Zampolli Celebrates His Birthday at Provocateur NYC." *Haute Living*, March 14. https://hauteliving.com/2011/03 /zampollis-world-paolo-zampolli-celebrates-his-birthday-at-provocateur-nyc /139181/.

Zelizer, Viviana. 1994. *The Social Meaning of Money*. New York: Basic Books.

———. 2005. *The Purchase of Intimacy*. Princeton, NJ: Princeton University Press.

———. 2006. "Money, Power, and Sex." *Yale Journal of Law and Feminism* 18 (1): 303–15.

———. 2012. "How I Became a Relational Economic Sociologist and What Does That Mean?" *Politics & Society* 40 (2): 145–74.

Ziff, Sara. 2014. "Yes, You Should Feel Bad for Models: We're Being Told to Diet—Or Go Broke." *Guardian*, September 9. https://www.theguardian.com /commentisfree/2014/sep/09/models-diet-go-broke-modeling-industry.

Zorbaugh, Harvey. 1929. *The Gold Coast and the Slum: A Sociological Study of Chicago's Near North Side*. Chicago: University of Chicago Press.

INDEX

A NOTE ON THE TYPE

This book has been composed in Adobe Text and Gotham.
Adobe Text, designed by Robert Slimbach for Adobe,
bridges the gap between fifteenth- and sixteenth-century
calligraphic and eighteenth-century Modern styles.
Gotham, inspired by New York street signs, was designed
by Tobias Frere-Jones for Hoefler & Co.

DISCUSSION QUESTIONS

1. The club promoter Malcolm tells Ashley Mears, "I always said, in nightlife, it's not what you spend, it's what you get for free. That's real power. . . . If you don't spend a dime, that's power." Why does this concept not extend to the women of this world of "bottles and models"?

2. It's striking how hard the club promoters hustle to make a night feel effortless for the women they recruit. How does their work pay off in the long term?

3. Mears notes that "promoters who were men were far better positioned than women to capitalize on girls' beauty." Why do you think money mostly stays in the hands of the men who revolve around the women?

4. Though rare, there are female promoters. Discuss the ways female promoters develop their relationships with the models and beautiful women differently from the tactics the male promoters use.

5. Compare and contrast the concepts of "party girls" (women who are beautiful, young, and carefree enough to be out late and often) and "good girls" (women who are beautiful and serious enough not to be out often), and note the different ways they are viewed by men in this world.

6. For promoters, Mears observes that their success in the VIP world "escalated their aspirations to unattainable heights" and made it challenging for them to bridge the financial gaps between themselves and their richer clients, but many still believed it was possible. Discuss how the VIP world creates these illusions of possibility.

7. Mears writes that by joining a world that excludes and devalues others but certainly makes one feel special, women "strike a patriarchal bargain by gaining access in exchange for their own subordination as girls in the VIP world." Does this bargain seem worth it?

8. Mears speaks to several promoters about the double-edged sword of color capital in VIP society—the advantages and disadvantages a significant number of promoters encounter by being Black. What surprised you about how race operates in this world?

9. In this world of excess and waste, clients are paying for experience not goods—which are oftentimes marked up 1,000 percent. Throughout the book, Mears vividly describes countless dinners, parties, and vacations: do these experiences seem enticing to you? If you had the money, would you spend like this?

10. Has this book changed the way you view nightlife and the concept of being a VIP?